How to do Your Research Project

How to do Your Research Project

A guide for students in education and applied social sciences

Gary Thomas

SAGE

Los Angeles | London | New Delhi
Singapore | Washington DC

First published 2009
Reprinted 2009 (three times)

SAGE Publications Ltd
1 Oliver's Yard
55 City Road
London EC1Y 1SP

SAGE Publications Inc.
2455 Teller Road
Thousand Oaks, California 91320

SAGE Publications India Pvt Ltd
B 1/I 1 Mohan Cooperative Industrial Area
Mathura Road
New Delhi 110 044

SAGE Publications Asia-Pacific Pte Ltd
33 Pekin Street #02-01
Far East Square
Singapore 048763

Library of Congress Control Number 2008940279

British Library Cataloguing in Publication data

A catalogue record for this book is available from the British Library

ISBN 978-1-84787-442-9
ISBN 978-1-84787-443-6 (pbk)

Typeset by C&M Digitals (P) Ltd, Chennai, India
Printed and bound in Great Britain by
CPI Antony Rowe, Chippenham, Wiltshire
Printed on paper from sustainable resources

FSC
Mixed Sources
Product group from well-managed
forests and other controlled sources
Cert no. SGS-COC-2953
www.fsc.org
© 1996 Forest Stewardship Council

Contents

Preface

Research is useful and it is exciting to do and the expectation for students to do a research project is becoming more and more common in almost every area of applied social science: education, health sciences, social work, criminology, and so on. And this is happening at every stage in higher education: foundation, undergraduate and postgraduate. It is right that this should be the case – that students should be learning by doing – for the research project teaches skills that no lecture can teach. Not only does it enable learning about the particular topic chosen for research but it teaches students about having a questioning disposition, about evidence and about the frailty of knowledge, about methods of research and their strengths and weaknesses. It helps you to learn independently and to organise your time. With the skills and the awarenesses that it fosters, research provides an almost tangible platform for personal and professional development.

I don't like to think too long about how many hundreds of projects – undergraduate, postgraduate and doctoral – I have supervised because it reminds me of my age. But the more I supervise the more I realise that whether you are doing an undergraduate project, a Master's, a PhD or a major piece of research for a government department, you always go through much the same sequence of activity. All research contains the same basic ingredients – having a question, discovering what others have done, refining your question in the light of that discovery and then going out to answer the question yourself. That's the basic framework and beyond that there are better and worse ways of going about doing it. In this book I wanted to show the better ways, using examples (of mistakes as well as successes) from my own experience wherever possible, to those who are inexperienced in doing research: the ways that avoid pain and encourage satisfaction and pleasure. Yes, pleasure: research really can give you a buzz. There's an immense satisfaction that comes from finding out something new and presenting it in a form that other people can understand.

On the assumption that the basic ground rules for research are similar at whatever stage, I haven't attempted to pitch this book at one particular group: undergraduate or postgraduate. I've tried to keep it simple and straightforward in a way that I hope will appeal to all students in education and the social sciences, and whether you are an undergraduate or just beginning doctoral work I hope it will be relevant. While I realise that what emerges is inevitably a bit of a cookbook, I hope it is more of an Elizabeth David cookbook than any other – in other words, telling a story or set of stories, and containing opinions as well as recipes.

I'm aware that readers will come to this book with differing academic backgrounds and professional trajectories: some at an early stage in academic study, others quite experienced; some having no first degree yet, others having studied history, French, biology, engineering, or a hundred other subjects for their first degrees. What unites readers among this disparity, I guess, is the coming to a research project in applied social study for the first time. I know that readers will have experience and intelligence in bucket loads and I have therefore tried to inhibit any tendency to spoon-feed advice.

At several points in the book I discuss the importance of critical reflection and I hope that I have given a taster of this in my own writing. So, where there is methodological controversy I say so. Where the academic community seems to me to be pretentious, pompous or unsure of itself, I also say so, and try to explain why. To my mind, there is no purpose to be had in papering over the frailties of an academic area with verbosity, pretend-clarity or pseudo-scientific jargon, and where the academic community in applied social science seems to me to do this I say so. I hope that in communicating a critical disposition I have presented the book more as a series of conversations than as a set of lectures.

I've wanted to write this book also because in my experience students undertaking projects often don't think hard enough about the questions that they want to answer. As a result, those projects are less interesting than they might have been, looking at a question that is much too hard to answer given the time available, or restricting the focus onto something perceived to be easy to measure such as attitude or experience. Often certain approaches to research are completely sidestepped: numbers or anything to do with statistics may be studiously avoided and this is partly because of the backgrounds of many students in education and the social sciences. They are cautious of using numbers, even though they have the ability and the wherewithal.

It seemed to me that many of the introductory textbooks didn't really help very much, focusing heavily on research methods rather than research processes, with too little information on how to knit together a story. Methods are not the end of research – they are simply ways of doing it, and it's just as important that a piece of research has integrity, coherence and meaning as it is that a particular method is successfully used. And those methods are sometimes described in scope and levels of detail that are of no interest to undergraduate or Master's students. There is, in the modern phrase, too much information. Stanislav Andreski, the perceptive commentator on social science, said that social scientists in the academy display an 'adulation of formulae and scientific-sounding terms, exemplify[ing] the common tendency ... to displace value from the end to the means' (Andreski, 1972:108–9). I think he was correct back then in 1972, and he is still correct now: we can become hypnotised by the elegance of our shiny instruments, and forget the integrity of the whole – the story we are telling.

I hope this book will be read, if not from cover to cover, at least in substantial sections. Much of the literature on research method seems to me to be dipped into by students, who emerge from their dip sometimes with inappropriate and half-digested notions (for example about reliability and validity), with little in the way of glue to stick the bits together. It seems to me that many of these readers have not been guided by the literature to understand what good research is – how it bonds together and why it is important for there to be a sense of integrity and narrative to the whole. I attribute students' hurried forays into the literature partly to that literature's emphasis on method and technique rather than on the balance of the whole research project.

The project should be seen as far as possible in its wholeness, and anything we can do to communicate this wholeness, this integrity, to the reader is of benefit. Fortunately, word processors enable us to undertake and write up projects almost seamlessly now. It is for this reason that I have omitted any section on 'writing up', because I think the notion of writing up belongs to a pre-wordprocessor era. In that era notes were collected, card file indices compiled and analyses separately undertaken: write-up could not happen until all parts were complete. That is no longer the case, which is wonderful: you can write as you go along. This is why it is possible to concentrate more on the process of thinking that is involved in writing rather than the writing up itself. I have tried to suggest how this can be done throughout this book rather than in a special chapter, concentrating on critical and reflective thinking and how to communicate this to the reader.

The following is a note to tutors. I have adopted what I think is a novel approach to the way that research methodology and design are discussed and handled, and I hope that you agree with me that this will be helpful to students. Everywhere I have looked I have found tensions about how to explain research design and method to students, with some quite serious ambiguities raised by overlapping vocabularies. This confusion was noted more than twenty years ago by Smith and Heshusius (1986), but textbook writers seem to have paid little heed. The confusion is not too troubling for you and me because we have a gestalt that lets us re-slot and reconfigure things when they are presented differently. What is an interview? Is it a method or a data-gathering technique? (You'll find it handled in both ways in the textbooks.) Are case studies, action research and experiments designs or methods? Again, you'll find them described as both. I think the reason for this ambiguity is apparent in this quotation from distinguished sociologists Schatzman and Strauss, where it seems to me they are unclear about what they mean by 'method':

> Field method is not an exclusive method in the same sense, say, that experimentation is. Field method is more like an umbrella of activity beneath which any technique may be used for gaining the desired information, and for processes of thinking about this information. (Cited in Burgess, 1982: 2)

Well, I'd venture that experimentation is not a method, except in the vernacular sense of the word: it is a design framework of such proportions that there is even a discrete branch of study dedicated to it, namely experimental design. And I have no idea what Schatzman and Strauss mean by an 'exclusive method'. They imply in 'exclusive method' that a discrete and limited range of techniques is used in experimentation (by contrast wiith field method). But this is clearly wrong, since experimentation may employ a wide range of data-gathering techniques, just as field study does. It's how the design frames handle the data that is different, and what I guess they are getting at is that this design (i.e. experiment) prescribes particular, well-defined processes – processes about, for example, control.

Though I differ with them on their explication of field method I do like the idea of the 'umbrella': much of our design rationale in social research, when you think about it, incorporates the umbrella. As they rightly note, field method is an umbrella, but so are action research, case study and evaluation – all use a range of methods and data-gathering techniques, and even envelop each other.

Before the metaphor of umbrellas and envelopment becomes overextended, I'll just lay out my thesis about research design for this book, which is that it proceeds from *purposes* to *questions* to *decision about approach*, then *design frame*, then *data-gathering methods*, then *analytical methods*. All of these elements, considered together, constitute the design route. Sometimes this design route will be straightforward, since certain methods almost always go with certain approaches, but usually in educational and social research it isn't simple (for umbrellas and other things interfere with the simplicity), and this is why I have taken time to outline paths of decision-making in design (for example in Figures 5.9 and 5.10 on pp. 92 and 96).

This orientation has influenced also my attitude to what my colleague Stephen Gorard calls 'the Q words': qualitative and quantitative. The division here sometimes seems to dazzle students in the QQ headlights so that they can't see beyond it. As Richard Pring (2000) has pointed out, while there is a *distinction* between these two types of research, they are not in *opposition* to one another, and it seems to be becoming clearer to all concerned with the teaching of research methods that these should not sit on either side of a fulcrum, dividing the whole world of social research into the one or the other. For this reason, I have tried to avoid using them, and thereby avoid the dichotomy they engender. Instead, I prefer to look first and foremost at the design frames – then at whether these use words or numbers in data collection and analysis (and of course sometimes they use both).

Back to students, and a word of advice. Every tutor has different expectations about what a research project should be about and look like. Some prefer the emphasis here, others there. One will want this kind of project, another will prefer something different. I've tried always in this book to indicate that there is no absolutely right way, that there are different avenues to follow. However, if I seem to be giving different advice from that given by your tutor (and there are places in social scientific study where there are real differences and unresolved issues, as I make clear in the book) listen to your tutor: your tutor is always right.

Look forward to your research project. When you have completed it you will have learned so much. You will have learned how to organise a major piece of work, how to get hold of information, and how to analyse and synthesise it. You will have learned sophisticated presentation skills and all the basics and more of the most common data management software. It is one of the most significant and productive things you will do in your time at university.

ACKNOWLEDGEMENTS

I'd like to thank all those who have helped in the reading of drafts and for encouraging and/or corrective comments of one kind or another. Special thanks for specific advice goes to Hilary Cremin from the University of Cambridge, Stephen Gorard and Ann Lewis from the University of Birmingham, and Geoffrey Walford from the University of Oxford.

Some people to whom I had sent drafts of the book have been enormously supportive in their commentary, bits of which are so lovely that I can't resist duplicating them here. Thanks to Gill Richards ('I loved this book! It brought research methods alive') from Nottingham Trent University and her Master's students: Alison Patterson ('brilliant'); Susan Allan ('love the visual models'); Anne Cowan ('filled me with optimism'); Viv Brown ('very entertaining as well as extremely useful'). Also to Neil Stott from Nottingham Trent University ('accessible and encouraging style') and Joy Jarvis ('unputdownable') from the University of Hertfordshire.

Many thanks to Helen Fairlie, who kept encouraging me to write a book that might be useful to students, rather than an academic one that 'only three people and a dog read' (I paraphrase Helen's actual comments, but this was the gist). Thanks also to all of Helen's colleagues at SAGE for their help. Thanks to Naomi Robinson for the thumbnail artwork, and to Sarah Wimperis for the portraits of key figures in social science.

Thanks to all my colleagues and to students (some of whom are mentioned in the book) whose ideas I have stolen and some of which have led to the examples used here. And of course I am grateful to all of those in our wider community of enquiry whose ideas I have borrowed and used, always bearing in mind playwright Wilson Mizner's comment: 'Copy from one, it's plagiarism; copy from two, it's research'.

A road map for your research project

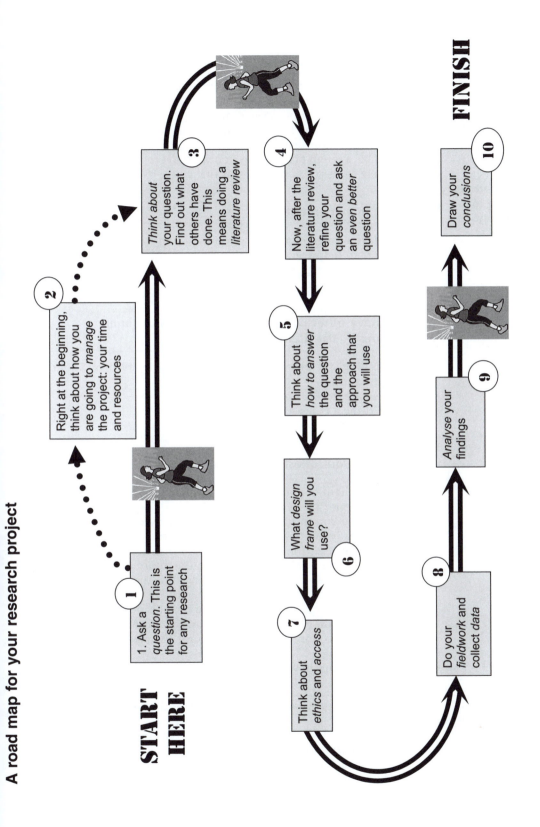

START HERE

1. Ask a *question*. This is the starting point for any research

2. Right at the beginning, think about how you are going to *manage* the project: your time and resources

3. *Think about* your question. Find out what others have done. This means doing a *literature review*

4. Now, after the literature review, refine your question and ask an *even better* question

5. Think about *how to answer* the question and the approach that you will use

6. What *design frame* will you use?

7. Think about *ethics* and *access*

8. Do your *fieldwork* and collect *data*

9. *Analyse* your *findings*

10. Draw your *conclusions*

FINISH

Rolling out the road map

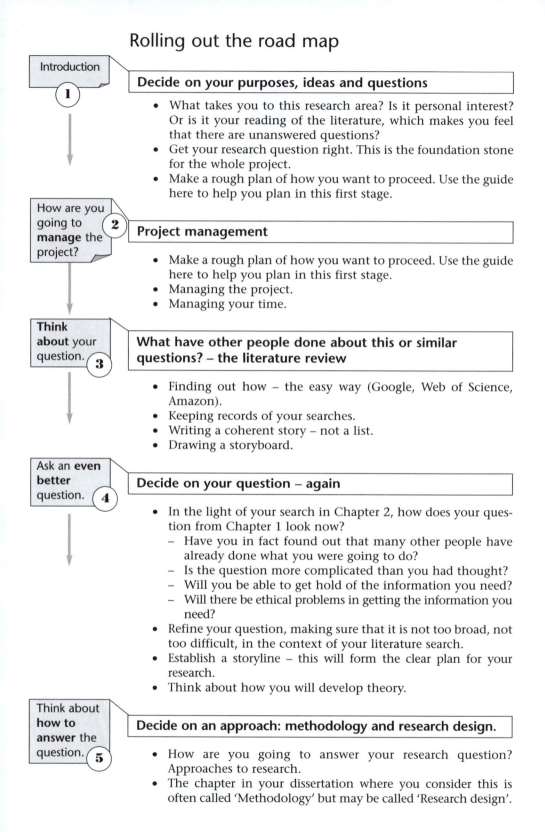

Introduction

①

Decide on your purposes, ideas and questions

- What takes you to this research area? Is it personal interest? Or is it your reading of the literature, which makes you feel that there are unanswered questions?
- Get your research question right. This is the foundation stone for the whole project.
- Make a rough plan of how you want to proceed. Use the guide here to help you plan in this first stage.

How are you going to manage the project?

②

Project management

- Make a rough plan of how you want to proceed. Use the guide here to help you plan in this first stage.
- Managing the project.
- Managing your time.

Think about your question.

③

What have other people done about this or similar questions? – the literature review

- Finding out how – the easy way (Google, Web of Science, Amazon).
- Keeping records of your searches.
- Writing a coherent story – not a list.
- Drawing a storyboard.

Ask an even better question.

④

Decide on your question – again

- In the light of your search in Chapter 2, how does your question from Chapter 1 look now?
  - Have you in fact found out that many other people have already done what you were going to do?
  - Is the question more complicated than you had thought?
  - Will you be able to get hold of the information you need?
  - Will there be ethical problems in getting the information you need?
- Refine your question, making sure that it is not too broad, not too difficult, in the context of your literature search.
- Establish a storyline – this will form the clear plan for your research.
- Think about how you will develop theory.

Think about how to answer the question.

⑤

Decide on an approach: methodology and research design.

- How are you going to answer your research question? Approaches to research.
- The chapter in your dissertation where you consider this is often called 'Methodology' but may be called 'Research design'.

- Different ways of viewing the world and different understandings about how knowledge is sought and gained in social inquiry: postivism and interpretivism.
- Thinking critically.
- Tying up your purposes and your questions with these considerations about knowledge and 'ways of finding out'.

How will your research be designed and framed? 6

Decide on a design frame

- Some general considerations in designing a piece of research.
- Which of the main 'frames' for research will guide the way that you do it?

Ethics and access 7

Practical matters

- Being ethical.
- Getting access.

Doing the research 8

Data gathering

- Interviews ⎫
- Diaries ⎬ mainly using words.
- Accounts ⎭
- Questionnaires ⎫
- Observations ⎬ using words and/or numbers.
- Tests ⎫
- Official statistics ⎬ mainly using numbers.

9

Analysing your findings

How are you going analyse the information you gather?

- Analysing words – constant comparative method: coding, sorting and patterns.
- Analysing numbers – how to analyse your results on Excel.
- Developing theory and discussing your findings.

Drawing your conclusions 10

Completing your analysis and drawing conclusions

- Drawing conclusions:
  - synthesising your findings;
  - reconciling your findings with those of others.
- Writing an abstract.
- Presentation and writing.

1

Your Introduction:
Starting Points

Introduction	Your introduction says why you have chosen to do your research project in this area. In it, you explain what you want to inquire into and why you want to do it, and justify your research question. This chapter considers:
Literature review	
Methodology	• what takes you to this research area? Is it personal interest? Or is it your reading of the literature, which makes you feel that there are unanswered questions, uncertainty or ambiguity?
Fieldwork and findings	• getting your research question right – this is the foundation stone for the whole project. Different kinds of questions will lead you to different kinds of projects;
Analysis and discussion	• what sort of evidence will you seek to answer your research question?
Conclusion	

You are here in your project

Very few people wake up one morning and think 'I'll do a research project!' If you are reading this book, the chances are that you have been told to do some kind of research project by your tutor on a course. Today's university education nearly always demands that students who are undertaking undergraduate or postgraduate work in an applied social field such as education or healthcare, or in any of the social sciences such as psychology, sociology or anthropology, do a research project. It may be a modest undergraduate project of around 10,000 words, or something more substantial such as a Master's degree project of around 20,000 words.

Question: Where do I begin? Answer: Begin at the beginning, with an introduction

'Begin at the beginning,' the King said gravely, 'and go on till you come to the end: then stop.' (*Alice in Wonderland*)

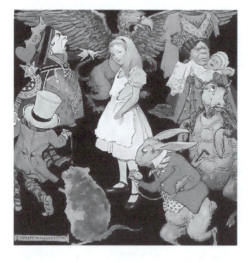

The King of Hearts's advice to Alice is wise not just for Alice, but for any storyteller. And your research project is like a story. Like a story, it has to hang together, so it needs to have a beginning, a middle and an end. So, as the beginning, your introduction is especially important: it needs to set the scene and outline the case for the whole project. While it is relatively short (just a few pages usually), it is centrally important for it sets the tone for the whole dissertation. It is probably the part that the people who read and mark your work will read most thoroughly for they will be looking for the rationale behind the project. As they read it they will be imagining you doing your research and asking themselves: Was this worth doing? Have you thought seriously about your questions – whether they are answerable and how you will answer them? And how are you beginning to make your case, to tell your story?

The introduction is a scene-setter, rather like Tenniel's illustration of *Alice in Wonderland*. It tells the reader in summary what is likely to be coming and, if it is good, manages to knit together elements of the story to whet the reader's interest. I hope your research journey won't be quite as surreal as Alice's, though you may indeed meet some odd characters and be forced to go through some bewildering procedures.

Your introduction has to do a number of things. It has to introduce the reader to your thinking behind the project: what interested you, and what was your *idea* at the outset? It has to outline the *purpose*: Pure curiosity? Evaluating something? Developing your practice? It has to translate your thinking, your interests and your purposes into *research questions*. And it has to summarise the ways that you are likely to go about *finding evidence and answering* these questions.

However, your introduction is not a summary of the whole project. Students often make the mistake of saying 'Chapter 1 is about … Chapter 2 is about … Chapter 3 is about …, etc.' Leave the summary for the abstract (see p. 237). Rather, it is the beginning of a story: it should capture the reader's interest. Most of all, it should say *why* you are doing it.

Thinking of a research idea

Once you know that a research project is part of the expectation for your course, you have to think of an idea for it – the 'why' that I have just spoken about – and this can be one of the hardest parts. It is what this chapter is about. It's worth reading it, because you really need to get this bit right. The right idea can lead to a good project, and the wrong idea will almost certainly lead to a poor project.

A research project begins with your curiosity – with an issue or an uncertainty, and this issue or uncertainty is reframed into the *research question*. You may want to know whether something is the case, or why it is the case. You may want to know what the consequences are of doing something. Your interest may stem from personal experience, from a discussion with a friend or colleague, from a lecturer's comment in a lecture, or from having read an article in the newspaper. There may be an 'angle' that needs investigating: you may, for example, want to resolve an apparent discrepancy between your own observation of the world and the situation that is reported by others. But whatever the inspiration, you should feel curious; you should feel that you want to know the answer.

Remember though that you are not out to prove something or to demonstrate that something is the case. Rather, you are looking to find the answer to a genuine question. It's a great privilege being able to research into a question of this kind with the guidance of a university tutor, and as you progress toward the end of your project you will realise that there is great satisfaction that comes from the analysis of your findings.

Other words for a project are thesis and dissertation. They all mean more or less the same, though 'thesis' usually applies to a longer piece of work.

Purposes of research

Of course, the purpose of your research is to fulfil the requirements of your degree, but let's put that aside for a moment. Why are you doing it? In other words, what *circumstances* encourage you to want to find something out? The idea that you have for your research (if you have one yet) does not exist in a vacuum. It exists as part of your curiosity, and your curiosity in turn depends on your own circumstances. Your circumstances affect the purposes of your research. They may mean that you want to ...

- *Find something out for its own sake.* Here you may just have an idea that you want to pursue. It is not related to anything other than your own curiosity. For example, you may have relatives who work in a social services department who may have mentioned disapprovingly how young and inexperienced in life all the social workers seem to be nowadays. This may lead you to look at (a) whether the perception is correct by examining the age profiles of different professions vis-à-vis social work, and (b) the possible reasons and potential consequences of any differences between age profiles in a few professions.

> There are different purposes to research. Ask yourself what your purposes are.

- *Evaluate something.* Here, there may be a programme or an innovation that is being introduced or that has already been introduced, and you want to see what its impact has been. What are its outcomes? In short, 'Did *x* work?' For example, an 'Active Kids' programme may have been started by a supermarket chain, with the provision of extra sports and PE equipment for schools if parents collect the supermarket's vouchers. You may choose to evaluate the project's take-up in schools local to you. As a follow-on (depending on the length of your project) you may wish to see what the impact has been locally and try to make some assessment of the costs and benefits of schools' involvement in the programme.
- *Find out if something works.* Here you may be interested in the consequences of bringing in a particular innovation and you may choose systematically to test this. For example, a publisher may have brought out a new series of reading books, which your school has decided to buy. You may choose to look at how effective these are by using them with half of your class while the other half use the existing scheme.
- *Improve your own or others' practice.* The aim here is to look in detail at your own practice or an element of it to see if it can be improved. Or, in your research, you may be helping others to do this. It will involve introducing new ways of working, thinking and talking about events and incidents as they happen, and collecting information about how these changes and this thinking and talking seem to be influencing things. This kind of research is often called 'action research'. Its main aim is to change practice – for the better.

Kinds of questions

Different kinds of questions will lead to different kinds of projects. This may sound obvious, but failure to recognise this represents one of the main problems for those beginning to undertake research: too often students get into trouble because they set off with a question that is not right and by the time they realise that this is the case it is too late.

> Remember the question asked of the supercomputer in *The Hitch-Hiker's Guide to the Galaxy* … 'What's the answer to the question of Life, the Universe and Everything?' After seven and a half million years the computer comes up with the answer: forty-two.
>
> > 'Forty-two!' yelled Loonquawl. 'Is that all you've got to show for seven and a half million years' work?'
> >   'I checked it very thoroughly,' said the computer, 'and that quite definitely is the answer. I think the problem, to be quite honest with you, is that you've never actually known what the question is.'
>
> Maybe social scientists' questions will never actually be posed as simplistically as this, but the story is a salutary warning to us all. It warns us that we should be aware of the complexities of the subjects we are studying.

The questions that educational and social researchers pose and try to answer aren't simple. And simplistic – that is to say, over-simple – questions lead to silly answers. It's very important in any inquiry where we are thinking about people, how they behave and interrelate, that we think about the *nature* of the questions we want to ask.

How, then, do you think of a good question? First you have to understand that there are many *kinds of questions*, and that these will lead us off into different lines of inquiry. Many kinds of questions have fairly simple answers. For example, if you ask whether there are more men teachers than women teachers, and whether the proportions of each have changed over the years, the answer will be quite easy to discover. However, if you ask a question such as 'Why do girls tend to do better than boys in literacy?' an answer – or a route to finding an answer – will not be so readily evident. In fact, to this question several possible answers immediately suggest themselves. It may be that girls' brains are better 'hard-wired' for language. Or the answer may be nothing to do with brains and hard-wiring: it may be because parents, friends and family of baby girls talk more to them than they do to boys. Eventually schools repeat the process. More is expected of girls in the way of language, and so girls get more feedback and training in the way that language is used. They therefore get better at it.

Each of these possible answers to this question comes with a perfectly valid train of reasoning behind it and we should be able dispassionately to work out which is correct. But that isn't possible. It isn't possible because ...

a) these answers aren't either/or – in other words, it is not one cause *or* the other. Both may be contributing to the phenomenon of girls' better literacy;
b) there are measurement issues involved – it may be that girls merely look as though they are better because of the ways that we use to assess performance;
c) we have no definitive way of answering the question – even if (a) and (b) didn't apply, there is no research design that could be set up which would enable an answer to be given once and for all.

Just because a question is difficult, though, it doesn't mean that we should not try to answer it, but we should be aware of the difficulties and, possibly, frame different, additional or more tentative questions.

So, if getting the right research question is vital, how can we decide on it? It is first necessary to acknowledge that there are different kinds of questions and it might be helpful to spend a moment categorising them. Broadly speaking, there are four kinds of questions involved in social research, all of them perfectly valid as starting points for a project, but each of them involving different kinds and degrees of complexity and each of them leading to different kinds of inquiry.

Four kinds of questions ...

1 *What's the situation ...?* You may have done some observation work in schools and noticed that there are far more teaching assistants there than you remember from your own time as a school student. This may lead you to be interested in the growth in the number of teaching assistants in schools over the last 20 years. It would lead to the first kind of question: *What's the situation ...?* The actual question may be something like: 'How have numbers of teaching assistants grown in schools over the last 10 years?'

Four kinds of question

1. What's the situation ...?
2. What's going on here ...?
3. What happens when ...?
4. What is related to what ...?

2 *What's going on here ...?* You may be a teaching assistant and note that a group of students in a class persistently flouts the rules and engages in more difficult behaviour than others in the class. Or you may note that one child in the class is always putting up her hand but has no idea what the answer is when the teacher asks her. These are specific instances that emerge from your own observation and in each case you may ask yourself why this is happening. You want to make an exploration into the issue. This leads then to the second kind of question: *What's going*

on here? The actual question may be something like: 'Why does Jade put up her hand when she doesn't know the answer?'

3 *What happens when …?* You are a teacher and your school plans to introduce a new policy on bullying. You decide to try and see whether it has any effect. This leads to a third kind of question: *What happens when …?* The actual question may be something like: 'What are the consequences of implementing an anti-bullying policy in Tower Hill Primary School?'

4 *What is related to what?* As a student in social work and taking a 'wild' module in economics, you notice from the latter that there seems to be a relationship between a country's gross domestic product and the amount it spends on education. Looking further, you see that while the relationship seems to be strong, there are interesting variations that seem to exist in the amounts spent on different phases of education (nursery, primary, secondary, tertiary and higher education). You decide to explore these relationships further, to see whether there are cultural or historical reasons that might explain them.

Though these categories may seem similar – they are all questions, after all – in fact they offer very different kinds of starting points and will lead to very different lines of inquiry. And within one study it may be appropriate to ask more than one kind of question, with several lines of inquiry, each intertwining with the others. Let's look at them in a little more detail.

Kinds of questions – and some nutshell-sized studies and their implications

What's the situation?

'How have numbers of teaching assistants grown in schools over the last 10 years?'

This question can be answered fairly straightforwardly by going to official statistics. Your analysis of these descriptive statistics will follow.

Here you are *describing* something that is happening. You are not making any significant *interpretations* about evidence. When you are describing, you are not trying to do anything much more complicated than saying 'This is the case'. Nor are you trying to find the *cause* of something – you are not, in other words, trying to see if *x* causes *y*.

But the researcher understands that to say 'this is the case', while relatively simple if compared with saying *x* causes *y*, is nevertheless not straightforward. Like an artist or a photographer, you are trying to present a faithful representation of the facts that you find, and this is harder than it seems.

Like an artist, you will be more or less successful at representing the world that you are trying to describe, depending on what you choose to focus on and depending on the techniques you use. The first problem the researcher faces compared with an artist is that while artists literally try to draw a picture, in research you are making your picture with words or numbers, and we all know (for example, from the way that politicians present their cases) that words and numbers are unreliable messengers of truth. We select the words and numbers that we use. Also like an artist or a photographer, your portrait will be vulnerable to pressures and prejudices of one kind or another and the picture you paint will be susceptible to distortion because of this. Artists' subjects want to look beautiful or handsome, and the subjects of research tend to be the same: they want to look good.

Like an artist or a photographer you will also be exposed to the risk of things going wrong: a photographer may have the picture go fuzzy or blurred or underexposed, or may have the wrong part of a portrait focused, or may make a beautiful person look ugly. A skilled photographer will know how to avoid these problems. Likewise, the photographer may be able to magnify the relevance of a particular facet of a scene by using a particular lens. These kinds of problems and opportunities are possible also when you are using words or pictures, and in the same way that skilled photographers can avoid problems, well prepared researchers can circumvent the traps that confront them when doing research.

While this represents a simple kind of question, it is perfectly acceptable and valid as a basis – a platform – for an undergraduate or Master's degree and can lead to a first-rate project or dissertation. But description on its own will not be sufficient for a project. You will be expected to make some sort of *analysis* of the increase in teaching assistants as well, and this may depend on further reading or on certain kinds of *fieldwork* – perhaps asking informed people (such as teachers) for their opinion on the growth of this group of employed personnel in schools.

> **Fieldwork:** The process of collecting data – so a place where data is being collected is called 'the field'. The field could be a classroom, a playground, a street, a hospital ward, someone's home – anywhere that you are collecting data.

What's going on here?

'Why does Jade put up her hand when she doesn't know the answer?'

How could you answer this question? You can't climb inside Jade's head. And asking her why she does it probably will not reveal very much. To try to answer it without recourse to a map of Jade's mind, you have to use your own knowledge of situations like this, and your own knowledge of people (including your knowledge of yourself) to make informed guesses. All of this is of course subjective, but it is none the worse for this, as long as you realise and acknowledge the boundaries that surround this kind of inquiry – and, as in all research, we must be sure that we do not make inappropriate claims for it. Deciding to judge the situation as a person makes this a particular kind of research: it is about two people – the observed and the observer, and we must be careful not to generalise from this very particular situation to others. You are trying to *interpret* the situation in order to *illuminate* what is going on. That is why a study of this kind may be called *interpretative* or *illuminative*.

When you are *illuminating*, you are shining a light on something. This implies that the subject is in the dark currently (or at least is badly lit): it's impossible to see what is going on. (If the sun were shining brightly, there would be no need for illumination – no need for research.) So you shine a light. What does this metaphor mean here?

First, it means that you are expecting to see something that you couldn't see before. Second, it implies also that you will be able to see because you are looking in a way that you weren't able to previously. Third, it implies that you are giving time and energy to looking hard (i.e. shining the light) and using *your own self* – your intelligence and experience – to make sense of the subject under study.

There's nothing 'unscientific' about this use of your own self, as some people who prefer more structured research proclaim: the famous mathematician George Pólya (1945/2004: 172) said that all kinds of discovery, in research or elsewhere, are determined by having 'brains and good luck' and by 'sitting tight until you get a bright idea'. In other words, the main part of research is not the cleverness or the specialness of the methods that you use, but rather your willingness to use your own head to look at something intelligently.

Don't, in other words, ignore your own ability to reflect on a problem, and don't minimise its significance in helping you to understand the problem. This is the case in all kinds of research, but particularly in illuminative inquiry you will be drawing on your own resources – your own knowledge of people and social situations – to make sense of what you find.

Extending the metaphor about illumination, remember that the object will look different when the light shines from different angles, and will appear different from various viewpoints and to different people. In remembering all of this, you will realise that you are doing something more than describing. In doing this kind of study, your aim will not be simply to describe the facts, because you will be interested in a social situation that is not usefully explicable simply within a framework of description. You will be involved in the kind of study that is about feelings, perceptions and understandings, and to get at these you will need to be listening to people and interpreting what they are saying, observing what they are doing and trying to understand their actions.

What happens when?

'What are the consequences of implementing an anti-bullying policy in Tower Hill Primary School?'

This 'What happens when?' question is accompanied by a particular kind of structure. This structure usually involves taking two or more observations or measures (e.g. before and after an imposed change) and then trying to *deduce* what any difference between those observations or measures may mean. So, in this example, you would have to have had a measure of the amount of bullying that took place before the policy and after the policy to see whether there had been a drop – which you might *infer* was due to the implementation of the policy. Clearly, the measures that would be taken about the subject under study, namely bullying, could be taken in a multitude of ways, and it is these different forms – and their satisfactoriness – that will be examined in Chapter 5.

Usually in this kind of study you are asking 'Does *this* seem to be causing *that*?' You are asking questions of the variety: 'Does *x* cause *y*?' or 'Is *a* related to *b*?'

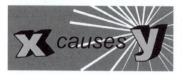

The situations here may have been engineered by you, for example by your setting up of an experiment, or they may be naturally occurring situations where you want to examine the influence of one phenomenon on another. Your observations of them may be more or less structured and your *inferences* more or less particular on the basis of this structuring.

Another example: you may be interested in changing the way that you, as a year tutor in a secondary school, address your Year 8s when you meet them in the morning. You may choose to be in class half an hour early, not take a formal register and instead ask the youngsters to sign in as they arrive. What effects does this seem to have? You will be making deductions about any possible consequences. You could make this observation informally by just watching and taking notes, or in a much more structured way by precisely adjusting the conditions (down to the length of time you are making the change) and also the outcome you are choosing to measure, and comparing the behaviour under the original condition and the new one. You might also compare what happens in a colleague's class where no such changes are made. Whether your observations are informal or formal, you will be making inferences about the cause and effect.

A particular kind of research design emerges from this sort of question, a design that promises an indication about the causative link. But, just as was the case in the consideration of 'What's going on here?' questions, we have to acknowledge the potential frailty of this kind of inquiry, and we must be sure that we do not make inappropriate claims for it. We'll discuss some of the things that might go wrong in Chapters 6 and 8.

What is related to what?

I gave earlier an example of the seeking of relationships – what is related to what – in official statistics. These relationships can also be sought, though, in questions that lead to empirical study 'in the field'. For example:

'What are the relationships between reading attainment, exclusion and non-attendance at Harley Green Comprehensive School?'

This is a question raised by a postgraduate Master's student, having noted in the educational press that children designated as having special needs were far more likely to be excluded than other children. Her study involved the collection of data in the school and inspection of school records. My interest in her comment on the press stories centred on the implication in those stories that in some way schools were picking on children with special needs to exclude – that special needs in some way or another 'caused' the exclusion. In fact, what seemed more likely to me was that 'special needs' as a category picked up young people who are failing for a host of reasons and this generic failure ultimately led to disaffection and exclusion. One did not lead to the other. Rather, the young people in each group were essentially being drawn from the same pool.

This inappropriate attribution of causation highlights the main challenge to the interpretation of a question that seeks relationships of any kind, as I shall discuss further in Chapter 9.

All of these four types of questions lead to their own routes of inquiry and will cause you to lean lightly or heavily toward a particular kind of approach and design for your research. Approach and design are facets of the research process that we shall examine in more detail in Chapter 5, but you should be aware at this stage where your initial questions are likely to take you.

> **Data:** This is rather a confusing word when you first come to social research, since you will probably associate 'data' with numbers. In social research, however, data means any source of raw information – 'raw' in the sense that no one has worked on it. So it may indeed be numbers (test scores, say) but it may also be the transcript of an interview, questionnaire responses, photographs, documents, videos, etc. All of these constitute data. By the way, 'data' is a plural noun (it's the plural of 'datum') so whenever you refer to data you should use the plural form, e.g. 'These data show …'; 'The data support the view that …' (not 'This data shows …', etc.).

A research question – or a hypothesis?

You may come across the term *hypothesis* and it may be suggested to you that your research should be framed around a hypothesis rather than a question. Research in the social sciences is framed less around hypotheses now than it was ten or twenty years ago for several reasons which are too knotty to go into here. However, if your question is of a particular kind it may well be appropriate to frame your research around a hypothesis – especially if you have been encouraged to do this by your tutor. Hypotheses are framed around 'what happens when' questions. The difference between a research question and a hypothesis is that the expectation surrounding the hypothesis is that the hypothesis is *precisely* testable. The emphasis is on 'precisely'. You have to be able to specify the conditions under which your hypothesis will be tested, and the expectation is that you will be able at the end of your research project to say: 'Yes, this is the case' or 'No, that is not the case'. (In fact, you can never say these kinds of things definitively, and hypotheses are problematic for this reason.)

But let's forget about the problems with hypotheses for a moment and assume that we can use them unproblematically. In order to be able to say 'Yes' or 'No' you have to be able to measure two or more features of a situation precisely and set up experimental conditions that will enable you to test the hypothesis. I'll explain further how you can test a hypothesis using an experiment in Chapter 6.

Coming up with a question

Your question will emerge from your interests and your observations. If you are having difficulty coming up with a question …

- Think of the situation in which you are working or the subject you are studying. Is there something novel, perplexing or unusual about it? If so, think about how you might look into it further.
- Ask a colleague, friend or relative who works in the field about a particular issue or problem in their working day. How might this lead on to research questions?
- Think of a story in the media about education, healthcare, probation or the field in which you are studying. Are there aspects of it that seem interesting or puzzling? What aspects of it could be followed up?
- Try looking at some websites on the Internet, such as those of the big government departments (Department for Children, Schools and Families, Department of Health, etc.). What is topical? School meals? Children's happiness? How could a project be geared around these topics?
- Look at Smith's www.secondarydataanalysis.com which gives access to a broad range of UK, US and international data. Scan through some of the data. See if it gives you any ideas.
- Go to the Campbell Collaboration or Cochrane Collaboration websites (see p. 35) for information on important current issues.

If you are still left wondering what to do, try …

- brainstorming (see box). From your brainstorming try to come up with three research questions, preferably from a situation you know something about.
- doing an A to Z of topics – think of anything at all, and see what it sparks off in your mind. For example:

> A – Adopted children – do they have special difficulties?
> Academies – what do parents think of them?
> B – 'Black history' – students' attitudes.
> C – Criminal justice and the young person.
> D – Diversity – how well are we doing?
> E – Early years education internationally.
> 'Every Child Matters' – how aware are parents of it?

> **Brainstorming:** This is a technique that was developed in the advertising industry (but let's not hold that against it!) for helping to produce interesting new ideas. Two or more people get together and say anything that comes into their heads on the topic in question. The ground rules are: (1) quantity (of ideas) rather than quality; (2) no criticism of the ideas of others; (3) unusual ideas are welcome.

Can I have more than one question?

Yes, though these will need to be related to one another, and don't start off with too many. It is best to start with fewer questions and see what these lead to as your project progresses. They may lead to subsidiary questions or completely new questions.

Is it feasible? Problems with research questions

When you have thought of a question, and have thought about how it maps onto the four types of questions I outlined above, consider it against two more important criteria: preciseness and 'doability' …

Is it precise?

The most common problem with a research question is that it is too *broad* or too *general*. 'What causes children to have reading difficulties?', for example, is a question that is almost impossible to answer. However,

> **Common problems with research questions**
> - They are too broad.
> - There's no clear way to answer them.
> - You can't get to the information you need.

'What are the characteristics of Sean's behaviour when he is reading?' is a question that can be answered. Remember that you have time and material constraints and some questions will not be answerable in the time you have available.

Is the research that will come from this question doable?

Sometimes there will be *ethical* problems about a research question. For example, if you were interested in how parents arguing affected children at school, it would not be ethical to ask children (or parents) about these intimate matters (ethics are discussed more fully in Chapter 7). Or there may be problems of *access* to the kind of information that you want. If your question would require observation in classrooms, are you sure that any school is going to let you in to observe?

Prima facie questions

Prima facie questions are questions that you start off with – the questions that you state in your introduction. That is to say, they are the ones that we are concerned with now. They change and become refined as your study progresses.

If you feel that your question is not quite right at this stage, don't worry. It is often the case – no, *nearly always* the case – that things won't be sorted out once and for all at the beginning of the study. I should state it even more strongly than that: *it is to be expected* that this (or these) will not be your final question(s). Especially in small-scale research of the kind that you are

> You will revise and sharpen your ideas as your work progresses. For this reason, your early ideas and questions are prima facie questions. These can be refined after your literature review.
>
> And social research rarely follows a blueprint. Plan for change as you progress.

doing, and particularly where there is any kind of practitioner bent to it, it is very likely that you will not be able to specify your questions exactly at the outset.

You may feel that you don't know enough about the area to make definitive choices at this stage about your questions or your plan of attack on the subject. This is fine. Or you may feel that you wish to do some practical groundwork that will in some way set the boundaries for the project, and in some way map out the channels down which your inquiry can run. Your reading of the literature will almost certainly enable you to refine your first questions.

The idea that we have to specify our course of action exactly at the beginning is something of a hangover from the days when social research aped the methods of the natural sciences, with experiments in which a blueprint of questions, procedures and methods would be drawn in detail at the outset and followed meticulously. In fact, it is doubtful whether that is actually the way that natural science researchers ever operated in real life, but it's what they *said* they did. As the renowned biologist Sir Peter Medawar put it in debunking this idea of cleanly planned and executed research, the special methods and

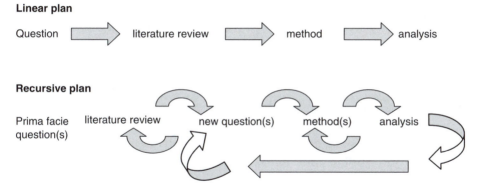

Figure 1.1   A linear or a recursive plan?

procedures that are supposed to be associated with scientists' work represent merely 'the postures we choose to be seen in when the curtain goes up and the public sees us' (Medawar, 1982: 88).

But social scientists, having a bit of an inferiority complex about their status as scientists, believed the natural scientists and tried to copy the folk-lore model of science that had been presented to the public. In the social sciences, though, it is nigh on impossible to set up a project of the kind you will be doing without stopping, rethinking, replanning, changing, starting again. And rethinking your *question* is the first part of this process of revisiting. It is to be expected, and is a necessary and integral part of the process of a research project such as yours.

All of this replanning and revisiting means that the kind of research that you do in investigating the social world is often called *recursive* or *iterative*. In other words, it turns back on itself and starts again, and a distinction is drawn between this pattern – involving reviewing and replanning – and what is sometimes called a 'linear' plan (see Figure 1.1).

So the idea that things won't go to plan is itself planned for. If the 'recursive' part of Figure 1.1 looks a bit of a mess, that's because that's what social research is often like. Your research in fact *may* follow an entirely different or simpler path but most likely it won't be a straight, blinkered path from beginning to end. Importantly, your reading for your literature review will inform your question and help you to refine it. Beyond this, you will see things to the side of the path; you will notice something over there and decide that that is more interesting than the original topic; you will find that you can't talk to the people to whom you wanted to talk, and so on. Always, what you discover and the way that the world treats you will influence the way that you proceed: it's like a game of snakes and ladders – you'll get knock-backs and sudden boosts and insights. And both knock-backs and insights will entail you in a lot of rethinking.

For this reason, the question or questions that you have at the beginning of your study are called *prima facie questions*. Prima facie means 'on its first appearance' or 'at first sight', so calling your questions prima facie is an acknowledgement of their status – an acknowledgement that they are tentative and will change. We will look at how you will revise your prima facie questions in Chapter 4.

Kinds of evidence and kinds of answer

Questions are easy to ask but often hard to answer. When we want to answer a question we are going to have to rely on *evidence* of some kind, and it is worth at this stage thinking about the kinds of evidence that might help to answer particular kinds of question. We talk of evidence being of varying kinds: strong, weak, circumstantial, primary, secondary, etc., but what do these mean and how are they likely to be related to your thesis? This is important to think about at this stage, since the assessment of your thesis by your marker will depend on your collection of evidence. If you have a question that leads to weak evidence, you will be marked down heavily for it. This is a good reason to get the question right at the outset.

Let's look at the simple questions given in Table 1.1 – none of them anything to do with education or social science – just to see what kinds of evidence might emerge and why you should be very careful at this stage.

Already from Table 1.1 you'll note several processes – you may be looking up facts in books or already published research. Or you may be collecting your own evidence 'out there' in the field: you may be asking people who are directly involved, or you may be making an observation, or trying something out to see what happens. What you get from each of these processes are different kinds of evidence, each kind acceptable. However, each has its own strengths and weaknesses and its own potential pitfalls, as you will have noticed from the examples.

Empirical: Strictly speaking this means something that has been found out from experience, from trial and error or from the evidence of your senses. 'Empirical' is often wrongly used, though, with the intimation of experiment of some kind, so when people talk of 'empirical evidence' they usually (incorrectly) mean evidence coming from some kind of trial or experimental study.

Usually (but not always), there will be an expectation that the kind of evidence you collect during a research project you undertake at university will be empirical. That is to say, you will be expected to go out into the wide world and collect data yourself rather than relying on information marshalled by others – for example in a book. (In fact, a research project as a literature review – that is, *just* as a literature review – is usually acceptable, but if you want to do a research project that is based solely on the literature you should check with your tutor.)

Table 1.1 Questions and evidence

Question	Ways of answering it with evidence	Is the evidence reliable and robust? (Stars out of 5)	Why the star rating?
How many colours are there in the rainbow?	Look it up in a book.	★ ★ ★ ★	The book is almost sure to be right. However, books aren't always right. There's always room for interpretation (e.g. what do you mean by 'colour'? Does ultraviolet count?)
	Wait for the next rainbow and count the colours.	★ ★ ★ ★	It's good to rely on your own observations rather than someone else's (e.g. in a book). However, be aware that your answer may not agree with another person's – because, in the case of this example, you may disagree on what constitutes one colour (where do yellow and blue become fused, and does the merging constitute a separate colour?).
	Ask someone else.	★ ★ ★	They may know; they may not. They may not know, but not want to tell you that they don't know – and make something up.
What is my best friend's middle name?	Ask her/him.	★ ★ ★ ★	You'd think this should be pretty accurate. But what if your best friend is ashamed of their name? Might they claim not to have one, or make up a different one?
What is the meaning of life?	Reflect on it yourself, or ask others. Read books.	★	No clear answer (ever, no matter how much research you do).
How can I get to Edinburgh from here?	Look it up on a map, or go on the Internet.	★ ★ ★ ★ ★	The chances of a published map being wrong in directions of this simplicity are vanishingly small.
How many legs does a millipede have?	Look it up – e.g. a book, or via an Internet search.	★ ★ ★	Doing an Internet search reveals reveals a suspiciously similar range of answers, giving 'between 80 and 400' rather too often for my liking, revealing that 'authorities' may

(Continued)

Table 1.1   *(Continued)*

Question	Ways of answering it with evidence	Is the evidence reliable and robust?(Stars out of 5)	Why the star rating?
			just rely on each other rather than find out for themselves (see the danger of secondary sources, p. 31).
	Dig up some earth, find one and count.	★ ★ ★	There's a good chance you'll lose count or in some way be inaccurate. And if you decide to check by counting the legs of another millipede and you come up with a different number you are into further questions about the possibility of different species or variation within one species.
What does this button do?	Press it.	★ ★ ★ ★	You should be able to see what the button does when you press it, but it may be the case that nothing happens (imagine a car dashboard, or a microwave oven control panel). However, if something observable *does* happen you can be fairly sure that the button did it. (But not absolutely sure – it might have been coincidence of some kind.)

Because of the potential frailties and weaknesses of one kind or another in evidence, it is useful to gather it in different ways, so that one piece of evidence supports another. When the police gather evidence at a crime scene they talk about *corroborative evidence* when one piece of evidence supports another piece. One piece of evidence on its own is often taken to be not enough, since mistakes can be made by witnesses or police officers; equipment may be faulty; witnesses may not understand what has been asked of them, or may be making something up for any of a host of reasons. So, if Mr Dorrit says that he saw his neighbour Mrs Nickleby go into her house at 10.30, he may be believed, but this on its own will not be taken to be satisfactory,

It's good to look for different sources of evidence, e.g. reading, observing, interviewing people.

for he could have been mistaken about the time, or may have confused Mrs Nickleby for someone else. But if another witness, independent of Mr Dorrit, says the same thing, you become surer about the fact that Mrs Nickleby indeed entered the house at that time. And if the video camera across the road catches a good likeness of Mrs Nickleby, timed 10.31, we're almost home and dry.

The same kind of thing applies in a social research project. It is much better to rely on several kinds of evidence rather than just one. There are many ways in which evidence can be sourced: from …

- personal experience
- the testimony of others
- documents or archives
- artefacts
- observation

… the list goes on. In social research, using more than one kind of evidence is sometimes called *triangulation* (see p. 111). Having noted the importance of corroboration (or triangulation) though, it is important to say that you will never in social research get conclusive evidence of something being the case. However, the more evidence there is – each piece corroborating the other – the surer you will be. This is why the noun 'evidence' is so often qualified with adjectives – for example, prima facie evidence, inconclusive evidence, weak evidence, strong evidence, conclusive evidence, and so on.

I have spoken about these issues of evidence in general, but it is important to think about them in particular in relation to the social sciences and your own thesis. Will you be able to collect evidence that will enable you to answer your question? Think about the evidence you are likely to collect when you answer a question. Suppose your question were something to do with the problems children have with maths. What kind of evidence could you collect? You could:

- Ask the teacher directly about the problems.
- Ask children what their problems are.
- Get children to talk to you while they are doing a problem.
- Get children to complete diagnostic tests.

All of these would garner evidence of some kind, and each would have its own strengths and weaknesses.

A final word about evidence: it is the way that you view, scrutinise and use evidence that is important. It is a matter always of looking at evidence, thinking about it *critically* and *assessing* it. The great philosopher John Dewey (1920/2004), in reviewing several kinds of thinking, argued that it is only 'reflective thought … [that] is truly educative in value' (p. 3). He distinguished this *reflective thought*, where there is a deliberate self-questioning about the grounds for a belief, from other kinds of thought where there is slight or no acknowledgement of the strength of the evidence or grounds on which it is held. He proceeded:

... [Some thoughts] are picked up – we know not how. From obscure sources and by unnoticed channels they insinuate themselves into accept-ance and become unconsciously a part of our mental furniture. Tradition, instruction, imitation – all of which depend upon authority in some form, or appeal to our own advantage, or fall in with a strong passion – are responsible for them. Such thoughts are prejudices, that is, prejudgments, not judgments proper that rest upon a survey of evidence. (pp. 4–5)

Dewey makes the important point here that we should be suspicious of certain kinds of thinking, particularly those arising from *tradition* and *authority*. We should think for ourselves. And we should be wary of any line of reasoning (in oth-ers or in ourselves) that comes from a vested interest or a strongly held opinion (a 'passion').

Show that you can think critically. When you seek evidence always be questioning about its value.

The *reflective thought* that he favours is about being sceptical about our thoughts and about always looking for evidence for a line of reasoning. He suggests that we should try to be almost instinctively critical. Such reflective thought is the hallmark of a good research project.

A title

You may want to have a precise title for your thesis right from the start, and while this may seem like good planning, this is one place (that is to say, the beginning) where it is probably good to be a little imprecise. In fact it is more important to be thinking about your *question* than your *title*. This isn't to say that a title is unimportant. It *is* important. It is vitally impor-tant, because your work will be assessed by reference to your title – in other words, the examiners will ask themselves 'Does this thesis address the title?'

But when you are doing a project in the social sciences, large or small, you will realise that the world isn't quite as you thought it was going to be. You can't get access to this place, there are ethical problems there, or better questions occur to you as you begin to read about the issue. (These changes will be addressed in Chapter 4.) The important fact to realise is that these changes will inevitably occur and that if you stick rigidly to a premeditated title you will be missing many opportunities to make your project more interesting or more manageable.

Or you might take notice of the necessary changes, but still stick unthinkingly to the title even though the project has changed substan-tially in practice. After all, *you* know what you are doing, and as your research gathers momentum the title may slip to a cobwebby corner of your reptile brain, never to be re-examined. But remember that while markers are reading your project they will be asking themselves if it is addressing the title. So if you have a title that doesn't match up to what is actually in the write-up of your project the marker will be disappointed and wonder why. One of the commonest causes of low marks is when a piece of work – essay or project – doesn't match the title.

So the best plan is to have a *working title* – something that captures what you originally set out to do – which you can then change once you have finished the dissertation. The new title – the one you decide on after you have finished – will match the completed product exactly. But

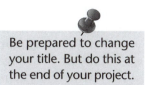

Be prepared to change your title. But do this at the end of your project.

always use the working title to remind yourself of what you set out to do, because you will always find when you are doing research that you will be tempted to follow a hundred different paths. It might be worth following one of them, but do you really want to? Always examine your motives and your likely outcomes. This is where the storyboard in Figure 3.1 will help. It will help you to decide which are the likely main routes that will emerge from your working title and what avenues of investigation may be opened up by each main route.

What research is – and what it isn't

It is worth closing this chapter with a word about what research is and what it is not. Research is about curiosity and inquiry, as for example journalism is. However, it differs from journalism in that it is governed by a number of expectations. There is the expectation that research will:

- aim to find new knowledge;
- be thorough;
- be balanced;
- be fair;
- be ethical.

These are some ground rules, and we'll look at them in more detail in Chapters 6 and 7. But it is worth reinforcing the fact that research is not journalism and it is not about campaigning for an issue. It's not about being committed to a position. Nor is it about 'knowing' something and trying to find 'proof' for it. You cannot assume that you already know the answer.

Research *is* about disciplined, balanced inquiry, conducted in a critical spirit.

Overview

Your introduction is important: it sets the scene for the reader. It should interest readers and make them want to read further. It tells them why you are interested in an area. It outlines what your first research questions are. You should have taken time thinking about the kinds of questions you will ask because your whole project will be geared around the way that they are constructed and the kinds of evidence you will need to address them. As you think about your questions, you should consider their nature and the likely paths of inquiry down which they will lead you. But you shouldn't become paralysed with fear about these early questions. At this stage, they are prima facie questions – questions that will be refined as you undertake preliminary work and as you do your literature review. They are working questions, in the same way that your title at this stage is a working title.

In fact, the whole of your introduction is really a working document, to be revised as your work progresses. It should not, however, attempt to airbrush out difficult aspects of your journey or places where you have decided to change direction. These are all part of your story. If you say where you started and where you have altered course it will help readers to understand why you went where you did. Do tell them about what you intended to do originally and how things have progressed as you have worked on your project.

Further Reading

Laws, S. (2003) *Research for development*. London: SAGE.
Focused particularly on development work, Chapter 5 is good on research questions and focus.

Thomas, G. and Pring, R. (2004) *Evidence-based practice in education*. Maidenhead: Open University Press.
A compilation looking especially at evidence and evidence-based policy and practice in medicine as well as in education. See Chapter 1 for a discussion of evidence, what it is and how it is used.

Thomson, A. (2005) *Critical reasoning: a practical introduction*. London Routledge.
Contains some good discussion and advice on evidence.

2

Project Management

Introduction

Literature review

Methodology

Fieldwork and findings

Analysis and discussion

Conclusion

Most projects conform to a similar structure, but this is quite complex, involving several different kinds of activity on your part. Your work therefore needs to be well planned and organised. This chapter considers:

- **managing the project – the main elements and how they fit together;**
- **managing your time;**
- **making a rough plan of how you want to proceed.**

Management is especially important for a project – even more important than it is for an essay or some other kind of assignment – because the project is such a large piece of work. It may comprise one, two or three modules worth of effort, with very little input from a tutor other than in tutorials, which may not amount to more than a few hours. All of the onus is on you to be organising your work. So it's a good idea to recognise this and prepare for it. It's not like an essay, where if the worst comes to the worst you can burn the midnight oil and polish it off (not very well) in a night or two. You really do need to 'project-manage'.

Once you have had an idea and decided on your question(s) you will have some notion about the sort of project you will be doing. You can now begin to project-manage it. Whatever kind of research project you do, there are several elements that will almost certainly be included in its composition:

- the introduction;
- the literature review;
- the methodology section;
- the findings;
- the discussion; and
- the conclusion.

We'll deal with each of these in more detail later in the book. For now, you just need to know that they exist and what proportion of the total dissertation each usually occupies. A very rough guide (and it is very rough – you shouldn't take it as 'gospel') is given in Figure 2.1.

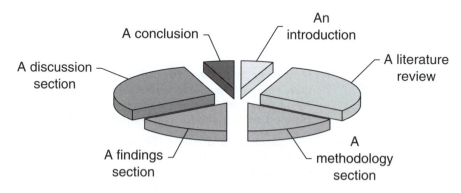

Figure 2.1   Elements of a dissertation

Thinking in terms of words and pages, the proportions in Figure 2.1 translate roughly to the numbers given in Table 2.1, with each A4 page taken to be written double-spaced and to contain around 300 words.

Table 2.1   Proportions of words and pages

Element	Proportion of words (very roughly)	In an undergraduate thesis of 10,000 words		In a postgraduate thesis of 20,000 words	
		Words	*Pages*	*Words*	*Pages*
Introduction	5%	500	2	1,000	4
Literature review	30%	3,000	12	6,000	24
Design and methodology	15%	1,500	6	3,000	12
Findings	15%	1,500	6	3,000	12
Analysis and discussion	30%	3,000	12	6,000	24
Conclusion	5%	500	2	1,000	4
Total		10,000	40	20,000	80

These can now be divided up into the time you have available. Suppose you have in total two semesters (or three terms) to complete a 10,000-word project – a piece of work that is sometimes said to be a double module's worth. Subtracting holidays and weekends, this probably amounts to around 80–90 days on which you can be putting some time toward the project.

You'll need to decide how to apportion time to each element of the project. It's helpful to plot this on a graph in some way. Suppose you decide as shown in Table 2.2.

Table 2.2   Apportionment of time

	Days
Read around the area	10
Write literature review	14
Examine methodology	7
Write methodology section	4
Do fieldwork	21
Analyse and write up results	21
Write conclusion	3
Finalise presentation	2
Total	82

Drawing a timeline

This can, for the sake of clarity, be presented as a timeline (sometimes called a *Gantt chart*), as in Figure 2.2.

If you can see the time available and the time needed for the various elements of your project it will be easier to make sure that you have enough time for each. The last thing you want is to get to a month or a week from submission date only to discover that you still have to do most of the literature review and the data collection.

How to draw a timeline using Word

1. From the toolbar at the top of the Word screen, click on Table.
2. Click 'Draw Table' – a little pencil ✎ should take the place of your cursor.
3. With the pencil, draw the shape of the table and draw in the numbers of rows and columns that you need.
4. Click again on the table so that the 'pencil' changes back to a cursor.
5. Click where you want to write in the table and start entering information about months, days and tasks to be fulfilled. *Hint*: for the tasks, you can probably copy the left-hand column of Figure 2.2.
6. Hover your cursor over the toolbars at the top of the Word screen and right-click. A list of all the different toolbars will appear. Left-click on 'Drawing' and the drawing toolbar will appear at the bottom.
7. From the drawing toolbar, click on the one that shows a 'line'. Take your cursor back to the table and it will appear as a horizontal cross +. 'Stretch' the cross across the rows of the table one by one to show the length of time you want for each phase of the project.

	Months									
	Oct	Nov	Dec	Jan	Feb	Mar	Apr	May	June	
	Days									
Days into project →	1–10	11–20	21–30	31–40	41–50	51–60	61–70	71–80	81–90	
Read around	▬▬									
Lit review		▬▬▬								
Find out about method			▬							
Write method				▬						
Fieldwork					▬▬▬					
Analysis							▬▬▬			
Conclusion									▬	
Presentation										▬

Figure 2.2   Timeline or Gantt chart

You don't have to use a Word table. You can just draw one in freehand. However, it's worth persevering with the Word chart because it is a useful presentation skill, and clear presentation of your findings is one of the skills on which you will be assessed – not just in the project but also in the rest of your degree. Show your timeline to your supervisor and discuss it with them: not only will they be able to offer useful advice, they will also be impressed.

It is worth remembering that the dissertation proportions given here are a guideline only – they are not set in concrete, and you can vary these proportions depending on the needs of your research. For example, one piece of research may contain a much longer findings section than another. Another may have a longer literature review. In yet another, it may be that there is very little need for a conclusion, which can be assimilated into the discussion. Don't feel as though you have to keep to a rigid formula in this regard. Look, for example, at the varying proportions between two dissertations in Figure 2.3.

Having said that you should be prepared to be flexible on the structure. All other things being equal, I personally like the balance of dissertations which are similar to Project 1 in Figure 2.3. If you adopt this as a guide – and you are prepared to be flexible – you won't go far wrong.

You may wonder whether this degree of preparation is worth it. It is. Preparation is a key skill and you are being assessed as much as anything on your ability to organise, prepare, think ahead and manage your work.

Just look at those fingernails! Time management

While discussing planning, it is useful to mention the thorny issue of time management. We all know we should do it better, because there is always a reason for not doing it effectively. I know the syndrome only too well: I sit down at the keyboard, nothing happens. I gaze at my fingers hopefully, but then … 'Just look at those nails!' Another half hour is wasted looking

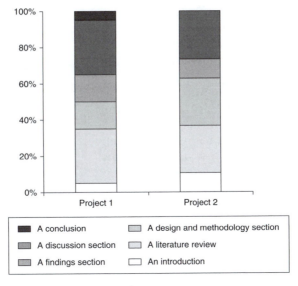

Figure 2.3 Not all dissertations are the same

for some nail scissors and then eventually getting round to carefully trimming the offending claws. Then I have to file off the rough bits. And by then of course it's time for a cup of tea, and then 'Oh, there's the postman', and the two hours I have carefully reserved for my work is gone.

Things you can do

Make a schedule

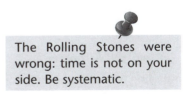

On the basis of the timeline you have drawn, and the apportioning of days to elements of the project, decide which days you are going to work during a week. Will

The Rolling Stones were wrong: time is not on your side. Be systematic.

it be just weekdays, just weekends, both, or what? Fit your timetable around your life, decide which days and hours you are going to work, and then keep to the plan (the last bit is important).

Little and often

Do a little every day. One of the commonest excuses for not being able to get on with work is 'I just don't get the extended periods of time I need to do the work'. Well, extended periods of time would be lovely, but they are difficult for anyone to find, and it is unrealistic to expect that a fairy godmother will present you with them. Modern life is chaotic and full of demands. It's more realistic to knuckle down to the understanding that you are going to have to compromise, and just do little and often. If it is often enough (that is, once every day or every other day) you will find that you are able to keep up the continuity – you'll be able to remember where you were. If it is less often than this (say, missing three or four days at a time) you'll find that you have forgotten what you were thinking and you will lose momentum and interest. So it is good to reconnect with your books and computer every day, even if you don't actually write anything. Even if it is 11.00 p.m. and you are absolutely exhausted, force yourself to turn on your computer and read what you were doing yesterday.

On the issue of little and often, and at the risk of getting whimsical, I'll offer my 'principle of the laburnum', to which I often refer when I want to prompt myself into working. Outside my study window is a laburnum tree. In May I notice that small buds appear on the branches. The next time I notice them, perhaps two or three weeks later they are magnificent long racemes of golden flowers. How did they do this without me noticing? They grew a tiny bit every day, and they carried on doing it. Little and often ...

Negotiate time

Set aside a time every weekday which you reserve for your work and which you and friends and family treat as sacred. Negotiate a time with them which is your research time. Make sure friends and family respect this: tell them your future depends on it, and tell them how guilty they will feel if you fail your dissertation. Tell them that if you fail you will probably descend into a depression from which you will never recover, and it will be their fault.

Set yourself targets

Keeping to your schedule, target yourself to write 250 words a day as a minimum for the days that you are working. Don't leave your desk until the 250 words are complete. (*Tip*: for a word count in Word, press Alt T W.)

Decide on a time period

You could get up early at 6 o'clock and work from 6 until 7. Or you can tell yourself that you will not watch TV between 8 and 9. Reward yourself with a little treat *after* your work period – a coffee or a glass of wine, or listening to some music, or going out or whatever, but keep these goodies for *after* the work, rather than *during* it.

If you still can't find the time

If you find that you are still not finding the time, draw up a blank timetable of a couple of days which shows every hour of every day. Then fill in the timetable with how you have actually been using your time over these days. Even if you have a busy life, you will be surprised at the time spent doing very little, pottering around or watching nothing very interesting on the TV. It's a salutary experience.

Overview

A research project is a major undertaking. If you don't plan systematically you will end up trying to do everything at the last minute, and it will show. You have to look at the kind of project you expect to do, divide up the time available and plan out how your practical work will fit into the timetable.

Further Reading

Burns, T. (2008) *Essential study skills: the complete guide to success at university* (2nd ed) London: SAGE.

Cottrell, Stella (2003). *The study skills handbook.* (2nd ed) Basingstoke: Macmillan.
This is very, very basic advice on study skills. When I say basic I mean basic: don't say I didn't warn you.

Walliman, N. (2004) *Your undergraduate dissertation: The Essential Guide for Success.* London: SAGE.

The Open University – Skills for OU Study http://www.open.ac.uk/skillsforstudy/
Another basic guide.

University of Birmingham Guide to Effective Learning – 'study skills elsewhere' http://www2.is.bham.ac.uk/gel/SSE.htm
This provides a list of links to Web resources that contain information at other institutions (mainly American) about study skills.

The Literature Review

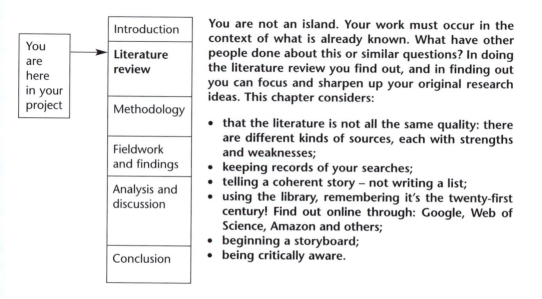

You are not an island. Your work must occur in the context of what is already known. What have other people done about this or similar questions? In doing the literature review you find out, and in finding out you can focus and sharpen up your original research ideas. This chapter considers:

- that the literature is not all the same quality: there are different kinds of sources, each with strengths and weaknesses;
- keeping records of your searches;
- telling a coherent story – not writing a list;
- using the library, remembering it's the twenty-first century! Find out online through: Google, Web of Science, Amazon and others;
- beginning a storyboard;
- being critically aware.

Once you have outlined the problem or issue that you wish to examine and you are happy with the expression of this in the form of an initial question or questions, you will need to find out about what other people have accomplished in researching this topic. Assuming that you have done your work properly in making sure that your research question is precise and doable, this review of the literature should lead you down some paths that will help you to define more exactly what you wish to do. Ultimately, you will be able to refine your research questions.

In thinking about a literature review, you first need to establish what's meant by 'literature'. Literature can be almost anything that represents the results of research or scholarship on a subject. It is written material that may appear in books, articles, conference proceedings, dissertations, websites, and so on. The shorthand for these kinds of information is *sources*.

Just running through these sources, you will see, even at first glance, that they are of different kinds, and they will be viewed differently by your tutors. Some have more credibility than others and you must be careful not to be taken in by something – or to present it to others – just because it is in print. Just because it is in written form doesn't mean that it is of unimpeachable quality as a piece of information. You will need to be clear about the status of the evidence that you are drawing on when you cite literature. You should ask yourself what kind of literature it is. Let's look at a few sources as shown in Table 3.1.

Primary and secondary sources

In Table 3.1, you'll notice that mention is made of primary and secondary sources, and I note that secondary sources are not usually as highly thought of as primary sources. It is worth spending some time looking at this distinction between primary and secondary, since tutors may place stress on using one (usually primary) rather than the other. Most of the sources mentioned in Table 3.1 will usually be primary (though textbooks are always secondary). Let's look at some others.

Examples of primary sources:

> A *primary source* is 'straight from the horse's mouth' – in other words, no other person has subsequently analysed or summarised it. A secondary source is a reworking of usually many primary sources, either in analysis or summary. The most common form of secondary source is a textbook.

- autobiographies
- diaries
- government documents and statistics
- letters and correspondence (including electronic kinds such as email)
- original documents (such as birth certificates)
- photographs and audio or video recordings
- reports from commercially produced surveys or other research (e.g. using focus groups)
- speeches
- technical reports.

Examples of secondary sources:

- biographies
- dictionaries and encyclopaedias
- review articles
- textbooks.

The main difference between a primary source and a secondary source is in the directness of the data or evidence being presented. Think of the primary source representing a first presentation or first analysis of the data, and the secondary source representing a second look, usually by someone other than the author of the primary source. In practice, it is difficult sometimes to distinguish between a primary and a secondary

Table 3.1   Sources of information

Kind of source	What is it?	☺ Good things about this source	☹ Not so good things about this source
Article in a peer review journal	This has been offered by the author to the journal to be judged. The peer reviewers (i.e. other academics in the same field) will ask themselves if it is good enough for publication. Only the best articles will be accepted, and for this reason the peer review journal is seen as the 'gold standard' for quality.	Only the best articles get published. You can therefore be sure of quality (in theory).	This material is published for the author's peers in the academic community, and may be difficult for anyone else to understand. Also, it will usually be on esoteric or cutting-edge matters and not necessarily straightforward issues. It may give little attention to explaining the wider context, or explaining in simple terms.
Article in a professional journal	A professional journal is similar to a peer review journal, and may be reviewed by peers. However, criteria for judgement will be rather different. It will be judged principally on its practical usefulness to the professional rather than on the satisfactoriness of the design of the study or the methods used.	Likely to be of practical relevance.	May be simply the view of the author. The work will not have been subject to such stringent scrutiny of research design, method, analysis, etc. It is difficult to assess the difference between a professional journal and a peer review journal, since both have elements of peer review. If in doubt, try to make an assessment of the article itself. Does it just seem to be a personal view? Is it well referenced? How thoroughly does it seem to have been done?
Authored book	Books vary in their 'scholarliness'. They will usually have been written as a major presentation of the author's work – research work or academic study – but they may be explanations of other people's work (see 'Textbook').	Books written by a single author represent an extended academic treatment of a particular topic. Because they are by one person they have integrity: they tend to 'hang together'.	Tend to be personal representations of a topic, unmoderated by the comments or views of others. So be cautious: this may be a very particular 'take' on a subject, or a personal view.

Table 3.1 (Continued)

Kind of source	What is it?	☺ Good things about this source	☹ Not so good things about this source
Chapter in an edited book	Edited compilations are books all on one theme brought together by an editor. These are like journals, but without the same degree of peer review.	Edited books are a good way of gathering related material on a topic. The editor will be an expert in the field, often taking an interesting slant.	Can be 'bitty', with some very weak chapters interspersed with good ones. The multiple authorial 'voice' may be confusing.
Textbook	A textbook is a bringing together of much work on one theme. This is not original work by the author, but work that she or he has summarised for the particular purpose of meeting students' course needs.	Saves a lot of time searching sources. It may, if the textbook is good, provide a very effective summary.	Because an author is reporting on others' work it is susceptible to distortion or misunderstanding (think of 'Chinese Whispers'). It is referred to as a 'secondary source' for this reason. When other people's work is brought together in this way by a textbook author it has to be summarised, perhaps not very well. Can become out of date quickly. For all these reasons a textbook is not valued highly as a source.
Conference proceeding	A paper that has been presented at an academic conference and that has then been printed in a collection of papers (called the 'proceedings' of the conference).	Usually right up to date, and often reporting on work that is still in progress.	Conferences vary in their status, and papers are often subject to only a minor form of peer review, if they are peer reviewed at all. Conference proceedings are therefore of very variable quality.
Thesis or dissertation	The theses and dissertations that you will be able to gain access to are written by students who have written Master's degrees or PhDs.	May be on a topic very similar to your own. May be very good (but may not – see the next column).	May be very weak. Do not use one as a model for your own. It may have only have scraped a pass.

(Continued)

Table 3.1 *(Continued)*

Kind of source	What is it?	☺ Good things about this source	☹ Not so good things about this source
Magazine or newspaper article	Like other forms of publication, newspapers and magazines (periodicals) take various forms, though the differences are more marked. Some periodicals and newspapers are as 'respectable' as some journals. Others are not.	Right up to date, and can be used as a starting point which leads you to a more reliable source.	Most of these publications depend on good sales and may be willing, even the 'high quality' ones, to distort material to make it more interesting. Reporters are subject to none of the peer review checking used in academic journals. It is not unheard of for reporters simply to make up stories.
Website	These are as varied as the sources of information above. A website is really just a medium for carrying a range of sources and has no inherent strengths or weaknesses. It's up to you to judge.	Most websites carry reliable information, some, for example, taking you directly to a publisher's site, where you can download peer reviewed articles.	Some websites, even quite well known ones, carry misleading information. Be particularly wary of those offering off-the-shelf answers to essay questions. Wikipedia can be helpful for giving you an impression of the breadth of the area, but is unreliable. Always verify from another source.

source, so you should not get too worried about strictly delineating one from another. However, you should be aware that an examiner may mark you down for using a textbook (definitely a secondary source) as your source of information.

You'll notice that I include *review articles* in secondary sources, and these are worth a special mention since they are taken to be rather more authoritative reviews of the literature than those that exist in encyclopaedias and textbooks. There are two kinds of review article: the *systematic* review and the *narrative* review. The systematic review uses particular methods to search for research on a topic in a wide range of peer review sources. Only studies of a predetermined type and/or quality are included in the ultimate review. A narrative review, by contrast, discusses and summarises the literature on a particular topic without conforming to a particular search formula. Narrative reviews often do not report on how they searched for literature or how they decided which studies were relevant to include. There are also *meta-analyses*. These are studies which use particular techniques for selecting and summarising the findings of many pieces of research.

Review articles and meta-analyses can be very valuable as sources, if you can find up-to-date ones which are relevant to your topic. While they appear in general academic journals, you can look especially for journal titles that begin with 'Review of ...' such as the *Review of Educational Research.*

A relatively new and increasingly important resource is the 'collaboration' that brings together high-quality evidence and then synthesises and summarises it for the reader. The most important of these for the social sciences is the Campbell Collaboration (www.campbellcollaboration.org/) This gives as its general purpose 'Improving decision-making through systematic reviews on the effects of interventions within the areas of education, crime and justice, and social welfare'. This is an example of one of its summaries on the impact of street lighting in the reduction of crime:

> This review of 13 studies of street lighting interventions in the United Kingdom and United States, spanning four decades, finds that crime decreased by 21% in areas that experienced street lighting improvements compared to similar areas that did not. The review also notes that street lighting appears more effective at reducing crime in the United Kingdom compared to the United States – a 38% reduction compared to 7%. In general, the American studies were older and several reported just nighttime crime, rather than both nighttime and daytime crime.

A similar resource is the EPPI-Centre (i.e. the Evidence for Policy and Practice Information and Co-ordinating Centre) at http://eppi.ioe.ac.uk/cms/.

Another of these banks of summaries is at the Cochrane Collaboration (www.cochrane.org/). This is a library of systematic reviews in healthcare. Also see the Educational Evidence Portal www.eep.ac.uk/DNN2.

Quality of sources

Aside from your judgement about the source that is being used, make a more general assessment of the work that you are referencing. Ask the following questions of it:

- Is this literature written following a piece of research? If so, what kind of research was being undertaken? Was it a large-scale or small-scale study? What was being claimed of the research? Usually research authors are 'up-front' about the limitations and weaknesses of their research, and work that is published in a good journal should not have been

Not all sources are equal. Think about the quality of the source. Is it primary or secondary? Is it based on research evidence? Has there been a peer review process?

accepted if it makes unrealistic claims. This is not to say that small-scale research is in any way inferior to large-scale research: each has its strengths and weaknesses. The main thing is to be aware of these and to show that you understand the limitations of any kind of research – to show that you are *critically aware* (see 'critical awareness' below).

- Or, if it is not a piece of research appearing in a journal, is it, by contrast, someone's opinion? Who is the person? What authority do they have? Do they have any vested interests that may have caused them to give the opinion or advice that they have given?

Your literature review should tell a story – it should not be a list

Your aim is to examine the literature for material that is relevant to your research topic. What have other people done that is relevant to your research question? You don't after all want to be reinventing the wheel. Your search will take you up against some disparate ideas and some interesting information, but your principal aim here isn't simply to make a list of everything that has been written on a topic. Such *summarising* and listing is necessary but is by no means enough. To conduct a good literature review, you also need to *synthesise* and *analyse*.

Summary is not too difficult, and this is perhaps why it tends to dominate student literature reviews. Analysis and synthesis are more difficult ...

When you *analyse*, you see what is going on; you see how one part relates to another; you see the wood for the trees. For example, political journalists don't simply write down everything that is said in Parliament: they analyse how one statement relates to another; they remember what was said last month and note

Your literature review should be a story with a beginning, a middle and an end. It is a synthesis that links ideas and finds differences. It is not a list.

whether it is consistent with this; they look for the vested interests that might be held by those making a statement.

When you *synthesise*, you bring things together, relating one to the other to form something new. When chemists synthesise a new molecule from two existing molecules, they don't simply glue one molecule to the next one. Rather, they put the molecules through some process that creates something entirely new and different, with different qualities from the two original molecules. This is what happens in the best literature reviews: there is an intelligent appraisal of a range of sources that in some way extracts the key messages and accounts for them in the context of an overarching statement or idea.

In the end, your literature review should make sense as a story with a beginning, a middle and an end, with lots of connections between one part and another. You outline the issues at the beginning; you provide the analysis and synthesis in the middle (always linking one bit with another: 'Sikes found more fluff in men's trouser pockets, while Cratchett discovered more in women's. The reasons for this may be found in …'); and you tie it up at the end by summarising the issues, differences, paradoxes, dilemmas and questions yet to be resolved.

Thinking around your question: drawing a storyboard

Now you can draw a storyboard. The aim is to find themes – or, by contrast, discontinuities, breaks, disagreements – that run through the literature: you are looking for a story or stories. When you have done a reasonable amount of searching you will be able to see these emerging and it is useful at this stage to draw a storyboard – a plan that sums up and brings together the ideas that are emerging from your literature review.

Let's look at the storyboard in Figure 3.1. The original question that has been posed is 'How do head teachers cope with difficult people?' This might be the sort of question posed by a head teacher or deputy head teacher undertaking a Master's degree in education. To draw your storyboard you will need to have done some reading already, and it will have helped if you have thought about or brainstormed on this reading.

Think of this process of combining summary, analysis and synthesis as telling a story or a series of stories. A story makes sense: it is not simply a list. A story has a beginning a middle and an end, and you can make your literature review take this structure. Try to build an interest in the area, rather like a novelist does. Start by establishing what the great educator Jerome Bruner (1997: 142) calls the 'trouble' in the story – not literally 'trouble', of course, but rather the issue, question or uncertainty. A good novelist begins a story by capturing the reader's interest with this 'trouble', and this is what you should do when you begin your literature review. You could begin by saying, for example, that although your area of interest is clearly a matter of national concern, researchers have tended not to focus on it, or have focused on an aspect of it that is not relevant to the teacher in the classroom. Or you could establish some 'trouble' by pointing out a major area of controversy, which still exists even after decades of research. You then need the 'middle' of the story – the establishment of what people are actually saying, and how they are disagreeing or agreeing. The end will come with a summing up and a moving on to the reasons for doing your own thesis.

Do authors concentrate on a particular theme? Do they disagree? Are there areas of controversy? Are there surprising areas of agreement or similar findings? Are there gaps that no one seems to be looking at?

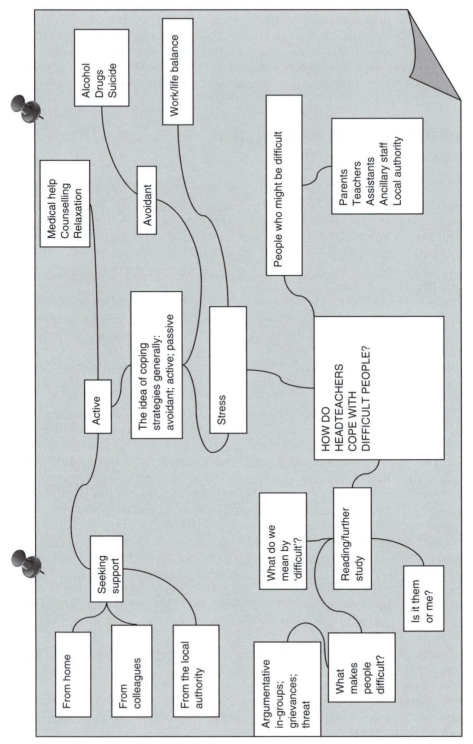

Figure 3.1 Storyboard

Table 3.2 Useful linking words

When there is a difference	When there is agreement	When one idea leads to another
however; but; notwithstanding this; although; yet; conversely; in spite of this; nevertheless; on the other hand; despite; then again	moreover; further; furthermore; additionally; likewise; also; similarly; equally; and; what is more	hence; because of this; thus; as a result; consequently; therefore; accordingly; so; for this reason; this is why

When writing your literature review, try to make links between different areas of work and make those links explicit with the words that you use at the beginning of sentences or paragraphs. For example, if Smith has found something different from Brown, don't simply list one after the other. Instead, show that you recognise the difference in their opinions by simply inserting a 'however', and relating one with the other: 'Smith (2006) found that boys in Year 9 were significantly below the level of girls in reading ability. However, Brown (2007) found no such difference.' Useful linking words are given in Table 3.2.

In Figure 3.2 I give a few paragraphs from the literature review of my own PhD thesis, which was about additional adults in the classroom – people such as classroom assistants and parents. In this particular bit, I was looking at how difficult it seems to be for adults to work together there and was making connections with similar kinds of situations that had occurred earlier, during the 1960s and 1970s, in team teaching. This excerpt is useful, I think, since it shows how different ideas can be linked.

In this excerpt you can see that I was trying to do two things as far as telling a story is concerned. I was trying to *link* the work of the researchers (Geen and Cohen) that I had located, and I did this by using words and phrases such as 'similar' and 'like Geen'. I was also linking the ideas that seemed to be coming through from the literature, ideas that were linked with the kinds of observations I had made myself and which had made this an area I wanted to research. I had noticed that working together in classrooms seemed to be difficult, and here were researchers saying exactly the same, and proffering reasons for the difficulties. So those difficulties were a thread I could pull out of the review. It wasn't simply a question of summarising what was found by the researchers, but rather a question of finding a theme or themes. For me, the theme was about teams being much more difficult to operate in classrooms than anybody seemed to be assuming.

And this is where your own research fits into the review. Would you be aiming to add some weight to one view or another? It is here that

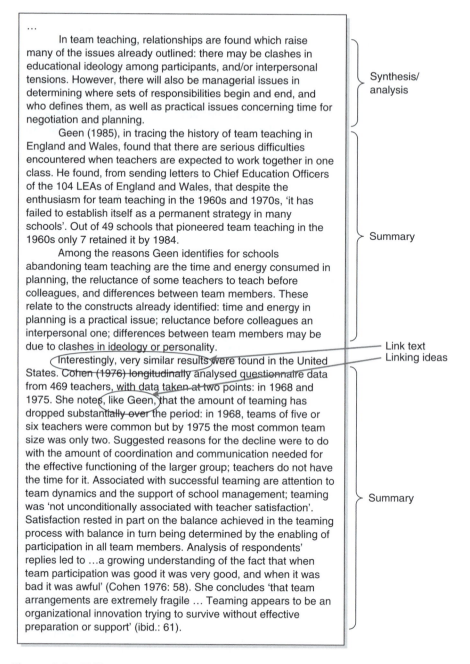

...

In team teaching, relationships are found which raise many of the issues already outlined: there may be clashes in educational ideology among participants, and/or interpersonal tensions. However, there will also be managerial issues in determining where sets of responsibilities begin and end, and who defines them, as well as practical issues concerning time for negotiation and planning.

Geen (1985), in tracing the history of team teaching in England and Wales, found that there are serious difficulties encountered when teachers are expected to work together in one class. He found, from sending letters to Chief Education Officers of the 104 LEAs of England and Wales, that despite the enthusiasm for team teaching in the 1960s and 1970s, 'it has failed to establish itself as a permanent strategy in many schools'. Out of 49 schools that pioneered team teaching in the 1960s only 7 retained it by 1984.

Among the reasons Geen identifies for schools abandoning team teaching are the time and energy consumed in planning, the reluctance of some teachers to teach before colleagues, and differences between team members. These relate to the constructs already identified: time and energy in planning is a practical issue; reluctance before colleagues an interpersonal one; differences between team members may be due to clashes in ideology or personality.

Interestingly, very similar results were found in the United States. Cohen (1976) longitudinally analysed questionnaire data from 469 teachers, with data taken at two points: in 1968 and 1975. She notes, like Geen, that the amount of teaming has dropped substantially over the period: in 1968, teams of five or six teachers were common but by 1975 the most common team size was only two. Suggested reasons for the decline were to do with the amount of coordination and communication needed for the effective functioning of the larger group; teachers do not have the time for it. Associated with successful teaming are attention to team dynamics and the support of school management; teaming was 'not unconditionally associated with teacher satisfaction'. Satisfaction rested in part on the balance achieved in the teaming process with balance in turn being determined by the enabling of participation in all team members. Analysis of respondents' replies led to ...a growing understanding of the fact that when team participation was good it was very good, and when it was bad it was awful' (Cohen 1976: 58). She concludes 'that team arrangements are extremely fragile ... Teaming appears to be an organizational innovation trying to survive without effective preparation or support' (ibid.: 61).

Synthesis/ analysis

Summary

Link text
Linking ideas

Summary

Figure 3.2 Telling a story

your research will be beginning to take shape, since you may now see that original research question you posed in a different light as you start to uncover what other people have already discovered.

Being in a research area is a bit like being told to go into a room in which pieces of a jigsaw puzzle have been scattered around the furniture, with half of the pieces missing: not only do you have to find the pieces you have been given and how they fit together; you also have to under-stand what is missing. Doing the literature review is like being at that first stage; doing your own research is the second – filling in the bits that are missing. In the first stage you have to discover what is already there and how one bit of the puzzle relates (or doesn't relate) to another. But when you embark on a literature review you are not only looking for pieces, you are also seeing how they fit together and interrelate. Does this piece go here, or there? What can we tell from these several pieces that seem to fit together? What do they tell us about the gaps that are in the area that is missing?

You will not find a stock of books and articles that are on the precise subject of your project. You will, however, find literature that is related and you must do what you can to see the relevance of this.

When you are reading, try to develop a skill of speed reading, 'gutting' an article or book for the material that you need. Keep an eye out for key words or phrases and ignore what is irrelevant. You cannot read an academic book in the same way that you read a novel or even a newspaper. Academics write in strange prose that is sometimes meaningful only to the limited group of people who work professionally in that area, and if you spend your time trying to decipher it all you will go mad.

So, as you are speed reading, keep a Word file of notes from your reading. Call it 'My project notes' (or something more imaginative). To this file you can add downloaded material from online copy or from websites. The Internet material is easy to copy by cutting and pasting, so paste straight into your 'My project notes' file. Then create a new folder into which you can put this file. If you don't know how to create a folder … click Start (bottom left of screen), click My Documents, click File, click New, click Folder, then name the folder 'Lucy's project folder' (only if your name is Lucy, obviously), and your folder is made – and it didn't cost you a penny. Now drag 'My project notes' into 'Lucy's project folder'. Now, into this folder you can add all of the files that you download. Your main file in this folder will be 'My project notes' but it will also comprise all of the files of articles and webpages that you have downloaded. It's worth noting that when you download a file from the Internet, it will be directed straight to 'My Documents', so drag all of these downloads from My Documents into 'Lucy's project folder'.

Critical awareness: be your own Jeremy Paxman

Critical awareness is a key phrase that will come up again and again in your university work, and despite the efforts of tutors to instil it in their students, it remains a rare commodity. You will get good marks for having it, and you will be marked down for not demonstrating it.

What, then, is critical awareness? The key thing about study in higher education is your *attitude* to knowledge rather than the *amount* of knowledge that you can show you possess. While at school the key thing seems to be to learn as many facts as possible and then reproduce them in a more or less logical form for an assignment, the attitude at university is rather different. Certainly there may be issues and knowledge with which you will be expected to be familiar, but it is your attitude to such knowledge that is more important: your approach should always be of scepticism – of suspicion and doubt. You will be expected to be aware there will always be different ways of interpreting some observation, different ways of arguing a case, different interests at play in any argument. In short you'll be expected to recognise, and to demonstrate that you recognise, that truth is hard to come by.

Why is this lying bastard lying to me?

You will usually be marked more for your *approach* to facts than for your knowledge of them. You should understand how someone comes to a decision, judgement or conclusion, and understand that there will always be other kinds of decision, judgement or conclusion that could have been drawn from data that have been gathered. As the great biologist J. B. S. Haldane put it, this is really about 'the duty of doubt'. Or as René Descartes (1647/1996) put it: 'Doubt is the origin of wisdom.'

Or as Jeremy Paxman put it, less elegantly though perhaps more straightforwardly, it is 'Why is this lying bastard lying to me?' Actually Jeremy Paxman claims that he never said this. He says of his reported use of this phrase:

> Do I think that everybody you talk to is lying? No I do not. Only a moron would think that. But do I think you should approach any spokesman for a vested interest with a degree of scepticism, asking 'why are they saying this' and 'is it likely to be true'? Yes of course I do. (Wells, 2005)

What Jeremy Paxman says is just about the best way of summing up critical awareness, and it applies not just to politicians and spokespersons. It applies to anyone who reports a finding or expresses an opinion, because everyone reports those findings and expresses those opinions in the context of their own experience. And this experience may be more or less valid, more or less loaded, more or less interested (where 'interested' means 'having a stake in'). You have to put out of your mind the idea that all researchers, indeed all people who write anything anywhere, are fair-minded, neutral observers. There may be any one of a thousand reasons why someone takes a particular slant on a research question, so they will go out and look for data in a particular way or analyse that data in particular ways to suit their purposes and end up with the sort of findings that they expect. They may simply start off with an involvement or personal investment in a particular area, or they may be sponsored by a particular company or government department which may have an interest in a particular finding being made. So, start with Paxman's axiom of 'Why are they saying this?'

Critical awareness, however, is not just about spotting bias or personal involvement of this kind. It is about an awareness that knowledge is frail, not fixed, and that you should approach everything you read and hear with a questioning mind, always asking yourself whether something could have been done differently.

For example, in August 2007 the respected survey research organisation ICM undertook a poll for the *Daily Mail* on the topic of the royal family (ICM, 2007). One of the questions asked: 'As far as you are aware, do you think that Camilla is carrying out too many royal duties, too few royal duties or about the right number?' The responses were: too many 10 per cent; about the right number 55 per cent; too few 12 per cent; refused to answer 1 per cent; don't know 22 per cent. With an uncritical eye, this all looks pretty straightforward: most people thought Camilla was carrying out about the right number of royal duties.

But how could you approach these findings more critically? You might first ask whether the political or commercial interests of the newspaper in question might have had an unspoken effect on the polling organisation. Both newspaper and polling organisation would of course strenuously deny any such connection (their reputation after all rests on their being honest purveyors of the truth) but there is a symbiotic connection between them and neither will want to alienate the other if it can be avoided. The polling organisation will know what kind of response the newspaper wants.

Then look at the categories that people have to fit their opinion into – too many, about right, too few, don't know. What about 'don't care'? Why isn't that there? This is a serious omission: the categories chosen imply that everyone has an opinion on the topic of Camilla's royal duties – even 'don't know' implies that respondents have carefully weighed up the alternatives and have come down on the side of 'insufficient evidence' or abstention.

The reality may be very different. It may be that the substantial proportion of people who are neutral or hostile to Camilla say 'about right' or 'don't know' simply to provide an answer. 'Too many', to a republican or a Camilla-hater, might be seen as too strong an opinion, or it might be taken to imply 'She should have fewer to give her more of a chance to settle into her role – she should be eased in gently'. No person who thinks that the country would be better off without a royal family would have wanted to give this impression, because it might be taken to imply some kind of generous endorsement of Camilla or the royal family.

So, however respectable the source, be questioning, be critical. Also, be tentative about any conclusions that you yourself feel you are able to make: avoid phrases such as 'this proves' and 'this shows' and instead use words such as 'this indicates' or 'the evidence suggests' or 'points towards' or 'implies'. Try to use moderating phrases such as 'tends to' or 'one might conclude that' instead of bolder ones. Academic writing is an area where it pays to be tentative: no one will give you high marks for making unwarranted claims about your own

> Demonstrating critical awareness, critical thinking, reflective thought is as important as anything else in your work. It's about being instinctively sceptical about claims to knowledge and truth.

research, or for gullibly believing the reports of others. Doubt everyone's findings, even your own. Remember again 'The duty of doubt'.

That duty of doubt, of *critical thinking*, has a long and illustrious intellectual tradition. Perhaps the most important philosopher of education of the twentieth century, John Dewey, put it this way:

> Men *thought* the world was flat until Columbus *thought* it to be round. The earlier thought was a belief held because men had not the energy or the courage to question what those about them accepted and taught, especially as it was suggested and seemingly confirmed by obvious sensible facts. The thought of Columbus was a *reasoned conclusion*. It marked the close study into facts, of scrutiny and revision of evidence, of working out the implications of various hypotheses, and of comparing these theoretical results with one another and with known facts. Because Columbus did not accept unhesitatingly the current traditional theory, because he doubted and inquired, he arrived at his thought. Skeptical of what, from long habit, seemed most certain, and credulous of what seemed impossible, he went on thinking until he could produce evidence for both his confidence and his disbelief. Even if his conclusion had finally turned out wrong, it would have been a different sort of belief from those it antagonized, because it was reached by a different method. *Active, persistent, and careful consideration of any belief or supposed form of knowledge in the light of the grounds that support it, and the further conclusions to which it tends*, constitutes reflective thought. (Dewey, 1920/2004: 6, original emphasis)

Click 'Search': finding information

Finding information is one of the areas that has changed most dramatically over the past few years. Before the mid-1990s, researchers had to rely on printed articles in paper journals and on abstracts and indices catalogued on paper, microfiches and cards. They had to go to the library to find these resources. Then at the end of the 1990s came the widespread use of the Internet, and researchers came to depend on big library databases using keywords to search them.

But then came Google. I'll say this very quietly so not too many of my colleagues hear (and I'm hoping you won't tell them) but when I am doing my own research I rarely use any other means of starting my searches. There is no point being snobby about Google. It works. Not only does it work but it works better than all of the posh library databases. Somehow (and it remains a total mystery to me how it does it) it seems to know what I am thinking and what I am wanting. It is free, reliable and quick. Not only is there Google, but there are also Google Scholar and Google Books. If you don't already know how they work, here's how …

Google

Unless you have been on Mars for the last ten years you will know how to use Google. Just a few hints:

- Type in as much or as little as you wish into Google's search box. For example, if you are interested in whether the Head Start programme produces beneficial consequences for primary school children, you could either type in the whole sentence (that is to say, just like this: *Does the Head Start programme produce beneficial consequences for primary school children?*) and click 'Search' or you can pick out the key words (*primary Head Start benefits*). Try it different ways and see what emerges.

> **Accessing material from home**
>
> You need access to a computer and the Internet to use resources such as this, and if you don't have them you will have to rely on your university or college computer terminals. It is much better to have your own though, so that you can work at home at odd times.
>
> If you use your computer from home you'll probably have restricted access to the range of facilities that your university library provides. There are clever ways around this if you want to be bothered with them. Ask your librarian about setting up a 'proxy service' on your home computer, which in effect makes your home computer browser into a monitor for your university system.

- Google searches for the words in your search in any order; it doesn't keep the words you type in as phrases. If you want to keep the words in the same order – as phrases – then put them in double quotation marks. So, for example if you wanted Google to search for the phrase 'Head Start' among the other words, you would type in *primary "Head Start" benefits*. It will then search just for the phrase 'head start' leaving out all other occurrences of 'head' and 'start'.
- If you want to search for something and you want the search to become narrower, so that it leaves out references to certain subjects or areas, you can put in a minus sign before a word or term that you wish to omit. So, if I wanted to find out about primary Head Start benefits, but I wanted only to look at children above reception age, I could type in *primary "Head Start" benefits – reception*. It's good to practise with many different ways of phrasing a Google query.

Athens

Some of the sources that you access on using Google will be journal articles. You will emerge with a publisher's journal page which provides an abstract and an invitation to buy a full download of the article. Don't be tempted to buy it, because you will probably have access to the journal through your university library and something called 'Athens'. If, on your introductory tour of the library you haven't been told about Athens, go along to one of the librarians and ask to be introduced to it. Don't be frightened to do this: in an information age this is what librarians are expected to do – to help you gain access to all kinds of information sources. It's what they get paid for. Remind them of this (that's a joke). Actually most librarians I know don't conform to the frosty stereotype at all; they are friendly and helpful. And Athens is easy to use: just be prepared to invest an hour or two playing with it and seeing what it can do for you.

You will be given a username and a password for Athens. Usually this is from your library or e-library access. Once you have entered your username and password details you will have access to an array of databases that carry the journal. Figure 3.3 shows the sort of page that emerges when you have done this. Figure 3.3 is from my own university library, and yours will be similar.

Type in the name of the journal that came up from your Google inquiry and press 'Go' (or whatever in your library's system) and you will come up with a page like the one in Figure 3.4. My library's system here gives you information about which databases hold access to the journal, and when I press 'Find It!' at the bottom of the page it gives me

Figure 3.3

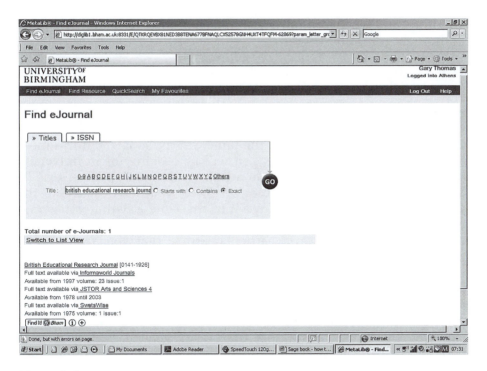

Figure 3.4

the choice of locating the article I want in one of several databases. It doesn't matter which one you use, but just check that the particular database (such as SwetsWise, which is the one I prefer) carries the journal for the year that you want.

If I now request the article I want from SwetsWise, the SwetsWise page asks me to log in via Athens at the top right of the page.

I can hear you saying, 'But shouldn't I already be in Athens?' Well, the answer of course is yes, but that would be too easy! It would be too easy to take you into Athens immediately you are in the e-library, silly! Maybe libraries and publishers will eventually get round to making their inquiry systems easier and producing something which is as easy to use as Google, but sadly it hasn't happened yet. In fact, because of these charming idiosyncrasies in 'information systems' you may have to devote a day to going to the library to familiarise yourself with these systems and asking a librarian to help you if you get stuck.

Because every university system is different, giving you more exact information from this point on in the process will not be of much use to you. So the next step is to make that library visit. Before you start asking librarians lists of questions, though, ask for the library's various leaflets and sheets on electronic access and try to make sense of them. Play around for a while on the computer and find what you can and can't do – what you can and can't access. Make a list of your

questions and when you have done this go to the librarian with a list
of more targeted questions.

Google Scholar

Google Scholar works in much the same way as Google, but it is more
targeted at the kinds of things you will be looking for in university
life. You can access it either from a link on the main page of Google
or from http://scholar.google.com/. Once you have accessed the
Google Scholar main page you use it in the same way that you would
have used Google. That is to say, you can type in a question or a more
targeted inquiry based on a particular article that you have already
identified.

For example, try typing in the same question that I used above for testing Google: *Does the Head Start programme produce beneficial consequences
for primary school children?*. When you do this and click on 'Search' you
will get many thousands of responses, as you do on ordinary Google.
However, these responses, rather than being general, will only be to
books and articles. The 'best' ones will usually be at the beginning, but
you will also find good ones lower down (though they will become pro-
gressively less relevant as you proceed downwards).

Figure 3.5 shows the first 'answer' I got when I typed that question
into Google Scholar. The figure shows the various elements of the
Google Scholar 'answer' page. As with all forms of electronic resource,
the key is to keep playing with it: click on links to see what happens.

Google Book Search

As if Google Scholar weren't miraculous enough, there is also Google
Book Search, which will find relevant books, point you to the page(s)
relevant to your search inquiry, and even show you the page(s) themselves. Type http://books.google.com into the address line and you
will arrive at the familiar Google front page, but orientated to a book
search.

Typing a general inquiry is less likely to be successful with the book
search than with a general Google search, so when I type *Does the Head
Start programme produce beneficial consequences for primary school children?*
as I did with Google and Google Scholar, it comes up with a dead end.
So I have to open up the search by using fewer words. Remember that
when you are asking Google just to look for books it is searching a far
narrower range of resources, so keep your options open by reducing the
number of words in your search.

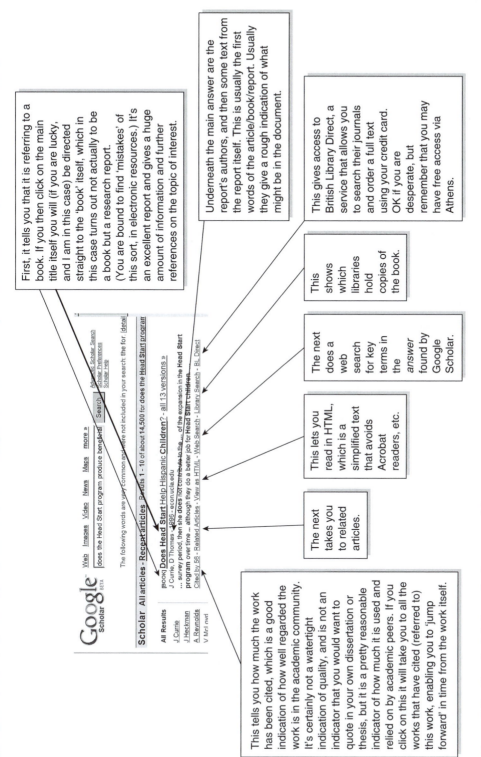

First, it tells you that it is referring to a book. If you then click on the main title itself you will (if you are lucky, and I am in this case) be directed straight to the 'book' itself, which in this case turns out not actually to be a book but a research report. (You are bound to find 'mistakes' of this sort, in electronic resources.) It's an excellent report and gives a huge amount of information and further references on the topic of interest.

Underneath the main answer are the report's authors, and then some text from the report itself. This is usually the first words of the article/book/report. Usually they give a rough indication of what might be in the document.

This gives access to British Library Direct, a service that allows you to search their journals and order a full text using your credit card. OK if you are desperate, but remember that you may have free access via Athens.

This shows which libraries hold copies of the book.

The next does a web search for key terms in the *answer* found by Google Scholar.

This lets you read in HTML, which is a simplified text that avoids Acrobat readers, etc.

The next takes you to related articles.

This tells you how much the work has been cited, which is a good indication of how well regarded the work is in the academic community. It's certainly not a watertight indication of quality, and is not an indicator that you would want to quote in your own dissertation or thesis, but it is a pretty reasonable indicator of how much it is used and relied on by academic peers. If you click on this it will take you to all the works that have cited (referred to) this work, enabling you to 'jump forward' in time from the work itself.

Figure 3.5 Google Scholar – the important bits

The Web of Knowledge

Your library should give you access to the Web of Knowledge (also called the Web of Science). Type http://portal.isiknowledge.com/ portal.cgi. At the homepage click

> **Citation:** A reference to a particular piece of work, usually by using the Harvard system (e.g. 'Smith, 2002').

'Social Sciences Citation Index' and follow the instructions on what to do. You can search by topic or author or a range of other criteria. I've given this only one 'thumbs up' since I find it clunky to use: it will obstinately refuse to find things where I know I have put the details in correctly. However, for those who are snobby about Google (and they are fortunately getting fewer in number) Web of Science provides the gold standard on citation information.

Zetoc

Your university library will provide a way for you to use to Zetoc, which gives access to the British Library's 20,000 journals and 16,000 conference proceedings published every year. Type http://zetoc.mimas.ac.uk/. Zetoc is particularly useful as it includes an email alerting service to help you to keep up-to-date with relevant new articles and papers – in other words, Zetoc will automatically send you an email when a new article appears that 'hits the button' as far as certain criteria that you specify are concerned. You could, for example, tell it to send you all articles by a certain author, or all articles with certain keywords in the title, or all articles in each new issue of a certain journal.

Zetoc will give you:

- a *search* facility, for citations of journal articles and conference proceedings – a bit like Google Scholar;
- the *alert* facility, to give you email alerts of new articles that may be of interest to you;
- *facilitated access* to full texts of articles and papers – Zetoc itself provides access to the table of contents rather than the full text. However, once you have found an article of interest, the full record page provides links to help you access the full text;
- *feeds* (also called RSS feeds – RSS stands for Really Simple Syndication), which help you to keep automatically up to date with what is happening in a journal. A feed is frequently updated content published by a website. Click 'Zetoc RSS' in Zetoc, and then click the feed you want to see. In the example in Figure 3.6 I've clicked on the feed for the *American Educational Research Journal*. When you subscribe to the feed, it will be

> **AMERICAN EDUCATIONAL RESEARCH JOURNAL - Windows Internet Explorer**
>
> http://zetoc.mimas.ac.uk/cgi-bin/rss?x=bX8AzI9E/JqjtPeX51isfQ39mrNwAHLKJTrzJdqoMI-UcPfF3Wr50/-brDBLcBc3S0qL5D!
>
> File   Edit   View   Favorites   Tools   Help
>
> Zetoc: Homepage   AMERICAN EDUCATIONA...
>
> **AMERICAN EDUCATIONAL RESEARCH JOURNAL**
>
> **You are viewing a feed that contains frequently updated content.** When you subscribe to a feed, it is added to the Common Feed List. Updated information from the feed is automatically downloaded to your computer and can be viewed in Internet Explorer and other programs. Learn more about feeds.
>
> Subscribe to this feed
>
> Displ
>
> ● All
>
> Sort
>
> ▾ Dat
>   Titl
>   Au
>
> **Editorial Team's Introduction: Special Issue on No Child Left Behind**
>
> 18 September 2007, 01:00:00 | Hollingsworth, S.
>
> Hollingsworth, S.; Gallego, M. A.; Clandinin, D. J.; Morrell, P.; Portes, P.; Rueda, R.; Welch, O.;
> AMERICAN EDUCATIONAL RESEARCH JOURNAL VOL 44; NUMB 3 No Child Left Behind pp. 454-459
>
> **Hidden Benefits and Unintended Consequences of No Child Left Behind Policies for Students Who Are Deaf or Hard of Hearing**
>
> 18 September 2007, 01:00:00 | Cawthon, S. W.

Figure 3.6   Example of a feed

added to your 'Favorites Center' in Internet Explorer (yellow star at top left of screen), which will automatically check the website and download new content so you can see what is new since you last visited the feed.

Amazon

The Amazon website is a useful resource for seeking out related information about books (but not articles). Type www.amazon.co.uk (or www.amazon.com for the US version). It's not as good as Google Book Search but it does have some useful features such as 'Search Inside!'™ which allows you to look at the contents pages and to read the first chapter, the index and some other information about the book. Also, it gives you information about what other customers who have bought this book have also bought – surprisingly useful, since many will, inexplicably, seem to be on much the same train of thought as you. There will also be a publisher's synopsis of the book and if you are lucky some reasonably informative reviews (but often also some spectacularly uninformative ones). Clearly, this is not data disinterestedly given by Amazon out of the love of knowledge – they want to sell you books, so be wary.

Something that the Amazon website is particularly useful for is when you are compiling your reference list. Unless you are absolutely perfect, you will have lost certain references, or you will have somehow missed off a key bit of the reference when making your notes. The Amazon website has co-authors, the publisher, the date of publication and dates of various editions, and this is often all you need to enable you to plug the holes.

Inter-library loan

I've been at pains to point out that you should be very wary about clicking on any link that asks you to part with money for a download of the article. This is partly because there is a very good chance that you will be able to access the article or book completely free through your university Athens account. Or you will be able to see enough of it to gain a sufficient impression of what it is about. If the worse comes to the worst and you decide that you simply must have a copy of the article and you are not able to access it by one of the means already explained here you can get the article via inter-library loan, either electronically or as a photocopy. Ask your librarian about this. There will probably be a charge, but it won't be as much as it would be from a publisher's website.

Hints on searching – separating the wheat from the chaff

Two common problems students come up with on doing a literature review are (1) that they can find no information, and (2) that there is just too much information.

Let's look at the first one: you can find absolutely no information at all on your topic of interest. The thing is, it is most unlikely to be the case in reality that there is no information to find on your topic, so if you are finding nothing on your various searches you should examine where you may be going wrong. It may be the case that you are not using enough search facilities, or, more likely, that you are making your search too narrow. You are pinpointing your search terms too finely, or throwing away related information that is not on the precise subject of your interest, but is connected and therefore useful. Remember that your literature review ultimately will not be on the exact topic of your research, but rather it will be on the more general subject *surrounding* your research. So, if you wanted to look, for example, at how head teachers cope with difficult people and you are coming up with nothing, it may be that you are searching too specifically. Your searches may need to concentrate on something broader, such as teacher stress, and you may wish to think about what 'difficult people' means. This will in turn suggest that

> Think like a search engine. Find alternative ways of formulating ideas connected to your research question.

Figure 3.7 Turning your question into alternative search terms

you think about the 'people' with whom head teachers come into contact: there are the other teachers in the school, other head teachers in the area, parents, pupils, teaching assistants, administrators, support staff, etc. Were you thinking of all of these when you posed your question, or just certain categories? So, think about the broader ways that your question may be framed. Think about alternative search terms.

You'll see in Figure 3.7 that the original question about how head teachers cope with difficult people has been reformulated into a range of terms that you might not have thought of originally, and you might, for example, ask why 'drugs' and 'suicide' are included as alternatives to 'coping'. The key is to try to think like a search engine. The search engine is sorting through words and phrases in an unimaginably large set of websites, a tiny fraction of which will contain, in some sense or other, 'stories' about head teachers and difficult people. But these 'stories' are hardly likely to be framed in these exact terms. They are more likely to contain words that are associated with the words you have identified. What are difficult people likely to do to a head teacher? To cause stress. What does stress lead to? Possibly drinking excess alcohol, taking drugs or even suicide. These may not be the coping strategies you were thinking of, but they will lead into stories that address the topic, perhaps comparing these routes out of stress with more positive ones. So the key is, if you don't at first succeed, try thinking like the search engine and formulating your question in a number of different ways using a range of related words.

And remember that your literature review is a general contextualisation. So stress in *teachers* as a *general* group is likely to be of relevance when you are thinking about stress in *head* teachers. Don't limit your search by a very precise word when you may find some very interesting information that relates to broader issues.

Now the second one: you are swamped with information on the topic. Suppose you are interested in the attainment of black boys and you enter *black boys attainment*. The search emerges with three quarters of a million 'answers'. If you now put in a term that is related to your interests – say *14–19* – it will reduce the number dramatically. Or you can put in a name of a key academic or a key commentator to delimit the search. Ask your tutor for key names. For example, if I put in the name of someone who I know is an expert here – *"Gus John"* – (in double quote marks because I want Google to find *only* references to Gus John, not to all the Johns and all the Guses in the world), it reduces the three quarters of a million to 155.

So, the key is to imagine that in your literature review the process is like sieving: with too coarse a mesh you let through too much; with too fine a mesh you don't get enough. Or imagine that you are trying to separate the wheat from the chaff. If you blow too hard you get rid of the wheat as well as the chaff. If you don't blow hard enough you don't get rid of the chaff.

Understanding how sources are cited: the Harvard referencing system

You need to understand the Harvard referencing system for two reasons. First, when you are reading, you need to understand the way that sources are referenced by authors in books and journal articles. Second, when you are writing, you need to know how to provide references yourself when you write up your literature review – in other words, how to give the full details of where others can find the work when you refer to a book or article. There are various ways in which referencing can be done, but the overwhelmingly preferred method in the social sciences is the Harvard system.

This is how it works. You find a source – let's say an article written by Jane Brown. If you then want to refer to the article you do so by using the author's surname, followed by the year of the publication in brackets – for example, by saying 'In a large study, Brown (2004) discovered that little bits of fluff accumulate in people's pockets.' You will then give the full details of Brown's publication in a list headed 'References' at the end of your report (not 'Bibliography', incidentally, which has the meaning of 'here are some interesting books that are related to my thesis' – by contrast, 'References' applies only to the works you have actually referred to in your text). We'll come on to how to compile the list in a moment, but first let's look at how you make reference to various kinds of sources in the text, since these will take a variety of forms.

How you make reference *in the text*:

- For a single author of a book or a journal article, use the author's name followed by the date of the publication in brackets, e.g. '... Sweedlepipe (2005) found that the fluff referred to by Brown (2004) is composed mainly of cotton fibre and dead skin ...'

- Where a work is by two authors, use both authors' names followed by the date in brackets: '... Sweedlepipe and Sikes (2007), in later work, showed that the ratio of cotton fibre to dead skin (by weight) is between 3:1 and 5:1 ...'
- For more authors, use the first author's name, followed just by et al. (et al. means 'and others'), e.g. '... Sweedlepipe et al. (2008) illustrated the mechanism by which cotton fibre bonds to dead skin ...'
- If you actually quote from the author, you must give the page number from which the quotation comes, with the page number given after a colon after the publication date: 'Sweedlepipe (2005: 134) sums up the importance of the topic this way: "The precise mechanism involved in the accumulation of fluff in the pockets is one of the greatest mysteries remaining for science to solve".'
- In the unlikely case of an author having two outputs in 2005 that you are referencing in the text, this is indicated by 'a', 'b', 'c', etc. after the date: 'Sikes (2005a) found that trouser pockets of male students contained significantly more fluff than those of female students, and in later work (2005b) hypothesised that lower amounts of fluff in female pockets were due to a higher frequency of personal hygiene measures (principally by washing and clothes laundering) among in the latter.'
- A book that has been republished long after the original publication may be cited with the author's name as usual, but followed by both the first publication and republication dates, e.g. Ryle (1949/1990).

And this is how you go on to reference the material *in the reference section* at the end of your thesis:

For a book:

Name(s) and initial(s) of author(s) followed by year in brackets, followed by book title in italics, followed by place of publication and publisher. For example ...

Sweedlepipe, P. (2005) *The Fluff in People's Pockets*. London: Sage.

For a journal article:

Name and initial(s) of author(s) followed by year in brackets, followed by article title, followed by name of journal in italics, followed by volume number, issue number and page numbers. For example ...

Sweedlepipe, P. and Sikes, B. (2007) Ratios of cotton fibres to exfoliated skin in trouser pockets of US males. *International Journal of Fluff and Allied Detritus*, 31, 1, 252–7.

For a downloadable Internet source:

Name and initial(s) of author(s) followed by year in brackets, followed by article title, followed by the words 'Available at' and the Internet source, followed by the date you accessed it. For example ...

Wells, M. (2005) Paxman answers the questions. *Guardian Unlimited.*
   Available at http://politics.guardian.co.uk/media/story/0,12123,140232
   4,00.html. Accessed 26 August 2007.

Formatting the reference list:

It looks good if each reference has a hanging indent – in other words,
the first line is formatted to the left, as normal, and the subsequent
lines are indented. You can produce the hanging indent in Word by
putting the cursor anywhere in the reference and pressing 'Ctrl T'. Or
do the whole lot together by selecting all the references (with your
mouse, left click at the beginning and drag down to the end) and then
pressing 'Ctrl T'.

   The list should be in alphabetical order. To alphabetise a list automatically in Word, select the whole list with your mouse, then click on
'Table', then click on 'Sort', and click 'OK'. The list will miraculously
appear in order. (If it doesn't, the settings on your copy of Word may
have been changed and you will need to look at the particular instructions under 'Sort' more carefully.)

   There are now several software systems for organising your references
automatically, such as EndNote, Reference Manager and RefWorks, and
your library will almost certainly offer support in using these through
leaflets, courses and email query and will provide a weblink on this and
related issues. My own library's (open to everybody), which also offers
detailed advice on the use of the Harvard method, is at www.i-cite.
bham.ac.uk/.

Taking notes and quotes

There used to be a time when people had to take careful notes of every
source they consulted on small cards that would be filed alphabetically.
(For people like me, who suffer from a mild variant of Asperger's syndrome, this was enormously satisfying.) Researchers had to be meticu-
lous about everything that they did, punctiliously keeping records of
references – because if you lost one or forgot to record it, it would take
hours or even days to track it down again. Things aren't like that any
more: you can now find a lost reference on the Internet in seconds. And
note-taking is different too: you can now be a lot more creative and
idiosyncratic in the way that you keep notes on your word processor.
The problem with the old card index file systems was that they almost
encouraged you to think of the literature review as a collection of
names and notes. Now, though, if you take notes more fluidly – as I suggest in the next section – you can add observations, make connections
and link one source with another through the notes that you take as
you are reading.

A notes file in Word

The software packages I have just mentioned (EndNote, etc.) seem to work for some people. However, I find a simpler system is just to paste everything that would conceivably be of interest into a Word file which I can then search for the keywords that I want. When I say 'keywords' I don't mean anything very technical. I just mean that I use Word's search facility to look for a word or part of a word that will find the topic I am looking for. So, for example, if I were interested in finding anything mentioning *science* or *scientists* I would ask the programme to find 'scie'. You can see in the box what this search locates in this small sample of my notes.

You can, of course, make your note-keeping file more sophisticated by adding specific keywords to each entry. I might, for example, have added the word 'theory' to the Schön reference.

So, as I am reading I copy quotations (and, importantly, the references from which they come) willy nilly into the file, as indicated in the excerpt from my own (considerably tidied)

Schön, D.A. (1991) *The Reflective Practitioner: How Professionals Think in Action*. Aldershot: Avebury.
When someone does something … 'He does not separate thinking from doing, ratiocinating his way to a decision which he must later convert to action.' (Schön, 1991: 68)

Wright Mills, C. (1970) *The Sociological Imagination*. London: Pelican.
Wright Mills (1970) quotes a number of Nobel-Prize-winning physicists on the nature of 'scientific method'; Bridgman, for example, says that 'There is no scientific method as such, but the vital feature of the scientist's procedure has been merely to do his utmost with his mind, *no holds barred*' [original emphasis]. (Wright Mills, 1970: 69)

Harré, R (1998) *The Singular Self*. London: Sage.
'Muddles are endemic in psychology largely because of the urge to find occurrent psychological properties of persons to explain what they think and do. But there are none.' (p. 16)

Foucault, M. (1989) *Résumé des Cours, 1970–1982* (pp. 13–14). Paris: Juillard.
'Knowledge … is produced not as a result of the harmony or happy equilibrium of these elements, but rather as the result of their antagonism, of their dubious and provisional compromise, of a fragile truce that they are always prepared to betray. Knowledge is not a permanent faculty, it is an event, or perhaps a series of events.'

Illich, I. (1979) *Deschooling Society*. London: Pelican Books.
'Some words become so flexible that they cease to be useful … Like an amoeba they fit into almost any interstice of the language.' (Illich, 1979: 32)

Crews, F. (1997) *The Memory Wars: Freud's Legacy in Dispute*. London: Granta.
'Algorithms for making something happen with maximum complication … [the] theory is a display of ingenuity unencumbered by recalcitrant data.' (p. 12)

Friedrich Nietzsche, *Die Fröhliche Wissenschaft*, Bk IV.
'Believe me! The secret of reaping the greatest fruitfulness and the greatest enjoyment from life is to live dangerously!'

Ignatieff, M. (1998) *Isaiah Berlin: A Life*. London: Chatto & Windus.
'In a dark century he [Isaiah Berlin] showed what a life of the mind should be: sceptical, ironical, dispassionate and free.' (p. 301)

Oscar Wilde: *The Portrait of Dorian Gray*. (2) (In relation to Ryle.)
'It is only shallow people who do not judge by appearances.'

Andreski, S. (1972) *Social Sciences as Sorcery*. London: André Deutsch.
'…an excessive preoccupation with methodology provides an alibi for timorous quietism.' (p. 116)

Box 3.1

reference file in the box. I always make a point of recording the reference as exactly as possible, and then the notes as I see fit at the time. I make it clear with the use of quotation marks which are my own words and which are the author's. This may not have the satisfying tidiness of the old card index, but the question arises how far that alphabetical imperative is still necessary. When you can now simply find what you need to find in a file such as the one in the box, why does it need to be in alphabetical order? You simply need to type a search word or phrase into the 'Find' box and the machine will do the rest. When you can easily fillet and sort a list alphabetically (see p. 56), why bother putting them in alphabetical order at the outset?

Many of the notes I take are copied directly from the Internet through using cut-and-paste. Cut-and-paste is particularly useful in copying reference details. However, you should always be very clear in your recording which are the author's words and which are your own. Under copyright law you are permitted to copy around 400 words from an author *as long as you make full and clear attribution to the author in question.*

Occasionally students are tempted to try to pass off the work and the words of others as their own. Your university will almost certainly have a policy on plagiarism, how it is defined, why you should not do it, how you can avoid it and the penalties for doing it. My own university defines plagiarism as:

> ... the submission for formal assessment of an assignment that incorporates, without proper citation or acknowledgement by means of an accepted referencing standard, the intellectual property or work of a third party.

Its policy, which is fairly typical of all, is given at www.as.bham.ac.uk/study/support/sca/plagiarism.shtml.

Having had the sense to read my book, you are not of course the sort of person who plagiarises. However, just speaking generally for a moment, plagiarism is a pity for a number of reasons. First, it is against the spirit of the thing: the aim is to learn, develop and improve – not just to get a certificate. So why pretend? Second, there is a real risk of being caught, and the likelihood of being found out is increasing as plagiarism software improves, and the penalties at any university are serious for those who are found plagiarising. Third, there is no penalty for drawing from others or using their ideas and words, as long as these are acknowledged. In fact, your marker will be pleased to see evidence of wide reading and the intelligent synthesis of this.

Although I have said that a marker will be pleased to see evidence of wide reading in quotations, you should avoid overdoing quotations. Generally, one short quotation per page would be the maximum I would want to see, with perhaps the occasional extended quotation. The aim in a literature review is to outline and demonstrate interconnections, not to present a list of other people's verbatim words. The key is analysis and synthesis, and quotations do not really play a role in either, unless with it you are providing an excellent illustration of a point that an authority is making.

Overview

Your literature review is not an add-on: it should be a major contributor to the development of your project. It should help you to shape your questions by enabling you to find out what has already been done. The literature exists in many shapes and forms and you should be discriminating in what you choose to include – even seemingly unimpeachable sources can be wrong. This is where critical awareness begins: show that you understand that there is always room for interpretation in the reading of any piece of work. Interpret and understand what others have done, and weave their contributions into a narrative. The literature review should be a narrative – a story – not a list.

Further Reading

Fink, A. (2005) *Conducting research literature reviews: from the internet to paper*. London: SAGE.
Systematic, with good examples on searching in health, education and business domains. Not just the process, but also good on evaluating the articles you select to review.

Ridley, D. (2008) *The literature review: a step-by-step guide for students*. London: SAGE.

Campbell Collaboration http://www.campbellcollaboration.org/ contains systematic reviews in education, crime and justice, and social welfare. Useful not just for the analysis and synthesis of studies, but also for examples of the way that evidence is balanced.

The Cochrane Collaboration http://www.cochrane.org/. This is a library of systematic reviews in healthcare.

The EPPI-Centre (i.e. The Evidence for Policy and Practice Information and Co-ordinating Centre) at http://eppi.ioe.ac.uk/cms/ is similar to Campbell, but tends to focus more on education.

4

Decide on Your Question – Again

	Introduction
	Literature review
You are here in your project →	**Methodology**
	Fieldwork and findings
	Analysis and discussion
	Conclusion

The literature review will have helped you to sharpen your research question. Your refined question enables you to proceed confidently. This chapter considers:

- how, in the light of your literature search in Chapter 3, does your question from Chapter 1 look now?
  - Have you in fact found out that many other people have already done what you were planning to do?
  - Is the question more complicated than you had thought?
  - Will you be able to get hold of the information you need?
- refining your original questions and ideas, making sure that the new, refined questions are not too broad, not too difficult, in the context of your literature search;
- moving from your storyboard to a more definite storyline – this will form the clear plan for your research;
- thinking about how you will develop theory.

Seeing the wood for the trees

When you came up with your first question after Chapter 1, it was from an idea in your head. It probably won't have been informed by much more than a feeling or an observation, or perhaps by a spark of inspiration that came from a lecture or an article in a newspaper. Because this was a question that came from this sort of 'top of the head' idea it is sometimes called a prima facie question, as I discussed in Chapter 1. It's now time to transform this prima facie question to a more refined, targeted question – a better question or set of questions.

The literature review will have given you avenues to follow, pockets of similar ideas from different authors or clashing ideas from others. If you have done it right you may be feeling at the end of your literature review more confused than you were when you started out, because you will have uncovered lots of new information and will have been set running on many new leads. Don't despair: this is normal. In fact, it *should* happen. These disparate ideas will form the basis both for a reorganisation of your literature review, for new ideas about how the project can proceed and for a reworking of your question.

You have to remember that the literature review is not simply a justification for your question. It is much more than this. It is a way of helping you to see your question from a distance – seeing the wood for the trees – and shaping it to something more meaningful. *Without* it, it's as if you are wearing blinkers, and walking straight down the first road you see. *With* the literature review, you can say, 'Shall I go this way or that way?'

So now you should be prepared to change your first question. Now that you have found what others have done you will very probably see your research question in a quite different light. I've mentioned that your literature review will give you a lot of information that will start you off on different lines of thinking. But there are also other reasons for rethinking your question: you may find out, for example, that someone has already done what you wanted to do – they have found the answer already. You may find that the research that has been undertaken in a certain area surrounds a particular controversy, and you may feel that you want to contribute to one aspect or another of the debate, rather than pursuing your original question. You may discover a particular gap in the literature that you feel needs filling. You will have got a feel of the area, where the most important lines of inquiry are and which are most interesting to you.

Perhaps even more importantly, the literature review will enable you to highlight areas that are irrelevant or too difficult to research ethically or in terms of getting access to relevant information. Remember one of the issues you had to face at the outset: 'Is it doable?'

So the first thing to do in reviewing your literature review is to go back to your storyboard (Figure 3.1). Let's think about that now.

> Your literature review has allowed you to refine your initial questions. Now, they can be sharper. Ask yourself what your purposes are.

From storyboard to storyline

The first thing that your storyboard will have done is to show you how broad the initial question could be. It will have shown you the directions that your research could take. More importantly, it will show you which of these directions you can now eliminate for any of a variety of reasons.

Figure 4.1 shows the redrawn storyboard shown in Figure 3.1 You'll see that I have taken out most of the brainstorming ideas from the bottom of the original storyboard and I have focused on the ideas from the top of the storyboard which related to the idea of stress. So the original question, namely 'How do head teachers cope with difficult people?', is already becoming more focused. Stress seems to be a key idea, and in examining it I will have looked at how stress is dealt with by people and the coping strategies that they adopt to manage it. In doing this I will have examined the concept of coping strategies generally, and I will have considered that psychologists claim that there are avoidant, active and passive coping strategies. All of this will have been discussed in my literature review.

On the basis of this literature review I now know a lot more about difficult people, what they are assumed to be, how they are defined by the individual who finds them difficult and what that individual does about dealing with them. Does that individual avoid the problem and turn to drink (the top right-hand side of the storyboard)? Or do they do something constructive and seek support (the top left-hand side)? And if they seek support, where do they get the support from?

Here we have the bones of a much more *targeted* project. From a fairly unspecific question about head teachers and difficult people we have something that travels along a clearly defined path. You have begun to get a more precise question about difficult people and how they may be described and defined, and you have the beginnings of a thesis about the connection of 'difficulty' with stress, and coping strategies around this. You understand that the coping strategies can be of various kinds.

The original topic has, then, developed many branches and you will have explored many of these in the literature review. The first thing you need to do now is to ask yourself which you want to pursue. This will be determined principally by your interest. You may not be attracted by certain lines of inquiry because they lead you along avenues that have no interest for you. On the storyboard it may be the case that you have no interest in the connections that head teachers have with the local authority. If, like me, you begin to feel yourself nodding off at the mere mention of local authorities then this is probably not a good line to pursue. It helps to be interested in the subject that you are researching.

Now you can also be asking yourself questions about 'doability'. If you have been led in your thinking toward the issue of coping strategies, will you actually be able to get information from head teachers about some of the avoidance phenomena that are flagged up in the storyboard? For instance, are head teachers likely to tell you honestly that they have turned to drink? The short answer is 'no', unless you are in a very particular position – perhaps as a head teacher yourself with the kinds of relationships with colleagues that would enable you to ask them about this kind of thing. And even if that is the case there are important ethical issues that you would have to consider in asking colleagues about this. How confident, for example, could you be that anyone reading your project would not be able to identify the heads you have interviewed,

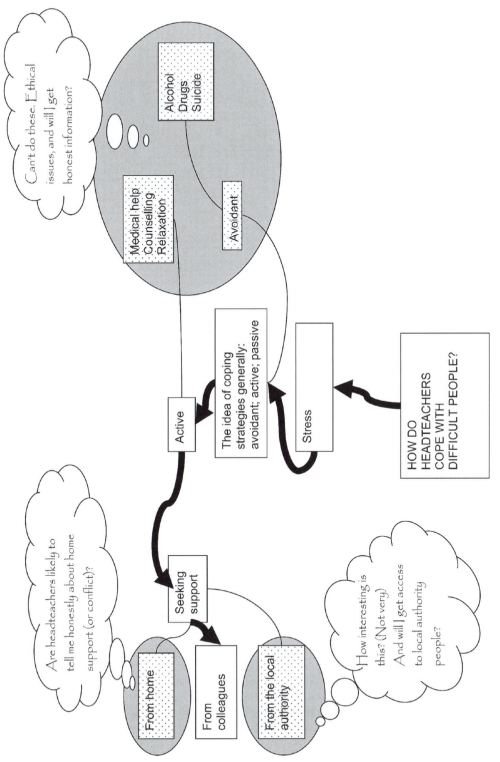

Figure 4.1 Storyboard from Figure 3.1 redrawn

even if you took great pains to make any write-up completely anony-mous? A reader who knows you may well know those colleagues with whom you have a close enough relationship to discuss this and will be able to put two and two together about their identity. So your expecta-tions about anonymity will not have been met.

You might also reject certain lines of inquiry because of the difficulties of getting access to the information that you want. It may be, for exam-ple, that you wish to do some observation in the heads' schools or to interview some of their teachers. This will be difficult to arrange without some prior connection with the schools in question. Allowing access of this kind will entail the staff in a great deal more work than normal and you may hit a brick wall in your attempts to set it up.

There are issues here then both about *access* to information (or data) and the *ethics* of collecting it. We will look at these in more detail later in the book.

So, unless you are absolutely sure that you have ways round these problems, you can remove them as potential avenues for you to follow in your project.

Having eliminated all the lines of inquiry that are either uninteresting to you or impossible to pursue, you can now draw your story line. In Figure 4.1 this is shown by the heavy arrowed line.

So the summarised storyline in Figure 4.1 now starts with the ques-tion about difficult people, the stress they cause, how people cope with stress as a general rule and the part played by colleagues in help-ing to deal with that stress. I've noted that having done the literature review you'll find that you have been set off on particular paths and the main one here is about stress. While 'difficult people' was the original spark of interest, the literature review revealed that 'difficult people' are difficult to define. Someone who is 'difficult' to me may be a charming eccentric to you, and someone who is 'difficult' to you may be a pussycat to me. You will have explored this as you have done more thinking and as you have read around the subject. The group of 'notes' at the middle-left of the storyboard in Figure 3.1 summarises a range of questions that you will have explored: 'What do we mean by difficult?', 'What makes people difficult?', 'Is "difficulty" caused by particular grievances, or by a perception of threat, or by one in-group in the staff room warring with another?' And there are various kinds of 'difficulty'?: one person may be bullying and brash; another quietly hostile or 'passively aggressive'. Is it legitimate to group those people together under the heading of 'difficult'? They will present different problems in your interpersonal relationships and you will surely find different ways of dealing with them.

So, the whole idea of 'difficult people' has become much more of a prob-lem after the literature review and you should be brave enough to grasp the nettle here. If 'difficult people' (or whatever your subject is) now seems too difficult to cope with you will have to change the question.

Ideally, you should at the end of your literature review be able to review the various storylines that have emerged, with an explanation of why you have chosen to take the route that you have. Your refined question will, in this example, be something like:

'How do head teachers use support from colleagues in coping with stress arising from interpersonal relations?'

This has grown out of 'How do head teachers cope with difficult people?'

There are a number of points to remember in this development, principally that the new question:

- is more specific on the issue of 'coping', specifying a method of coping, namely using support from colleagues;
- drops the mention of 'difficult people' which is impossible to define adequately – instead, it brings in the idea of interpersonal relations;
- brings in the concept of stress, noting implicitly that 'coping' is about dealing with a situation that is difficult to resolve – we tend to see such difficulties as stressful.

You should still be aware with this question, though, that it is appropriate only for a certain kind of project, or, rather, a certain kind of researcher. To research it you will need access to head teachers who are willing to talk to you about personal issues, and this is most unlikely to be the case if you do not know the individuals personally, either as a close colleague or as a personal friend or family member. The more head teachers you want to talk to, the more difficult the issue becomes, so do be aware of the access issue right at the start.

Theory

During and after the literature review you will also have a chance to think about *theory*. Theory is a key issue in educational and social research and many millions of words have been spent discussing its meaning. I personally spent the first twenty years of my academic life trying to work out what 'theory' was supposed to mean in social research and came up with some not very clear conclusions. If you are interested in my deliberations you can read my book *Education and Theory: Strangers in Paradigms* (Thomas, 2007). So, don't feel alone if theory perplexes you.

One thing is clear: everyone in academic life thinks theory – or at least the thinking that surrounds it – is vitally important, and 'He/she hasn't located his/her work in theory' is one of the most common reasons for a research project being marked down. So I'll forget my own hobbyhorse about the subject for a moment to explain to you why theory is thought to be important.

Five main meanings of theory

The first thing to be aware of when people talk about theory in the social sciences is that there is no *one* meaning. People mean different things when they talk about it. Perhaps the clearest statement that can be made is that it refers to thinking, abstraction and generalising. Having said this, the thinking, abstraction and generalising are different in different kinds of inquiry.

Theory can mean ... *A generalising or explanatory model*. Theory tries to distil a range of specific findings or observations into general propositions that explain these findings.

Theory can mean ... *The 'thinking side' of practice*. Especially in the applied side of the social sciences (such as teaching and social work) theory or 'theorising' means thinking and reflecting on practice. It is sometimes called 'reflective practice'. It has also been called 'personal theory' or 'practical theory'. When people talk about this 'personal theory' they mean conjectures, personal thoughts and insights that help practitioners to make sense of the practical world. Many people suggest that in practical fields (such as teaching, nursing or social work) the enhancement of this practical theorisation, coming from our own experience, is what professional development should ultimately be about. The idea is not new: the Greeks had words for this kind of practical theory: *phronesis* and *techne*.

Theory can mean ... *A developing body of explanation*. Here theory means the broadening bodies of knowledge developing in particular fields. A body of knowledge may be wide, as for example in 'management theory' or 'learning theory', or tight, based around a particular set of ideas, as for example in 'Piagetian theory'.

Theory can mean ... *Scientific theory*. Theory here is modelled on the idea of theory in the natural sciences. It may ultimately exist in the form of ideas formally expressed in a series of statements. With these statements you are able to predict and explain. As social science progresses it seems less hopeful of discovering this kind of theory.

Theory can mean ... *Grand Theory*. 'Grand Theory' is a term used mockingly by the great sociologist Wright Mills (1959) to describe social scientists' expectation that their disciplines should attempt to build a systematic theory of 'the nature of man and society' (p. 23). The theories of Marx and Freud are examples. Wright Mills saw this effort as an obstacle to progress in the human sciences. I take it as given that Grand Theory is not what is generally wanted in social and educational research nowadays. You certainly will not be aiming to develop Grand Theory in your own research, though you may use Grand Theory as a framework or stimulus for it.

Theory: tool or product?

One of the great debates of social science has been about whether theory should be a *tool* or a *product*. In other words, should theory be the *aim* of our endeavours, on the assumption that theory will enable us to explain and predict more. Should we be trying to develop more and better theory with this aim in mind?

Or should it be a tool, devised and used simply for the purpose of helping to explain something that we are currently researching. As the latter it will be fashioned and used for the purpose in hand. It will have been manufactured merely to explain a particular phenomenon. The sociologist Pierre Bourdieu favours this latter kind of theory. He says:

> There is no doubt a theory in my work, or, better, a set of *thinking tools* visible through the results they yield, but it is not built as such ... It is a temporary construct which takes shape for and by empirical work. (Bourdieu, in Wacquant, 1989, cited in Jenkins, 1992: 67)

So, for Bourdieu, theory emerges and disappears in order to help us do our research and explain the findings we are making. And it is temporary, like a shooting star. It should not, in other words, be the *aim* of research. Another great sociologist, Howard Becker (1998: 3),

Theory is about:
- ... seeing links;
- ... generalising;
- ... abstracting ideas from your data and offering explanations;
- ... connecting your own findings with those of others;
- ... having insights.

talking of his highly respected tutor Everett C. Hughes, explains Hughes's 'take' on theory, which is similar to Bourdieu's:

> His [Hughes's] theory was not designed to provide all the conceptual boxes into which the world had to fit. It consisted, instead, of a collection of generalizing tricks he used to think about society, tricks that helped him interpret and make general sense of the data.

This idea of *generalising tricks* is a key one in the theory of educational and social research. It is about your ability to suggest meaningful explanations concerning your findings and how these fit in with the other research that you have reviewed in your literature review. How does it all fit together? What insights can you come up with? What explanations can you offer? *'Generalising' here means 'finding the essence of', 'finding links between', and it is often what is meant by theory in social science.* Unfortunately, when you are at the beginning of an academic career and have little in the way of a broad resource of alternative viewpoints and ideas to make links *between*, this can be the hardest of all tasks. But you *can* show that you have done reading, that you have weighed up ideas, that you have looked at them critically, that you have seen links and themes. Often students make the mistake of under-taking this process only in the last few lines of an essay or the last page or two of a dissertation. Try to extend the process of thinking about what you have done and what you are finding beyond this minimal synthesis so that it becomes not just the concluding lines or paragraphs. If you can do this – if you can make it also at the centre of what you do throughout the process – you will have demonstrated something important to the reader. You will have demonstrated something not only about what you have discovered in your research and why you think it is important, but also about how you think about knowledge, and how you think knowledge can be used.

Overview

After your literature review you will have had an opportunity to climb the hill, look down and see the wood from the trees. You can look down on all of the other research and commentary and see where your prima facie questions stand next to all of this. Have those prima facie questions been answered already? Are there agreements or arguments in the literature? Now you can think about the area in detail, using the storyboard to emerge with a fairly definitive storyline for your research. If necessary you can rewrite your questions and you can think about how these new questions might be answered. This will form the backdrop while you consider the different approaches and methods that may be used to answer the kind of question you are posing. This is also a good time to be thinking about theory – about the ways in which ideas can be drawn together, links made, explanations offered. In doing this, in 'theorising', you are showing that you are more than a copy typist – rather, you are analysing and synthesising and already constructing potential explanations for your forthcoming findings.

Further Reading

Thomas, G. (2007) *Education and Theory: Strangers in Paradigms*. Maidenhead: Open University Press.
Detailed, critical discussion on the meaning of theory and how work can progress without recourse to 'formal' theory. I didn't really write this for beginners, though, so you may find it hard going if you don't have some sort of background in the area.

Deciding on an Approach: Methodology and Research Design

Introduction
Literature review
Methodology
Fieldwork and findings
Analysis and discussion
Conclusion

You are here in your project →

Your literature review and your storyboard will have enabled you to sharpen your research question(s) and understand what they involve. You can now think about the means of answering them. This chapter considers:

- how are you going to answer your research question? Approaches to inquiry;
- the chapter in your dissertation where you consider this is often called 'Methodology' but may be called 'Research design';
- different ways of viewing the world and different understandings about how knowledge is sought and gained in social inquiry: postivism and interpretivism;
- thinking critically;
- tying up your purposes and your questions with these considerations about knowledge and 'ways of finding out';
- deciding on a 'design route' that takes account of your purposes, questions, approach and methods.

Once you have decided on your question you have to think of the best way of answering it. This is an important point in the project, for the question you have decided to ask will determine the whole approach that you take in your work. It is now, at this point, that you will make decisions about the form that your research will take. How will your purposes, research questions and methods for collecting and analysing data all knit together? A successful research project depends upon the integration of all of these elements (purpose, questions, approach and methods), and you will be marked up or down on the way that you demonstrate your understanding of the need for this integration.

This chapter in your dissertation or thesis is often called your 'methodology' or your 'research design' chapter, and it is important to be clear what methodology is and why methodology and research design are often bracketed together. Methodology is *the study of* method. ('...ology' means to talk about or study something, so 'method*ology*' means to talk about or study *method*.) So you must be aware that your methodology chapter is not simply the presentation of the method that you are going to be using in your research. Rather, it is a *discussion* of the methods that you will be using and, more importantly, why you are using them. This 'why' will relate back to the purposes of your inquiry and the choices you have made about the approach you intend to take to your research. This is also the reason that this chapter is often called 'research design': it is about thinking about why you are doing this research, how you intend to go about it and the 'shape' it will therefore ultimately take.

Research design

The research design is the plan for the research. In being a plan, it has to take into account your expectations and your context. If the idea of research design is unfamiliar, imagine another kind of design: that of a new kitchen. In designing your kitchen you will not (if you are sensible) just draw a plan completely off the top of your head and stick to it rigidly, come what may. You will first think what you want a kitchen for – whether you have a large family and are always cooking, or whether you rarely cook; whether you have gas in your property; the position of the drains, water, electricity, natural light. How much money do you want to spend? What sort of 'feel' are you comfortable with – traditional or modern? Will you want to eat in the kitchen as well as cook there? You will want to look at friends' kitchens to see what has and hasn't worked. You will want to consult catalogues and kitchen design specialists.

And so on – you get the idea. Once all of these questions have been answered and you have done all of your fact-finding you will be able to draft out a sketch of your plan. The first few drafts will have to be discarded as you realise things that you didn't include in your plan – the units are 600 mm wide and don't fit in the space, so you have to re-jig things and move them around on the design. Finally, you get to build the kitchen, but even now, as you are building it, you will come up against snags – the tap you wanted is out of stock so you have to order another, or you discover when the electrician arrives that it's against building regulations to put an electricity socket so close to the water. Eventually, the kitchen is made, and you're pleased with it, but it will have involved a great deal of planning and re-planning.

The design for a research project has to bear similar considerations in mind. What is it you are trying to achieve? Will you want any findings to be used practically? If so, how? What resources – time, money – do you have available? What kind of access do you have to the people or the situations you will focus on? What kind of expertise can be called on to support you? What are your own strengths and skills and could you realistically develop these in ways that will enable you to do a certain kind of research? What kind of formal and informal regulations of one kind or another will you have to adhere to.

All of these questions will lead you ultimately to the kind of design route shown towards the end of this chapter in Figure 5.9, taking into account the possibility of using a number of *design frames* that are examined in more detail in the next chapter. Importantly, they will also lead you to consider the approach that you take to your research.

It is worth saying that in educational research and in research in the applied social sciences research design is taken to mean something broader than that in 'pure' social science, for example in psychology. In psychology, research design is often taken simply to be a part of the method, and is often just a synonym for 'experimental design'. In applied social research it means something much wider.

Research approach

When I talk about the *approach* that you adopt in your work I mean something quite fundamental, and something about which social scientists continually agonise and argue. The *approach* isn't just about whether you use this method or that method, but rather about how you think about the social world. The issue here is that education and the social sciences are hugely varied and complex, with our interests ranging across all kinds of individual and social behaviour. One of the main difficulties is that we are not sure what to focus on in this broad vista. Should it be individuals or groups? Should we measure closely defined variables (things that can be counted) – or should we forget about variables and try to understand the meanings that people invest in the encounters they have with one another? These are big issues to disentangle. By contrast, rocket science seems straightforward.

In this chapter I am going to talk about frameworks for thinking about these issues, about the difficulties of knowing anything, and about the need to be cautious in any claim to knowledge. In the light of this I am going to revisit questions about the different kinds of research that we might do.

Scientist or spy?

The way social scientists react to the complexity of social research differs. Some have suggested that it should be like the research of natural scientists – people such as chemists and physicists – asking very precise questions, identifying relevant variables (like gender, class, school funding or reading age), coming up with ideas and hypotheses about how these might (or might not) be related to one another and experimenting to discover the answers. They use their inquiries to try and explain and pre-

dict the social world.

Others have said that we should behave more like spies, infiltrating ourselves into the social worlds of those in whom we are interested to observe and describe in rich detail what happens there, behaving as naturally as possible while doing this. Yet others have suggested that we might behave more like historians, listening to the accounts and narratives of the people with whom we are concerned and constructing explanations of events on the basis of these.

A common view now is that social researchers should be eclectic and do all of these, depending on the kinds of questions that we pose.

Eclectic: Taking a broad view; using a variety of methods; taking the best of many methods; not following one tradition; using complementary insights.

Frameworks for thinking about the social world – paradigms

I have talked about scientists and spies, and while this will do as a simple metaphor for different frameworks about thinking and researching, it is something of an oversimplification.

The technical word used to describe the ways that we think about and research the world is *paradigm*. In common parlance (as distinct from technical parlance), paradigm has come to have several meanings. For example, it may mean 'an example of the best', as in 'David Beckham is the paradigm

Paradigms are …

- shared ideas in a particular community of inquiry;
- 'thinking habits' of researchers;
- 'rules' of procedure.

Paradigms …

- *shift*, as the old one proves to be inappropriate.

of a midfielder', or it may mean a particular kind of mindset. But you should forget these uses of the word, for when it is used in the social sciences it refers technically to two particular approaches to knowledge – how we seek knowledge and how we use it. These two approaches – these paradigms – are *positivism* and *interpretivism* and I'll discuss them more in a moment, but it is useful for you to know a little more about what 'paradigm' means before explaining them.

The word comes from the Greek *paradeigma*, meaning, broadly speaking, an unchanging model. The word was used by the philosopher of science Thomas Kuhn (1970) to mean a fixed set of assumptions about the way inquiry should be conducted. Kuhn's focus was physics and the way that physicists work with certain fixed methods (which they hate to consider changing), but his ideas have been readily taken up by social scientists, who see a clear relevance of the notion of paradigm to their own work.

Figure 5.1 Thomas Kuhn, the Big Daddy of paradigms

The idea of the paradigm is particularly relevant to social scientists because Kuhn suggested that traditional paradigms – familiar models and ways of working – eventually give way to new ones, which are better, more accurate frameworks for thinking about the world under study. But this giving way, he suggested, happens only after much resistance from the old guard who cherish their traditional ways of thinking and working. In short, people don't like change, and scientists – even hard-nosed physicists – are as irrational as the rest of us when it comes to being faced with new thought and new ideas. Eventually, though, as evidence gradually reaches overwhelming proportions for the success of the new ways of thinking there is acceptance and change. He called this process of change *paradigm shift*.

Now, in the social sciences the dominant paradigm for many years was a way of thinking called *positivism* (of which more below), and this has been challenged by a more recently developed framework for thinking called *interpretivism*. So – using the Kuhnian model – it seems as though one paradigm is giving way to another. In fact, the process has been going on for so long (since the 1920s and 1930s) that it is by no means clear that there is a process of paradigm *shift* actually happening in social science. What appears

Positivism as a paradigm:

- The social world can be studied objectively.
- The methods of natural science are appropriate in social science.
- General accounts inform the specific.
- The act of trying to know ought to be conducted in such a way that the knower's own value position is removed from the process.

Interpretivism as a paradigm:

- Knowledge is everywhere and is socially constructed.
- All kinds of information are valid and worthy of the name 'knowledge', even things 'of the mind'.
- Specific accounts inform each other.
- The act of trying to know should be conducted such that the knower's own value position is taken into account in the process.

rather to be the case is that the two paradigms, positivism and interpretivism, are coexisting with each other – each recognised as having its own part to play in social inquiry. It depends on what you want to find out: it's horses for courses. One paradigm will be right for one kind of question, the other right for another. In this sense, the paradigm model doesn't quite work in the social sciences, but it does nevertheless provide a useful way of thinking about our main frameworks for thinking – positivism and interpretivism – about the questions that confront us.

Positivism and interpretivism

Positivism

For positivists, knowledge about the social world can be obtained objectively: what we see and hear is straight-forwardly perceived and recordable without too many problems. The things of the social and psychological world can be observed, measured and studied scientifically, in much the same way that physicists study levers, atoms and pulleys.

Figure 5.2
Auguste Comte – the 'father' of positivism

It was the French philosopher Auguste Comte who, in *A General View of Positivism* (1856), suggested that the most advanced form of thinking was the scientific form – in other words the science of natural scientists should as far as possible be emulated. Even before this, the Scottish philosopher David Hume had come up with what he called a *principle of verification*. We should ask of any learned work, said Hume (1748/1910):

> *Does it contain any abstract reasoning concerning quantity or number?* No. *Does it contain any experimental reasoning concerning matter of fact and existence?* No. Commit it then to the flames: for it can contain nothing but sophistry and illusion.

Figure 5.3   David Hume

This was stirring stuff in the eighteenth century, when the predominant world-view was simple: all things are planned for and provided by God. Questions could be answered with the simple 'It is God's will'. Here, with Comte, was someone saying that this wasn't good enough, and that social matters could be studied in the same way that scientists studied physics and chemistry where there had been such success with scientific method.

We should therefore try to isolate variables, measure the ways that they varied, look at the relationships between the variables, develop hypotheses about these relationships, perhaps manipulate the variables for experimentation to test a hypothesis, and draw conclusions on the basis of these studies. In doing all of this – in following 'scientific method' – we should try to be as objective and as neutral as possible. We should watch from outside as disinterested observers, trying not to 'contaminate' our findings in any way. The world view underpinning all of this is sometimes called *realism*, namely the view that the world we perceive is straightforwardly the one that is 'out there'. There is not much room for interpretation about it.

> **Disinterested:** Detached, without bias. A piece of academic research is supposed to be seeking the truth without taking sides or coming from a particular angle. Is this ever possible? Probably not, but it's expected that you should be striving to conduct your inquiries as disinterestedly as possible. (Note that 'disinterested' doesn't mean 'uninterested'.)

Interpretivism

An alternative view developed. It was that the social world – that is to say, the world in which we are interested as social scientists – is *not* straightforwardly perceivable because it is **constructed** by each of us in a different way.

It's not simply 'out there'; it is different for each of us, with words and events carrying different meanings in every case. It cannot therefore be adequately studied using the methods of physics and chemistry, with talk of variables and quantification: an entirely different mindset and set of procedures is needed to inquire into it. This view is called **interpretivism**, and started (more or less) with the American sociologist George Herbert Mead (though there were several strands to the line of thinking that we now call interpretivism, and no clear beginning).

Figure 5.4 George Herbert Mead – interactionism and interpretivism

The main point about interpretivism is that we are interested in people and the way that they interrelate – what they think and how they form ideas about the world; how their worlds are constructed. Given that this is the case we have to look closely at what people are doing by using our own selves, our own knowledge of the world as people. We have to immerse ourselves in the research contexts in which we are interested – for example talking to people in depth, attending to every nuance of their behaviour, every clue to the meanings that they are investing in something. So we attend to their blinks, winks, hums and hahs, their nods and nose-blowings as well as listening to the actual words that are coming out of their mouths. The key is *understanding*. What understandings do the people we are talking to have about the world, and how can we in turn understand these?

You will realise that this talk of understanding is at cross purposes with the method of the positivists. There is no talk of *variables* in interpretivism, because it is considered artificial to fracture the social world into these categories and there is no expectation that you should be objective in your study. It is the opposite in fact – you should use your own interests and understandings to help interpret the expressed views and behaviour of others. You should be a *participant* in your research situation and understand it as an insider. In doing this, you have to recognise your position – your social background, likes and dislikes, preferences and predilections, political affiliations, class, gender and ethnicity – and how this position (sometimes called 'positionality' – see p. 109) is likely to be affecting your interpretation. So you shouldn't deny this position. On the contrary, you should use it, but in using it you should also be fully aware of it and acknowledge it – aware that it is likely to be affecting your interpretation in particular ways.

Because of these starting points, research undertaken in this tradition is sometimes called 'naturalistic'. In other words, as a researcher you are behaving as naturally as possible in the social world in order to try and understand it properly. You will be listening and watching naturalistically, and in all of this listening and watching you will be using your own knowledge of the world. You will not necessarily be trying to be objective; rather, you will be accepting the centrality of subjectivity. But this is not a second-best to objectivity; it's simply a different 'take' on research. You won't, in other words, be saying 'Well there's not much I can do about a certain amount of subjectivity so I'll have to live with it'. Rather, you'll be acknowledging that in doing this kind of illumination, our personal selves – our opinions, intentions, likes and dislikes – are an essential part of what we hear and see. So you will start with the assumption that there is no clear, disinterested knowledge – people have feelings and understandings and these affect the ways that they perceive and interpret the world. Not only is it impossible to eliminate these but these are the stuff out of which interpretation is made.

Remember that being objective is not the same as being thorough and balanced. You can be thorough and balanced without pretending to objectiveness. Imagine that you are interested in the representation of disability in children's comics, with a question of the sort: 'How was disability represented in children's comics in the years 1950 to 2000?' With such a question, you have to use your own knowledge of the world, as I have just discussed: you read, interpret, put into context and so on. And you do this, as far as possible, by using what the great anthropologist Clifford Geertz (1975) called 'thick description'. Thick description refers to understanding a piece of behaviour – a nod, a word, a pause, etc. – in context, and using one's 'human knowing' to interpret it when one describes it. Geertz forcefully notes that in interpreting meanings one cannot be a 'cipher clerk' (1975: 9). You cannot, in other words, simply report things 'thinly' without context. The example he uses is the one originally used by philosopher Gilbert Ryle (from whom he borrowed the idea of thick description) of three boys moving the muscles of their eyes. With one it is a twitch, with another a wink and with the third a parody of the second one's wink. What turns the twitch into a wink, and what makes the mickey-take a parody? As Geertz puts it: '... a speck of behaviour, a fleck of culture, and voilà! a gesture'. The trick is, in reporting your observations, to make clear what is going on in a social situation to turn the twitch into the wink, or into the parody of the wink. How do you know which is which? The interpretative researcher has to tell the reader.

The fact that you read, interpret and put into context in the ways that I have described does not absolve you, though, from the imperative to approach the question in a fair and balanced way. It might be the case, for example, that you come to this question with a particular viewpoint about disability – a viewpoint that says that disabled people are marginalised and oppressed by society. Would this give you licence simply to pick on particularly offensive representations of disability in comics and to ignore positive images of disabled people that you find there? Opinions differ on this, and some advocate research that is 'emancipatory', that principally makes a case – that is campaigning. I do not share this view. My own opinion is that there are many legitimate kinds of activity in life and that *research*, as an activity, is governed by some fundamental ground rules, which include a duty of balance, fairness and thoroughness. Research, in this respect, is different from campaigning.

A good example of interpretative research is to be found in James Patrick's (1973) *A Glasgow Gang Observed*. Here, the author, a young sociologist, infiltrated himself into a gang of young men in the Maryhill district of Glasgow. By becoming a participant in the gang's activities, Patrick (a pseudonym, wisely, since he didn't want subsequently to be knifed) paints a fascinating (and entertaining) picture of the way that the gang worked and its motivations, intentions and modus operandi. It helps us to understand gangs, but there is no pretence that this is a representative picture, or that all gangs are like this. In researching in this way, Patrick is not pretending to be objective: on the contrary, he is using all of his personal self to help him infiltrate, engage with and understand what is going on among the young men.

One of the attractions for researchers in the applied social sciences, and I include practitioner-researchers in this group, is the humility of interpretative research – the fact that it makes no grand claims about generalisability or causation. What it does instead is to take from the local experience and illuminate and influence the local experience: it helps to influence the practitioner-researcher's own developing practice.

Paradigms and research approach

Actually, paradigms are not straightforwardly 'views about the world' as I perhaps implied earlier. Rather, they are positions on the best ways to think about and study the social world – the world in which we are interested as social scientists. Table 5.1 indicates how these paradigms differ in respect of what they say about how research should be conducted.

What planet are you on?

How can you use this knowledge of paradigms in your own research? Actually, if you look at any write-up of social research in an academic journal or in a research report for a commissioning body you will not find mention of positivism or interpretivism. It is taken as 'given' that there are different ways of looking at and thinking about the social

Table 5.1   Paradigms: positivism and interpretivism (loosely adapted from Oakley, 2000)

	Positivist	Interpretivist
The researcher aims to …	predict and explain, usually generalising from carefully selected samples	understand the particular, contributing to building a framework of 'multiple realities'
The researcher uses (for example) …	survey, experiment, structured observation	unstructured observation, case study, unstructured interview, participant observation
The researcher aims to be …	independent, an outsider	an insider, interacting with participants
The researcher looks at …	things that can be quantified and counted	perceptions, feelings, ideas, thoughts, actions as heard or observed
The researcher analyses …	variables, decided on in advance of fieldwork	emergent patterns
The design of the research is …	fixed	flexible
Other words sometimes used (often inaccurately) to sum up these approaches …	scientific, quantitative, nomothetic	naturalistic, qualitative, idiographic

world and that these will have structured the research. However, in a dissertation or thesis from a research project at university you will have to show that you understand the broad principles that guide the way that social research is conducted – the ways that questions are answered and data is gathered and analysed. This does not mean that you should have a section on positivism or interpretivism, but it does mean that you should explain the principles that are guiding your research.

What does this mean? Well, positivism and interpretivism are such different ways of thinking about research that one could liken them to being on different planets. To borrow a metaphor, positivists are from Mars and interpretivists are from Venus. On Mars everyone counts everything and talks in numbers, but on Venus they don't know what numbers are (no one has ever seen one) and they just talk to each other non-stop, everyone always asking each other about how they are: 'How *are* you? What do you *mean* by that? Really? Tell me more.' In fact, the Martians have a joke about the Venusians: 'How many Venusians does it take to change a light bulb? Answer: 19 – one to change the bulb and 18 to share the experience.'

Now, if you are a positivist writing about research on Mars, you don't begin every sentence with 'Here on Mars ...', just as on Earth newspapers do not begin every story with 'Here on Earth ...'. It's just part of the background noise. We *know* that we are on Earth and have Earthly experiences every day. We don't need to say it. In the same way, you don't need to say that you are working in a positivist or an interpretivist tradition. You just have to be aware of it. It's part of the air you breathe when you do a particular kind of research.

And, as a student, you have to demonstrate your awareness. This presents something of a dilemma for student researchers, who do realise that they have to show that they know about these things but without having a rather gross reference to them in the text. (Some students write pages about positivism or interpretivism, which is unnecessary and distracting.) It's a bit like the dilemma you feel when you are on your driving test and you feel you should *show* that you are looking in the rear-view mirror by making an exaggerated movement of your head. Though you want to do this, a good examiner will be watching for your eye movements – you don't in fact need to extend your neck to giraffe-like proportions to convince the examiner that you are looking in the mirror. And you don't usually need to explain about positivism and interpretivism in your dissertation. But what you *do* have to do is to be aware of the ways that they are structuring your research.

How can you demonstrate your knowledge of them without the giraffe syndrome? The key is in the argument you make for the approach that you take in your research, though the need for this argument will be more or less pronounced depending on the question/s that you ask. The key to all research – whether you are thinking as a positivist or an interpretivist – is describing, interpreting and analysing and what you need to do is to say why you think it is a good idea to describe, interpret and analyse in this way or that. In making this argument, you may make reference to positivism or interpretivism and this may need to be more or less extended. So your methodology chapter will begin with the reasons why your questions have led you to the approach you have decided to take in answering those questions. In explaining these reasons you may begin by saying something such as:

> My questions (*a, b, c,* etc.) call for straightforwardly descriptive answers and I shall provide these answers through an examination of government statistics and from my own structured observations.

or

> My questions (*x, y, z,* etc.) stem from a wish to understand the reasons for Shaquille's persistent failure and 'blocking' in maths.

In both instances, you would then go on to say how you proceeded from these starting points to your choice of approach and method. In the first case, it would be possible to move from the statement about an examination of government statistics to an examination of those statistics relatively unproblematically. (There is no need to say that statistics have been collected in a positivist paradigm.) However, you may want to spend more time on explaining the reasons for choosing to use structured (rather than unstructured – see p. 182) observation. In the second case you will need to explain how you are going to understand Shaquille's difficulties – By asking him questions about what he is doing when he is calculating? By watching his behaviour? By relating his difficulties to your own when you were a child studying maths? In doing this, you will wish to outline the background to an approach that accepts as valid the thoughts, imaginings and empathies that are involved here. And in so doing you will draw on methodological literature that discusses such an approach. You may also give examples of such an interpretivist approach to understanding behaviour, such as Oliver Sacks's (1996) *An Anthropologist on Mars* (the Mars connection is coincidental).

So, getting back to paradigms and how they structure our thinking for our research, I think the best and simplest way of distinguishing one kind of describing, interpreting and analysing from another is to remember the epithet I earlier gave from Hume: *Does it contain any abstract reasoning concerning quantity or number? … Does it contain any experimental reasoning concerning matter of fact and existence?* It was 250 years ago that Hume came up with this 'principle of verification'. This was before the word 'positivism' was coined, but it led indirectly to Comte's positivism and it serves us well now, for it can lead to the continuum in Figure 5.5. This, I hope, is a way of not getting trapped in a mindset that says that we have to be either positivist or interpretivist. Rather, it's horses for courses.

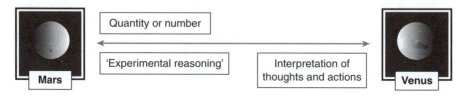

Figure 5.5   Positivism or interpretivism

I don't want to extend the metaphor too far, but of course Earth is midway between Mars and Venus, and here in the real world we use all kinds of reasoning to come to our conclusions about the evidence that we collect. It is not a question of one *or* the other.

But is it science?

Much of the debate about positivism and interpretivism hinges around whether a study can be called scientific. In fact it is very difficult to define what a 'scientific' study is. Chemists work differently from biologists who work differently from physicists, who work differently from doctors, who work differently from astronomers (… you get the idea), yet few people would have difficulty in agreeing that they are all scientists. Imagine for a moment the work of palaeoanthropologists – the

> There is no single way of being scientific. You should be open-minded about the methods that you use to answer your research questions.

scientists who try to understand how our human forebears evolved. They work by collecting fragments of bone and other material and piecing together stories – plausible accounts – of the way that this pre-human may have led to that one. They use information from a whole range of sources in doing this. For example, they use knowledge from geology about the age of rocks in which materials are found; they use carbon dating; they even use knowledge from psychology and physiology: the palaeoanthropologist Louis Leakey described how he worked out that a particular pre-human, for whom he had a skull, had quite advanced language facility by looking at the roots of the specimen's teeth. It transpires that a particular physiological construction – a little depression in the jaw-bone called the *canine fossa* – can be shown to be associated with the production of speech: the little dip makes room for a muscle used in language production. None of this work – depending on inference and intuition – is formally experimental, yet few would doubt that it is science.

In the same way, much of what we do in social research is a mix of forms of inquiry: an idea from here, a hunch from there, a searching for evidence – then a putting together of hunches, ideas and evidence and a 'Eureka!' There is no formal method to follow that will lead you to the right answer. It is always a matter of finding the right information and using your head.

Starting points can come from anywhere: from a need, from curiosity, from serendipity, from surprise. The philosopher Paul Thagard (1998) has offered the diagram in Figure 5.6 to explain the relationship of these beginnings of inquiry with forms of questioning to lead to discovery. There is no formal route that could be branded 'Scientific Method®'. As Einstein put it, scientific method is no more than trying to find '… in whatever manner is suitable, a simplified and lucid image of the world … There is no logical path, but only intuition' (in Holton, 1995: 168).

Sometimes, this requires a shifting of perspective as far as our ideas about causation are concerned. The commonly understood method of science is to look for causes, and this is certainly one legitimate avenue to follow in social science too. But, as Thagard's diagram indicates, it is sometimes more complicated than this – even in the natural sciences.

This complexity is no less true of the social sciences. The world-famous sociologist Howard Becker suggests that the complexity is such in social research that the notion of 'cause' is almost a misnomer (Becker, 1998: 60–1). He suggests that we should see ourselves searching for *narrative* rather than cause:

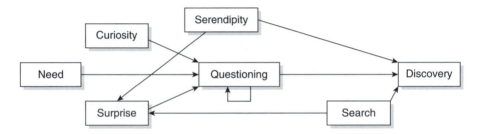

Figure 5.6   Ways to discovery (Thagard, 1998)

> Assume that whatever you want to study has, not causes, but a history, a
> story, a narrative, a 'first this happened, then that happened, and then
> the other happened, and it ended up like this.' On this view we under-
> stand the occurrence of events by learning the steps in the process by
> which they came to happen, rather than by learning the conditions that
> made their existence necessary.

Educator Jerome Bruner puts it this way:

> The process of science making is narrative … we play with ideas, try to
> create anomalies, try to find neat puzzle forms that we can apply to
> intractable troubles so that they can be turned into soluble problems.
> (Bruner, 1997: 126)

If the question demands description, one avenue will be sign-
posted; if it demands illumination, another; or if it demands inference, yet another. It's the same in any field. Police officers investigating
Dr Black's murder will seek evidence not just at the simple physical
scientific level – was there blood on the lead piping, and whose was it? –
but also evidence about motives: did Mrs Peacock stand to gain in
some way from Dr Black's demise? How *well* did they know each other
(exaggerated wink)? Was she a beneficiary in his will? So they will
need not just to send material to the labs for DNA analysis but also to
question Mrs Peacock skilfully and observe her demeanour for signs of
lying. Likewise, the research team at FastFood Inc., when developing
Speed, its new sparkling drink, will want not simply demographic statistics to see which groups of the population seem to be growing or
declining, but also rich information from small groups of people –
focus groups – about the image portrayed by artwork on prototype
cans of Speed.

All kinds of evidence will be needed and employed, and we need to
piece it all together. In Bruner's terms, we need to play with ideas; in
Becker's, to view the story. Of course, there is always the danger that we
may add 2 and 2 and make 5. Our 'Eureka!' may be wrong, and there is
a real danger of this in the social sciences. This is why it is essential to

understand the importance of humility in your claim to have found something out – why it is important to think reflectively and critically.

The Q words – qualitative and quantitative

Quantitative research refers to research using numbers, and qualitative research refers to that which does not use numbers. To characterise these 'types' crudely by paradigm, I could say that positivism, which you'll remember all started with Hume's principle of verification, lends

> Quantitative and qualitative research are not in opposition to one another. Rather, they can complement each other.

itself to quantification, while interpretivism lends itself to words, thoughts and images: it is qualitative.

I've tried to avoid the Q words in this book because I think that their use makes for unnecessary and unwelcome oppositions between different kinds of research. It is absolutely the case that qualitative and quantitative research differ, and that they are governed by different assumptions and ground rules. But it is not the case that they are incompatible. Indeed, they complement each other. Nor can social and educational research be divided neatly into one or the other type, for much analysis can depend on plainly descriptive words or numbers – words where there is remarkably little in the way of interpretation going on, and numbers doing no more complicated a job than counting. Such analysis eludes the divisions of the Q words and the positivism–interpretivism continuum, employing both words and numbers and slipping effortlessly between the one and the other.

To create a stark division between qualitative and quantitative sometimes engenders a cart-before-the-horse mentality. Sometimes people are tempted to think of types of research first (quantitative or qualitative) and then think of a research pathway that will lead into one of these. This is entirely wrong: your research approach should be the servant of your research question, not its master. Always start with your research question, and think of ways of answering it. This may lead you to a design frame where you use numbers, or it may lead you to one where you use words.

The important thing is that you use the design frame that is right for your question, and this is why I have organised the chapter that follows this one into *design frames* rather than invoking any quantitative–qualitative division.

Thinking critically – how the 'ologies' help

One of the most frequent reasons for the marking down of a project (or indeed any piece of work in the social sciences) is that a student has not demonstrated an ability to *think critically*. This is about your ability to think-about-thinking and always to be sceptical about claims to knowledge, given the complexity of the subject matter in which we are interested.

I've been at pains to hammer home the point that education and the social sciences are complex – they are about a wide range of interrelating issues and if we want to ask questions about these different issues we have to think seriously about the best ways of answering them – and there will be many of these ways, with no single 'right' way. Behind all of this are some very basic issues that are at the root of all inquiry – about what it is that we should be studying, and about knowledge, what it is and how we come by it. It is these issues that really frame our research – even frame the paradigms that shape the way that we work. Considering these matters in depth helps you understand that knowledge is hard to come by and why we must be critical about claims to knowledge – whether they are the claims of others or our own. Thinking about all of this is where the 'ologies' come in: ontology and epistemology.

What are the 'ologies'?

The 'ologies' strike fear into the hearts of many students, but it is useful to think about them because they help you to decide on the kind of research that you will be doing. Thinking about them helps you to consider more deeply what you are asking in your research question and – even more importantly – how you will go about answering it. Perhaps most importantly they help you to realise that knowledge is frail, and that claims to knowledge, in your own findings or those of others, should always be scrutinised closely.

Don't be frightened of ologies

If you are old enough, you may remember the advertisement in the 1980s in which a grandma (actress Maureen Lipman) is on the phone to her grandson Anthony who has just completed his GCSEs. It's clear that Anthony is unwilling to tell his grandma his results. Sulkily, he tells her about two or three mediocre passes – in vocational rather than academic subjects. Then, almost worse than the performance in woodwork and metalwork, he glumly admits to a 'C' in sociology. *Sociology* – embarrassing. For Anthony this all amounts to utter failure and he confesses this to his grandma.

But hearing the word 'sociology', Grandma puts the phone to her chest, turns round and calls out loudly to Grandpa: 'An *ology*! He gets an ology and he says he's failed!' Turning back to her conversation with her grandson, she declares: 'You get an ology, you're a scientist!'

Anthony's grandma is partly right about scientists, because 'ology' is often associated with science (biology, geology, etc.). But it means more than just scientific endeavour. Words ending in 'ology' come from the Greek suffix 'logia', which means 'speaking'. So, when we add 'ology' to a word, it usually means 'speaking about ...', or to think about or to study something. So, for example, 'sociology' means to think about or study the social world; 'psychology' means to think about or study the psyche.

The 'ologies' we are interested in here, though, are not sociology and psychology. They are rather more unusual ones, and are usually associated with philosophy. They are:

- *ontology* and
- *epistemology*.

Some people would say that we spend too much time bothering about these. They would say that it is only because social scientists are so unsure of their status that they spend so much time gazing into their navels about how they know what they know – and surrounding themselves with all sorts of fancy-sounding words (such as epistemology and ontology) that are difficult to understand. The more unsure you are of your academic credentials, after all, the more likely you are to puff yourself up with all the paraphernalia of science – the more you need ologies: 'You get an ology, you're a scientist!'

This is *partly* true of the social sciences and their use of jargon, but *only* partly true. Some of the navel-gazing is actually necessary, because the issues we confront as social scientists really are knotty ones.

That 'knottiness' – in other words, the difficulty of framing the key questions of the social sciences – is what the ologies are about and where they can help out. They are about the fundamental issues, the basic questions. *What* is there to study? How can we *know* about it? How do we find what we are looking for?

Ontology

Much of the confusion about what methods we should use in educational and social research comes from head-scratching about the nature of the world. What *is* it that we are studying? This question is not so difficult for physicists, since it is clear that they study electrons and neutrons and Higgs bosons. No one disagrees. It's similar for biologists: they study life processes in things that are alive. But for social scientists there is a problem, since we are studying people, on their own or together, and people do strange, unpredictable things, gather themselves in peculiar ways, act irrationally, learn and change. Is it their observable behaviour that is the focus of our deliberations, the way that they gather together, or what? As social scientists we can become especially concerned with ontology because it is not at all clear what kind of world we should be studying.

The trouble is that when you start looking at people and the things that they do, one of the major issues that confronts you is how those things are perceived by us: how those things 'come to life' and how we should look at them. For example, when people are in any kind of relationship with one another – whether as teacher and student, as life partners, as friends, colleagues or anything else – it is undeniable that they create to a greater or lesser extent some kind of 'chemistry' that comes from shared understandings and outlooks (or the lack of these). Now, how do we begin to understand what this 'chemistry', this meaningfulness and mutual understanding, might be? In other words, *what* is it that we are looking at?

Ontology is about this question of what we are looking at. In philosophy, where we borrow the idea from, ontologists have posed questions such as 'What is existence?' and 'What are physical objects?' These questions are clearly not social scientists' focus in their everyday work. But in the broadest possible sense they do have central relevance because there are various kinds of 'existence' and 'objects' or phenomena in which we could be said to be interested in the social sciences. An awareness of the issues of ontology makes us wary, for example, of what is sometimes called a *correspondence view of knowledge*, meaning an assumption that what you see and hear correspond to facts 'out there' in the real world. This is more or less the view held by the person in the street: what you see is that which is there, and what happens in your head more or less corresponds with what is in the 'real world'. In fact, this turns out to be a lot more complex an issue than you might assume, even for quite straightforward matters, but it is multiplied hugely when we are talking about things to do with human behaviour and interaction.

So, the issues to be encapsulated in the word ontology concern the kinds of things that we assume to exist in the world, and how those things should be viewed and studied. Is the social world in which we are interested best seen as comprising simple *variables*, or matters such as the *interaction* among people? Should we start our inquiries with theories of social behaviour or should we aim to develop our own theories as we progress?

For example, if a boy is biting the other children in the class, how should we look at this problem? Should we treat the issue as a natural scientist might, concentrating on what we can see (the biting) and the variables we can manipulate (perhaps rewards or punishments) to influence his behaviour? Or should we see the problem as a complex of social interactions wherein meanings are made out of the expectations, connections and interactions that occur in the artificial environment of the classroom? Or could we see it in both of these ways?

This is where awareness of ontology helps in the construction of research. It helps us to understand that there are different ways of viewing the world – of viewing what there is to study. In other words, things may not be as simple as they at first appear, and there are different ways of seeing and understanding a problem or an issue. You will understand, if you have read the section above on paradigms, that it is different ontological positions which lead on to the different paradigmatic positions.

Epistemology

If *ontology* is the study of what there is or what exists in the social world, *epistemology* is the study of our knowledge of the world. How do we *know* about the world that we have defined ontologically? Epistemologists ask questions such as:

Ontology is about *what* you are looking at – the kind of events that exist in the social world. Epistemology is about *how* you look and find out about these.

- What is knowledge and how do we know things?
- Are there different kinds of knowledge?
- Are there good procedures for discovering knowledge?

Rumsfeld on knowing ...

If all of this stuff about existence and knowledge is making no sense at all, cheer yourself up with the reassuring thought that you are not alone. In 2002, Donald Rumsfeld, the US Secretary for Defense, gave a now-famous news briefing. In talking about weapons of mass destruction, he brightened a gloomy world when he came out with this statement:

> There are known knowns. There are things that we know we know. There are known unknowns. That is to say, there are things that we now ***know*** we don't know. But there are also unknown unknowns ... there are things we ***do not*** know we don't know. So when we do the best we can and we pull all this information together and, and we then say well that's basically what we see as the situation that is really only the known knowns and the known unknowns, and each year we discover a few more of those unknown unknowns and ... and I, I ... it, it sounds like a riddle ... (Department of Defense news briefing, 12 February 2002)

How true. And it makes a lot more sense when written down than it did when he said it. His brief speech on knowing illustrates some of the difficulties of describing what we know and how we come to know it.

In education, we are interested in all of the knowns and unknowns of Mr Rumsfeld's speech. And one thing that the speech correctly suggests is that nothing is certain. If there is one single thing that you need to absorb from the whole debate about ontology and epistemology it is that knowledge is a frail thing. You can't be *certain* of anything. The main consequence of this for your research project and how you write it up is that you should always make it clear that you understand why it is hard to know something – that you understand why you should be tentative and not over-confident in your conclusions.

Let's look a little at that frailty – at why it is hard to know something, or at least to be sure that we know it. Put differently, why do we have to be careful about asserting something to be true? In Chapter 3 I made the point that you should always avoid phrases such as 'this proves' and 'this shows' and instead use words such as 'this indicates' or ' the evidence suggests' or 'points towards' or 'implies'. You should use phrases such as 'tends to' or 'one might conclude that …' instead of bolder ones. Remember again that maxim from the great biologist J. B. S. Haldane (who appears rather dapper in his blazer in Figure 5.7): 'The duty of doubt'. Haldane concluded his famous essay *Possible Worlds* (Haldane, 1928: 224) with the words ' … science has owed its wonderful progress very largely to the habit of doubting all theories'.

Figure 5.7   Haldane, who spoke about 'The duty of doubt'

It's all very well to be doubtful and tentative, but what would social scientists say to epistemologists about how they know? …

How can we know something in the social sciences?

We know things because we *experience* them: we see them, hear them, touch them. *Empiricism* is the word given to the idea that knowledge comes from experience. To know something *empirically* is to know it from experience.

But how do we get from seeing, hearing and touching (experiencing) to knowing something? To explain the process of moving from experiencing to knowing Wolcott (1992) draws a diagram of a tree, wherein the experience is absorbed by the tree's roots, to be transformed into the knowing that comes via various analytical strategies. Those analytical strategies employ *reasoning* of one kind or another, and there are taken to be two main ways of reasoning that lead us to knowledge …

First, there is *inductive reasoning* …

With inductive reasoning we proceed on the basis of many observations gathered from experience to derive a general principle. So, if you see lots of swans and they are all white, you may come up with the general principle that all swans are white.

The sun has risen this morning, and has from the beginning of the time, so you may infer that the sun rises every morning.

The more observation the better and, clearly, the more observations you take, the more sure you can be that your general principle is true. Inductive reasoning's central point is that lots of similar experience leads to general principles.

But there is a big problem with the confidence that comes from this kind of inductive reasoning. This is that just because your observation is always that something is the case, it doesn't automatically follow that this will continue to be the case. For example, when Europeans first went to Australia they discovered that swans could be black as well as white. And while the sun has risen every morning, we now know that there are a variety of astronomical horrors that could end up with it not happening tomorrow. So, our knowledge from induction is not perfect, and never can be. This is particularly so in the social sciences where we very rarely, if ever, find clear-cut evidence of this kind.

Second, there is *deductive reasoning* ...

Deductive reasoning concerns argument. An argument proceeds on the basis of statements (or premises) which are assumed to be true, to conclusions which must be true if the premises are true. Problems arise, of course, because of assumptions that the premises are true when they are not.

Inductive and deductive – they are both forms of reasoning. So, we know things because we think about them and *reason* about them. *Rationalism* is the word given to the idea that knowledge comes from our reasoning. That reasoning depends on both inductive and deductive strategies.

I hope I have explained that these processes of reasoning are far from perfect. Scientists, whether natural scientists or social scientists, try to improve processes of reasoning by being methodical in the way that they seek and acquire experience – seek and acquire evidence. Natural scientists, physicists and chemists are able to control their experience using carefully contrived experiments and manipulating variables methodically in those experiments. However, in the social sciences it is far more difficult to do this – and, indeed, all sorts of questions arise (as I indicated in the section on ontology) about what exists to be experienced. Knowledge here is said to be *provisional*, and by provisional we mean that it is taken to be the best in the circumstances, but may always be superseded if other information or insights come to light.

As with paradigms, you will not be expected to include dedicated sections on epistemology and ontology in your thesis. They may be mentioned in the discussion of the approach to your research but, as with the non-discussion of paradigms (see p. 79), the trick is to reveal your awareness of their importance with subtlety. Epistemology and ontology are not, after all, at the centre of your inquiry; the only reason that they concern us is in your appreciation of their significance in *shaping* your inquiry – their importance in moulding the nature of your work. You have to show that you haven't stumbled bleary-eyed into the first set of methods you have come across. Rather, you have understood that knowledge is construed in different ways and that there are different ways of coming to knowledge. So you may include sentences such as, 'I recognise the competing world-views that frame social inquiry, and in this recognition I have chosen to ...'. Or, if you want to be more explicit – perhaps for Master's, and certainly for doctoral research – you could expand this. You might begin a discussion with something such as:

In considering an inquiry into the topic of stress in nurses, I am faced with two alternatives about the nature of my research. I can make assumptions about the world that faces me being divisible into quantifiable elements that I can measure and manipulate. Or, rejecting the validity of the ontological assumptions on which such division is based, I can see the social world in which I am interested as fluid, as constructed by individuals in myriad ways, as not amenable to quantification …

This would lead on to a discussion of stress being examined in fundamentally different ways given differing ontological, epistemological and paradigmatic stances. But the discussion of ontology, epistemology and paradigms is always secondary to the topic: you'll notice that in those three sentences there is only a passing reference to 'ontological assumptions'. The topic is the important thing, and what you have to show is that there are different ways of looking at it and studying it.

Critical awareness (again)

I discussed the importance of critical awareness on p. 41. Having looked at all of the rabbit-holes you can stumble into (to continue the *Alice in Wonderland* analogy) when thinking about something and trying to know about it, it is worth restating the significance of criticality and scepticism. But this uncertainty about knowledge should not leave us dithering in a heap of anxiety about what to do. Doing research is about finding out and trying to know things in the best possible way. While the important thing to remember about inquiry is that knowledge is tentative and provisional, we should stay optimistic …

The three Bs:

- **Be** doubtful.
- **Be** sceptical.
- **Be** critical.

And a fourth B:

But remember that doubt is nothing on its own. It is a prelude, a stimulus to action.

From purposes to questions to approaches to data gathering

Having looked at research approaches, paradigms and ways of thinking and knowing, let's go right back to the beginning of the chapter and think again now about research design. All the time during a research project you should be considering how the various elements of your research fit together: *purposes*, together with *questions*, together with *literature review*, together with *approach*, which leads on to decisions about design frame, methods and *analysis*.

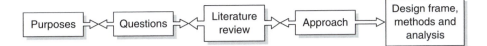

Figure 5.8   Knitting it together

Each part should be informing the others (see Figure 5.8). How has the purpose (for example, evaluation, or improving your practice, or describing) led you to a research question? And how has the research question led you to a particular approach or approaches? As your findings emerge you may wish to ask further, subsidiary questions, or you may wish to go back to your literature review to see if light can be cast upon an unexpected aspect of your findings.

In social and educational research there is always this toing and froing back and forth from one element to another. You will constantly be revisiting and revising your views, and this is perfectly proper and to be expected for it means that there will be a logic and a progression to the shape of your research project. This logic needs to be evident to the reader so you need to be able to show how it is emerging.

What does all of this mean for you and the way that you proceed to your design frame, methods and analysis? It means that you have to think about the interrelationship of these issues in relation to your project. Figure 5.9 sums these up

If we look at Figure 5.9, the process of going from questions to approaches can perhaps be illustrated with some examples. In Chapter 1 I talked about different kinds of research question to try to clarify the different trajectories on which research could be set by different kinds of question. These were questions that demanded description, interpretation, deduction or inference. As the book has proceeded you will have realised that it isn't quite as simple as this. A question that looks as if it will require only description in the answer may be a lot more complex, for description can happen in a wide variety of forms. You can describe in words or in numbers. You can describe one situation or many. Let's imagine that you are interested in hospital education services for children who are chronically sick. You could pose questions such as the following:

1. How many children are educated in hospitals in England, how have trends changed in postwar years and what are the possible reasons for this?
2. What is the experience of children educated in hospital today?
3. What are attitudes to hospital-educated children when they return to school?
4. If a rest period is introduced into the hospital school day at mid-morning, what will be the consequence on children's lunchtime behaviour?

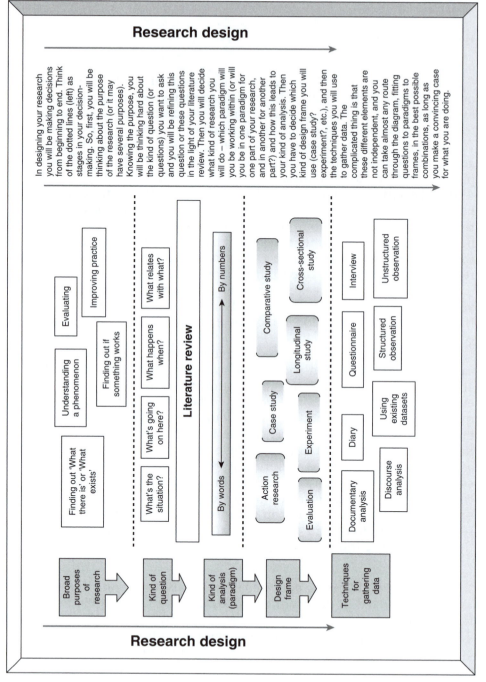

Figure 5.9 Process of research design

Question 1 leads you into a project that is unequivocally concerned with description and descriptive statistics. You will be seeking answers in official statistics and looking to relate these statistics to social movements, events and changes in policy. *Question 2* leads you to examine children's experience. You can choose how you try to gain access to this experience and how you interpret it, but interpretation will certainly be involved. You might choose to observe the experience of children by placing yourself in a hospital education setting, or you might ask the children themselves or their parents or staff. *Question 3* leads you to consider attitudes – the attitudes of children in ordinary mainstream schools – when children return from sometimes long stays in hospital. This could be done by interviewing individual children or a group of children in a focus group, or it could be done by giving a questionnaire to children, or even by observing a class. Whatever, some kind of judgement about their attitudes will be required from the researcher: interpretation will be needed. *Question 4* involves some kind of assessment of consequence: 'What happens when?' While this could be answered narratively, in words, it is more usual in this kind of question to try to be able to say 'This does (or doesn't) seem to be associated with this' – not only are they related, but x seems to be causing y. For this, some kind of measure of y may be helpful.

So, particular kinds of question lead to particular kinds of study. However, the relationship is by no means one-to-one: you cannot map one approach and one method to one kind of question, even though sometimes certain kinds of question will lead more obviously to one route than another. At each stage choices will be required from you, and rather inconveniently there are no right or wrong answers when it comes to research design. It's a question of thinking intelligently about it, and then accounting for the choices that you have made.

Let's take a more detailed example of a research study in the context of Figure 5.9. Which route through the diagram would be taken from beginning to end, and what kinds of choices might be made?

Designing research: an example

Angharad is a newly-qualified teacher in a rural primary school in North Wales where most of the children are bilingual in English and Welsh. A small minority of the children are fluent only in English, while the other children are familiar with what is called 'bilingual code-switching' – in other words, regularly and unthinkingly switching between two languages in which they are fluent. This is not discouraged in the school, though Angharad realises from her reading that the practice of allowing this has aroused controversy in the education community generally – some believing that the different languages should be kept separate to avoid confusion.

Angharad is aware that the group of five English-only speakers in her Year 3 class is becoming isolated; they are increasingly playing together and there are signs that they are not being integrated into the group and are even beginning to be bullied by some of the bilingual children. Angharad's observation here has emerged out of curiosity and interest: she has become curious about the behaviour of the children and her reaction is to try to find out whether her perception is ...

(a) an accurate one of what is actually happening – in other words, is she imagining it, or is there more evidence for it than just her gut feeling?
(b) that it is a common one in her school and in other schools locally, nationally or internationally where bilingualism happens, and
(c) that if the situation is as she perceives it to be, whether there is anything that she can do about it.

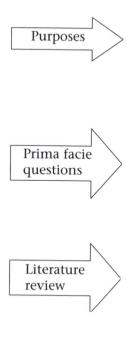

Purposes

There are two simple purposes in her research, then. The first purpose (related to (a) and (b)) stems centrally out of curiosity (emerging, in turn, out of concern for the isolated children) – curiosity to know whether her feelings are accurate. The second purpose (c) stems out of a desire to improve her practice if it is the case that the monolingual children's experience at school is becoming more separate and segregated from mainstream activity.

Prima facie questions

Two kinds of prima facie question emerge from this. The first leads to a 'What's the situation?' question, while the second leads to a 'What's going on here?' question.

Literature review

Her literature review will focus on bilingualism and code-switching not only in Wales, but also in the US where there is a substantial literature on code-switching in Chicano and Puerto Rican communities. What do school staff in these communities do? Do they have special procedures and policies? Are these similar to those operating in schools in the UK?

Her literature review will lead her to be better informed about the issue of bilingual code-switching and to realise that positive action could help her to resolve some of the issues that had emerged for the

Revised
thinking in
light of liter-
ature review

Revised
questions

Design frame
and data-
gathering

children in her class. Before doing that, though, she would need first to assess properly the level and extent of any problems that existed, and second to understand the likely consequences for the mono-lingual children. The latter had to be seen in the context of the school's and the local authority's policies on code-switching, and whether anything could realistically be done to influence code-switching or the consequences of it.

Her first question involves some fairly simple data-gathering about what is happening, for the question seeks to describe something: to state the current situation. If Angharad believes that she can make observations of the classroom to verify (or otherwise) her informal observation, these may involve both structured and unstructured observations: the former assuming that there are things that she can count and the latter relying more on impressions, gathered more systemati-cally in a diary. Her second question is rather more complex and involves (i) the collection of documentary data from the school and the LA, and (ii) information from the children themselves on how they are being affected.

She then decides that her design frame (of which more in Chapter 6) will be a case study. She also decides on methods for gathering data within this frame (Chapter 8).

Mapping this process through our design trajectory would look some-thing like the series of routes shown in Figure 5.10.

Overview

I've tried to show that much discussion in social research agonises over the purposes of research and what research can and cannot do. What are we trying to study? What counts as knowledge? Can social research explain things? Or does it just help our understanding? How is expla-nation different from understanding? Is descriptive research without numbers of any value? How far are the methods of *natural* scientists (such as chemists and physicists) appropriate in *social* science? Who can define what science is anyway?

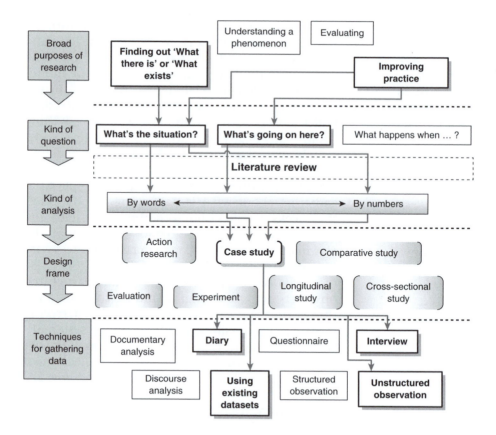

Figure 5.10   Angharad's course through the design maze

These, among others, are the Big Questions of social science and many million words have been written about them without anyone coming to any firm conclusions. Reading about research method in the social sciences, leads you to words such as 'epistemology', 'positivism', 'structuralism', 'interpretivism', 'postmodernism', 'quantitative', 'qualitative', each of them describing different frameworks within which these issues are thought about.

Don't worry about these rather frightening words. More important is an understanding that there is an increasing awareness of the need for different approaches in answering the questions of the applied social sciences, particularly if there is a practitioner focus to these questions. The positive side of this as far as you are concerned is that a broad spectrum of research activity is perfectly acceptable. The most important thing is to make sure that the methods that you use are appropriate for the questions you pose.

You will decide on your research approach after having considered the nature of your question and what you want to find out. Having said that different approaches are acceptable, it is important to remember that the choice you make about your approach is a choice between fundamentally different ways of viewing the world and equally different methods of discovering knowledge. But these different 'takes' on discovery are not in opposition to one another: they can complement each other. Different puzzles demand different thinking strategies. Questions needing formal description in the answer, or questions about what causes what or what is related to what, will usually need an approach that calls for the isolation of variables and the quantification of their variation. Other questions – perhaps about specific systems, institutions or people – demand insight, empathy and understanding. They need a more naturalistic approach that takes cognisance of the person of the researcher.

To labour the point, it's not a choice of one or other of these approaches; they can be used side by side. The key decisions that you make about the approach (or approaches) of your inquiry will depend on its purpose and the nature of your questions: what kind of knowledge do you ultimately want? Or do you want different kinds of knowledge, each associated with a different kind of data, for different strands of your research? It is these issues that determine the design of your research.

Further Reading

Brookfield, S.D. (1995) *Becoming a Critically Reflective Teacher*. San Francisco, CA: Jossey Bass.
A thoughtful book on reflective teaching, encouraging readers to question the implicit assumptions they hold.

Etherington, S. (2004) *Becoming a Reflexive Researcher: Using ourselves in research*. London: Jessica Kingsley.

Fuller, S. (2007) *The Knowledge Book: Key Concepts in Philosophy, Science and Culture*. London: Acumen.
An A-Z of key concepts, refracted through Fuller's refreshingly unusual mind.

MacIntyre, A. (1985) *After Virtue: a Study in Moral Theory*. London: Duckworth.
See Chapter 8 of MacIntyre's book for his devastating critique of the social sciences.

Oakley, A. (2000) *Experiments in knowing: gender and method in the social sciences*. Cambridge: Polity.
Ann Oakley is a feminist scholar and this book includes her take on gender bias in social science. She looks at the historical development of methodology in the social and natural sciences and argues that they have been subject to a process of 'gendering'. Arguing, like so many others, that the divide between quantitative and qualitative should be played down, she says that we should not play down experimental ways of knowing in the social sciences.

Pring, R. (2000) *Philosophy of educational research*. London: Continuum.
Excellent – especially on the invalidity of a quantitative/qualitative divide in inquiry.

Sacks, O. (1996) *An anthropologist on Mars*. London: Picador.
A lovely collection of essays. Sacks is in fact a neurologist, not an anthropologist, and the people he talks with and observes (for example, people with autism and Tourette's) are particularly interesting for those researching with people who are in any way different.

Savin-Baden, M. (2004) Achieving reflexivity: moving researchers from analysis to inter-pretation in collaborative inquiry, *Journal of Social Work Education*, 18 (3), 365–78.

Schön, D. (1983) *The reflective practitioner: how professionals think in action*. London: Temple.
This is *the* key text on reflective thinking and practice.

Seale, C. (2003) *Social research methods: a reader*. London: Routledge.
A fine collection of classic papers on method, including pieces from Wright Mills, Durkheim, Flanders, Feyerabend, Kuhn, Geertz and others.

Thomson, A. (2005) *Critical reasoning: a practical introduction*. London: Routledge.
This is industrial strength critical thinking, but clearly explained. If you can use and understand this, you are up in the premier league of critical thinkers.

If you are interested in the kind of research Angharad is doing, see:
Wei, L. and Moyer, M. (2008) *The Blackwell Guide to research methods in bilingualism and multilingualism*. Oxford: Blackwell.

The Design Frame

Introduction	
Literature review	
Methodology	
Fieldwork and findings	
Analysis and discussion	
Conclusion	

You are here in your project →

Once you have decided on your general approach to answering your question, you can think about the 'scaffold' or 'design frame' within which you will plan and execute your research. This chapter considers:

- **some general issues in designing a piece of research;**
- **the main 'frames' to guide the way that you carry out research:**

  - **action research;**
  - **case study;**
  - **comparative research;**
  - **ethnography;**
  - **evaluation;**
  - **experiment;**
  - **longitudinal, cross-sectional studies and survey.**

Design is about plan and structure, and as Figure 5.9 in Chapter 5 indicates, the whole programme of your research, from purposes to execution, constitutes the design. One particular part of the sequence of decisions you make will be about what I am here calling the *design frame*. I have called it this because it constitutes the most important element in the way that your research is structured: it's like a chassis or superstructure that supports your research. The design frame provides the framework for your research – connecting purposes with questions with the ways in which data can be collected – though it does not *prescribe* how that data will be collected.

I will be concentrating on seven types of design frame here. There are others, but these seven are the most common structures used in small research projects. They are:

- action research;
- case study;
- comparative research;

- ethnography;
- evaluation;
- experiment;
- longitudinal, cross-sectional studies and survey.

It is important to reiterate that these are not designs for research in themselves. The design itself is the plan for research that you adopt from the beginning of your project. The reason I have called these design *frames* is that they provide the defining structure within the design. By choosing one or more of them you are consolidating decisions that you have made about the purposes of your inquiry, the kind of research that you are doing and what you want to achieve from it.

The design frames are scaffolds within which to structure what you do. But it is important also to say that these design frames are not in any way similar as structures, nor are they mutually exclusive. They can exist in combination. So, for example, action research could take shape in most of the other forms, or a case study could include a survey. This will become clearer as we look at the frames themselves.

The idea of research design per se – the idea that you plan research at the beginning and carry on according to the blueprint you have drawn until the end – is a bit of a hangover from the days when social research was expected to be as similar as possible to natural scientific research. As such, it would be mainly experimental and it would come complete with very specific instructions on procedures, methods and apparatus, with the idea that anyone could come along after you and repeat the experiment you were doing. The key idea behind all of this was *replicability*, or in other words the ability for someone else to repeat what you were doing. If then, after many repeats of your experiment, many others had the same finding as you, having followed the same design and procedure, the scientific community could be sure that the finding was secure.

Nowadays, social scientists working in an applied field such as education, social work or criminal justice are particularly aware of the difficulties of conforming to these kinds of expectations for our research. For a start there are now recognised to be difficulties, sometimes insuperable, of managing a social situation in the same way as a chemistry experiment, but there is also now less certainty that there is one best way of organising research. As I tried to show in Chapter 5, if we are trying to research something in the social world we don't even necessarily even have to adopt the position of neutral, disinterested observer. By contrast, we can be open, involved interpreters of events, responding and changing as new information appears.

The latter point is particularly relevant as far as 'research design' is concerned, since it implies that there should be far less rigidity about such design than had hitherto been expected. This ties in with the expectation of a recursive plan (rather than a linear plan) that I talked about in Chapter 1. The design, it implies, should not be set in stone, ready to be replicated exactly by the next researcher. Given that this is the case, some have spoken about *emergent design*, in other words letting the design 'happen' as you find out more about the situation in which you are interested. This idea of emergent design is an important one for social research in the interpretative tradition, and though the word 'design' is still used, it really turns the idea of 'design' on its head, since something that 'emerges' cannot be 'designed'. We should perhaps look for a new word for the process.

However, I'm not going to do that now, since 'design' is the word we are stuck with and everyone knows what they mean by it – or at least they think they do. The trouble with using 'design' is that it implies all of the traditional features of experimental design that I have talked about (e.g. specification of sample, apparatus and so on), and these features carry with them other expectations. There are, for example, expectations about sample size (the bigger the better), reliability (you have to be sure of getting the same result if you do the same again) and validity (you have to be sure that you are finding out what you set out to find). But these are not the ground rules for interpretative research.

Yes, I said *not*. It is *not* expected that you can generalise from interpretative research: your 'sample' gives you insights rather than generalisations. So your 'sample' is small – even as small as one. Be happy with that. In fact the notion of the sample is a misnomer in interpretative research since your informant (or whatever) is not a sample from a wider population. They have integrity in their own right. It is *not* expected that if someone else does the study they will find something identical to what you found. Quite the contrary: someone else will almost certainly find something very different from what you found and this is to be expected. They will be interpreting with their personal history, interests, predilections and idiosyncrasies, you with yours.

So, the word 'design' should be interpreted with caution in social research. In certain kinds of research it will be more fixed; in others less. Expectations about it in one kind of research will not always apply in another.

Some general issues in design

As I have just tried to indicate, design is something of a misnomer and leads people to have cast-iron expectations about the structure of research, ignoring the tenets of different types of research – the presuppositions that ground it. Given these different types of research, there can be no expectation that the ground rules and methods of one kind of research will be appropriate in another. It is as well to be aware of this since a major error committed in many dissertations is the use of one set of expectations with a form of research that does not carry these expectations. It is with this warning that I discuss now some general issues in designing a research project.

Sampling

The notion of sampling really belongs in experimental research (see p. 124) and research that seeks relationships among variables. There is the assumption that you are taking your group or groups for your research from a manageable sample which is representative of a larger population. A population in experimental design means something rather more than the one we speak about in everyday parlance (e.g. 'The population of the USA is 350 million'). It means the total number of all possible individuals relating to a particular topic which *could* (if we had all the money and resources we wanted) be included in a study. So, there is a population of teaching assistants, a population of school-aged children, a population of people on benefits, a prison population, and so on. Assuming that the sample is truly representative of this wider population, the findings of your well designed research can then be generalised to the population.

Of course, the sample may not be representative: there may be *selection bias* of one kind or another. There are many ways in which one can ensure that the sample is representative of this wider population. One is by taking a *random sample*. This is what it says on the tin: it is a sample that is randomly taken –

> **Selection bias** is a distortion of evidence arising from the way that the data is collected. It usually refers to the selection of people in a sample, but can also refer to bias arising from the ways in which other kinds of data are selected.

in the same way that names could be picked from a hat: the process is random. However, it is not good enough for the sample *just* to be randomly taken. If you took as a random sample of university students the first dozen people you found in the bar on Wednesday night, your sample would be susceptible to various sources of distortion – how do you know that bar-dwellers are representative of the student population generally? It may be that those who go to the bar are less likely to go to the library, or that they tend to be representative of one ethnic or religious group more than another. That is why this kind of sample (the first dozen in the bar) is called a *convenience sample*, and why a convenience sample has many problems associated with it if you are expecting to generalise from it. To take a true random sample, you would have to ensure that you were drawing a large enough subset of the population so that the chance of getting a distorted picture was reduced to the minimum. You may have noticed that polls from market research organisations, when they are looking at voting intentions, take a sample of around 1,000 people, and this may (or may not, given that the voting population of the UK is over 40 million people) be a satisfactory sample.

A way of improving a sample's representativeness is to *stratify* it. In taking a *stratified sample* you ensure that the sample you are taking reflects in important ways the characteristics of the actual population. So, suppose you were interested in the views of heating engineers, you could ensure a simple form of stratification in the sample you collected

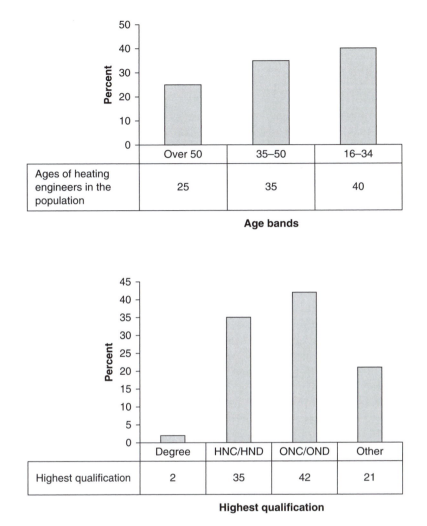

Ages of heating engineers in the population	Over 50	35–50	16–34
	25	35	40

Age bands

Highest qualification	Degree	HNC/HND	ONC/OND	Other
	2	35	42	21

Highest qualification

Figure 6.1   Stratifying your sample

by matching the sample with facets of the (whole) population of heating engineers nationally. You could make sure that your sample mirrored known features of the population – say, with regard to gender, age, and highest qualification, as shown in Figure 6.1.

What's wrong with the idea of samples?

Professional researchers have extended the notion of sample to all kinds of study, not just experimental research and research concerning the collection of data from groups of individuals. So, sometimes people will speak of a 'sample' in relation to a case study where only one case is being studied. But this is a quite unnecessary extension of the use of the word 'sample' and is clearly ludicrous. For even in a colloquial definition, there is the expectation that a sample will be in some way representative. Chambers dictionary gives as its definition of sample the following:

sample *säm'pl, n.* a specimen, a small portion to show the quality of the whole.

So, even in everyday usage, 'sample' carries the meaning that the sample is in some way reflective of the whole. But often when the word 'sample' is used in social research it carries none of this 'reflective of the whole' notion. So, a *snowball sample* – which involves the respondent telling the researcher who the next respondent might be, and that respondent doing the same, and so on – does not pretend to any kind of representativeness. Likewise, a

In experimental research 'sample' refers to a subset that is representative of a larger population. In interpretative research it does not carry this connotation.

purposive sample, which involves simply the pursuit of the kind of person in whom the researcher is interested, professes no representativeness. For this reason, these kinds of 'samples' are sometimes called *non-probabilistic* samples, because they do not lend themselves to the kind of design on which inferential statistics using probability estimates are used. Personally, I think it would be easier if they weren't called 'samples' at all.

As I indicated earlier, this carrying of experimental meaning of 'sample' to other kinds of research is accompanied by dangers since it carries with it the quiet assumption that all of the other paraphernalia of experimental research goes along with it. This should not be the case.

Sadly, this mixing of tenets and ground rules has sometimes been deliberate rather than merely accidental and of course the confusion transmits itself to you as a student – and you have no idea what to make of it. It's only someone who is as old as I am who can realise what has happened. What has happened is that when interpretative research was trying to establish its credentials as authentic 'social scientific' research forty or fifty years ago, researchers went to great lengths to ape the language of traditional experimental and relational research. They did this to boost the status of interpretative research. So Glaser and Strauss (1967), for example, drew a distinction between what they called the *theoretical sample* and the *statistical sample*. By a 'theoretical sample' they meant the amount of sampling that would have to be done in order for the researcher to be sure that no more categories were being encountered as they went through more and more data. They say: 'As he sees similar instances over and over again, the researcher becomes empirically confident that a category is saturated' (Glaser and Strauss, 1967: 61). If this sounds a little vague, it's because it is, with the word 'empirically' thrown in just to make things sound more scientific. (When do you think, 'Ah! I am now empirically confident!'? When do you feel that warm, gooey glow of empirical confidence?) If you are interested, I have explored elsewhere (Thomas and James, 2006) the reasons why interpretative researchers sometimes seem to think that they need to parrot the language of experimentalists. My feeling is that it is not only unnecessary to do this (particularly in relation to the sample), but also that it leads to misunderstanding about the nature of interpretative research. Sadly, the feeling that one has to use the language and methods of experimentalists is a relic of the days when interpretative research was felt to be not quite good enough. Even more sadly, it leads inexperienced researchers to inappropriate research designs.

Variables

Things that we want to measure in the social world *vary*. (If they were always the same – didn't vary – we wouldn't be interested in measuring them!). So, *variables* are measurable attributes of things that change. Age changes, so it is a variable. Scores on tests vary so they too are variables. Anything that can be counted could be a variable: age, class size, time spent sitting down, hair length, reading age, level of stress, number of words written on a page, and so on. We can also treat what could be called 'on–off' matters as variables. Thus gender, of which there are of course only two varieties, can be a variable. The amount of a variable is called its value.

Reliability

Reliability refers to the extent to which a research instrument such as a test will give the same result on different occasions. Really, the idea of reliability has been imported into applied social research from psychometrics – the 'science' of testing people's individual characteristics such as ability, attainment and personality. In my opinion, psychometrics is where the notion of reliability should have stayed. It is far too heavily drawn on particularly by student social researchers, who spend too much time thinking about it and writing about it in their reports. Because it is something quite concrete (complete with bullet-pointed sub-varieties) in the rather difficult area of methodology, students sometimes fall on it with eager relief: 'Ah, here's something I can get my teeth into!' and spend two or three pages writing about the sub-varieties of reliability in a wholly irrelevant way.

Certainly if you are collecting data you want your measuring instruments to be consistent from one time to the next. In other words, if you are giving a test to a group of children and then give it again soon after, you would expect it to provide much the same results each time: this is called *test–retest reliability*. Or if two different people gave the same test to the same group, you would expect the test to provide very similar results each time: it should have good *inter-rater reliability*. Or you may devise some kind of measure of classroom activity, such as being 'on task' (see the example of Karen on p. 127). If this is the case, you will want to know that the measure you are using is accurately assessing the feature or activity on which you are focusing.

Of course, it is as well to be aware that biases can occur in the use of any instrument – such as teachers giving a test 'helpfully' because they like the new teaching programme which is being assessed by the test. But if teachers were craftily or unconsciously introducing bias in this way it would not be a technical matter; it would be a matter for intelligent appraisal. We should be alert to matters such as this (e.g. giving a test 'helpfully') and try to minimise their effects. The compiling of types of errors and biases into technical taxonomies (observer error, observer bias, subject error, subject bias, etc.) diverts attention from the real subject of the research, and it suggests that there are technical 'fixes' to the problems of any kind of individual or social assessment. There aren't. Worse, the idea that these fixes may exist may even distort the construction of instruments, so that they may be 'reliable' but in fact tell us nothing useful.

It is possible to use formulae to help you to establish a coefficient of agreement across times and/or observers which will give a figure representing the reliability of the instrument being used. However, in my experience, in applied social research done by students at undergraduate and postgraduate levels, these are rarely if ever used – nor do they need to be in most cases. It is far more important that you pay attention to whether the instrument is doing what you want it to do and isn't picking up something irrelevant or something that is simply easy to measure (such as 'out of seat' as an indication of being 'off task' – but are pupils necessarily 'off task' when they are out of their seats?). Does it matter if, given on two occasions, the same instrument says something rather different? Surely it is almost bound to, given the nature of people (as distinct from the nature of nitrogen).

As in the case of sampling, there is a confusion that sometimes exists between different kinds of research, with an assumption that reliability should apply in all kinds. It shouldn't. In interpretative research you are interpreting on the basis of you being *you*, interviewing someone else being *them*. Who you are – your 'positionality' (of which more below) – will affect this interpretation and you would not expect someone else to emerge with the same interview transcripts as you. So reliability is, in my opinion, irrelevant in interpretative research.

Validity

There are two meanings to validity in social science research, but before giving those, I should preface my comments by saying that everything that I have said about reliability applies also to validity: it is a concept imported from psychometrics and from experimental design; it is discussed far too often; it can distract you from the proper purpose of your research.

> Reliability and validity are important only in certain kinds of research. Don't let consideration of them derail your progress.

What are the two meanings? I have separated these meanings because, as with reliability, some students appear to latch on to the notion of validity and beyond this latching fail to understand the basic differentiation of types of validity (partly because in test construction several subtle differentiations are enumerated). The two types I am enumerating here are *instrument-based validity* and *experimental validity*. Unfortunately, the types have become hybridised and confused in such a way that it is now nigh-on impossible to understand what validity means. Here is my simplified version.

Instrument-based validity

With a measuring instrument such as a test, validity is the degree to which the instrument measures what it is supposed to be measuring. *Construct validity* is the Big Daddy of instrument-based validity – the sun around which all the other little instrument-based validities spin. Construct validity is the extent to which the results of a test (or another instrument) correlate with the theoretical construct for which it is seeking to act as an assessment. So, do the results from the test for *x* correlate with the actual *x*? If, for example, someone devises a test for extraversion, scores on this should largely parallel judgements made by a psychiatrist making judgements about extraversion – the latter being taken to be an unimpeachable assessment of this personality trait (and this is of course in itself questionable, but we won't dwell on this). All the other forms of validity you will find are offshoots, really, of construct validity. There are, for example, *content validity* (does it cover all of the necessary content?), *predictive validity* (does a test in intelligence, say, predict the kinds of outcomes for how intelligent people are supposed to fare?), *face validity* (does it look as if it's doing what it should be doing to the person being tested – has it, in other words, got street cred?) and *ecological validity*. They all really are facets of construct validity and there is no real need to try to disaggregate them in your mind unless you are constructing a psychometric test.

Again, the taxonomy of types here is an example of social scientists becoming more interested in the methodology than the subject, and the existence of such a complex taxonomy of types in my opinion distracts from an intelligent case-by-case appraisal of an instrument's use. For example, an IQ test could be constructed that had high marks for construct validity, but this would disguise to the lay reader the extent to which the concept of IQ is itself challenged as a notion – a construct. It's the danger of technical considerations taking precedence over others.

Experimental validity

There are many things that happen in psychological and social life that can mess up an experiment. The extent to which the design of an experiment attends to these and eliminates them is reflected in its 'internal validity'. (Why 'internal'? Don't ask me, ask Campbell and Stanley (1963) who came up with the term.) Chemists (lucky them) can pressurise some nitrogen in a bell jar and see how much it contracts to demonstrate Boyle's Law. They don't have to worry about the nitrogen getting older, or having been exposed to the test before, or deciding to quit the experiment for family reasons, or being a particular kind of nitrogen that doesn't like bell jars. No such luck for social researchers. If we construct an experiment we have to keep all of these things (and more) in mind. If an experiment is somehow constructed (designed) in such a way that it manages to eliminate all of these threats to the conclusions being taken seriously we can say that it has good internal validity.

One particularly important threat is that of mistaking causal direction. Is the wind caused by trees shaking their leaves? Are eggs the right size for eggcups because of good planning by hens? I have explored the latter elsewhere in relation to how research on reading difficulty is interpreted (see Thomas, 2002), and it is of course always necessary to consider direction of causation. What causes what? To you and me it's daft even to suggest that the wind is caused by mass leaf-shaking by trees, though a visitor from another planet which experienced no wind, not even a gentle breeze, might be tempted to explore the proposition. It becomes more difficult, though, when an association is found between something like skill in auditory memory and early reading success. It is easy to run away with the idea that the memory is the cause of the reading skill. In fact, though, it may be that reading 'trains' the auditory memory, and that better reading therefore is actually the cause of the better memory.

However, as is so often the case, the problem is not technical. The problem is usually *not* that no one has considered the possibility that *y* may be causing *x* rather than *x* causing *y*, but rather that they do not *want* to consider the possibility, for any one of a variety of reasons. (The sinister implications of this are discussed very nicely by Gerald Coles (2000) in *Misreading Reading: The Bad Science That Hurts Children*.)

Generalisation and generalisability

In everyday life, when we make judgements about the future – predictions – these are usually on the basis of generalisation from experiences we have had in the past. Events that repeatedly occur in certain circumstances enable you to generalise – to say to yourself that these events will tend to occur in these same kinds of circumstances in the future. You notice that when there are no clouds it doesn't rain, so you make a reasonable generalisation about the low likelihood of precipitation when there are no clouds in the sky. While such generalisations serve us well most of the time, they do not match up to the expectations that science has when it seeks to offer laws and theories – which are also based on generalisation but, one might say, generalisation-plus. Scientists cannot proceed *simply* on the basis of common-or-garden generalisation. As the great philosopher Bertrand

Russell (1956: 91) put it, the person who says that unsupported bodies in air fall 'has *merely* generalized, and is liable to be refuted by balloons, butterflies and aeroplanes' [italics added].

What Russell is saying here is that while generalisation is important, it has to be more than a mere rule of thumb based upon everyday observation of life's patterns. Science's generalisations have to have a bit more oomph about them than that. Good generalisations – generalisations that provide accurate predictions – are at the cornerstone of scientific progress. It's just that we have to find ways of making our generalisations more than the 'mere' generalisations Russell was talking about. And it is even more difficult to make sensible, accurate generalisations in social science than it is in physics or chemistry.

In social research, generalisability is about the extent to which research findings can be applied in settings other than the setting in which the original research took place. To make such a generalisation requires that some quite strict criteria are met about the way that the study is set up. In the main, the extent to which you can generalise hangs on the extent to which your sample is representative of the population. As I noted above in discussing sampling, the whole idea of taking a sample is that it is a sample of a wider population.

Remember that generalisability is of importance only when you want to generalise. If you are conducting a case study with only one subject, it is more or less meaningless to worry about generalisation (though people do worry about it, I can assure you). You cannot generalise from one case. The Germans have a phrase, *Einmal ist keinmal*, which means 'What happens only once might as well not have happened at all'. I personally wouldn't go quite that far, but I would agree with a watered-down version of this, namely that we can learn no general lessons from things that happen only once. But how many more do we have to study before we can say that we can generalise? This depends on a great many factors, not least the adequacy of your sample as a representative sample.

As with so much in social science, there are no hard and fast rules about generalisation. Many would no doubt go along with the short-story writer Damon Runyan and his comment in *A Very Honourable Guy*: 'The race is not always to the swift, nor the battle to the strong. But that's the way to bet'. In other words, one's generalisations may be far from perfect as ways of judging the future, but one can, to varying extents, rely on them as rules of thumb in ordering our lives or in interpreting the findings from our research.

Positionality

In interpretivist research there is an assumption that knowledge is situated in relations between people. This is sometimes called *situated knowledge*. With this assumption taking the foreground, the person doing the research takes a central role in the interpretation – in the discovery of this situated knowledge. The researcher therefore has an undeniable *position* and this position affects the nature of the observations and the interpretations that they make. There is an acceptance in this of the importance of the person – their likes and dislikes, their backgrounds and their pastimes, their vested interests and expectations. The researcher is an active, not passive, agent in acquiring knowledge of the processes, histories, events, language and biographies of the research context. Because of the importance of the nature of the relation between the researcher and research participants, the researcher's biography – including class, gender, ethnicity, ideas and commitments – needs to be made explicit.

There is also the assumption that in doing research you are in some sense serving a certain set of needs, and these needs are not necessarily unequivocally good or altruistic. They will not necessarily be about the good of education (in the widest sense) or the child. They may be self-serving or benefiting a particular group. This should be made explicit.

The explicit acknowledgement of this may present some dilemmas. Let's imagine that you are a newly qualified teacher having completed your PGCE recently and you wish to study now for a Master's in Teaching and Learning for which you have to complete a research project. You discuss it with Zena, your Head of Year, and she suggests that you use your research project to evaluate the school's new inclusion policy. You already know from staffroom discussion that the policy is thought to be a joke – devised to keep Ofsted and the local authority happy but serving little purpose in practice. You are therefore faced with a predicament. Given that you intend to undertake an interpretative study, how would you construct your eventual write-up, for the university will be expecting a discussion of positionality – of your interests, uncertainties, allegiances, and so on – while Zena and the school management may expect something entirely different, something that pretends a cleaner, more dispassionate and supposedly 'objective' assessment of what they assume to be 'the facts'. So, for you, this idea from Zena is non-viable as a potential research project because you would have to make all of this explicit in the write-up. And the issue now becomes 'How will I find a way to reject the Head of Year's suggestion?', given that the school is giving you some time in your timetable to complete your project. The problem here is about the conflict between your integrity as an interpretative researcher and the expectations and interests of the school.

In presenting interpretative research you should accept your subjectivity and not be ashamed of it or afraid of it. Given that it is central, your dissertation or thesis should be written as if you realise the underpinning principles that guide the conduct of this kind of research. An interpretative study will therefore be reported in an entirely different way from an experimental study. You should begin – right at the beginning, in the introduction – with a full discussion of positionality: of *yourself*, why you are interested in this topic, what your personal circumstances are, and so on. You will always write in the first person, saying, for example,

'I believe that ...' rather than 'The researcher believes that ...' This may seem obvious, but it is a common mistake for students conducting interpretative research – research that demands that they put themselves at the centre of the analysis – to report their work as if they have just conducted an experiment and to omit any information about themselves. If you do this kind of research, readers need to know who you are and where you stand, metaphorically as well as literally.

Triangulation

Triangulation is a term that has been borrowed from surveying and geometry, where it refers to the use of fixed reference points organised in triangles. By knowing an angle and the length of two sides of a triangle, the third can

> **Positionality:** Saying who you are and 'where you are coming from'.
>
> **Triangulation:** Seeing things from different angles.

be accurately calculated and distances can be checked and cross-checked.

In social science the term is used simply in a metaphorical way, based on its origins in geometry and surveying. There is no intimation that triangles should be involved, or that things have to be done in threes. Rather, the term is used to indicate that viewing from several points is better than viewing from one. Given the instinctive uncertainty – the critical awareness – that should be the hallmark of the good social science researcher, another viewpoint or another analytic method may make you decide to reject an explanation that you had come up with from your first analysis of findings. Or it may encourage you to have more confidence in the explanation you proposed on the basis of your first analysis. For this reason, using several methods, or viewing things from several directions, is sometimes built into a piece of research at the beginning.

Denzin (1978) outlined several types of triangulation, including *investigator triangulation* where more than one person is involved in interpretation and analysis, *theory triangulation* where more than one theoretical framework would be involved and *methodological triangulation* where more than one method would be used to collect data. The last of these is the most common meaning, though the emphasis on method (that is to say the data-gathering method) should not be taken to imply that the use of more than one design frame is excluded in the concept of triangulation. So I would add to Denzin's categories *design frame triangulation*. In other words, you would be triangulating if you used both a case study and a longitudinal study together in the same piece of research.

Opinions differ on the need for triangulation. Some interpretative researchers argue that a piece of interpretative research has value and completeness in itself. It doesn't need any verification from other kinds of research. It has integrity as a singular inquiry. The argument for the integrity of the singular case, singularly done, is a powerful one. But the argument for corroboration, for the need for alternative kinds of evidence, each corroborating the other, is to my mind even more powerful, and triangulation is really simply about corroboration. I discussed the importance of corroborative evidence on p. 16.

The design frames

Action research

Action research is research that is undertaken by practitioners (for example, teachers, social workers, nurses or doctors) for the purpose of helping to develop their practice. It is usually done at the same time as performing that practice. The central aim is *change* and the emphasis is on problem-solving in whatever way seems most appropriate. It is flexible in design: the assumption is built in firmly at the beginning that as the research proceeds you will go back to revisit your aims, assumptions, beliefs and practices, think about all of these critically and then revise them.

It may be done by an individual or a group, perhaps in collaboration with a consultant such as a university tutor. For this reason it is sometimes called 'participatory'. In other words, the assumption is that it is different from the way that traditional social research has sometimes been conceived: that is to say, as research done *by* researchers *on* subjects. It is research primarily done by the 'subject' or practitioner, with the aid of others.

The idea of action research came from the great social psychologist Kurt Lewin. In his paper 'Action research and minority problems' (Lewin, 1946) Lewin was critical of social research, saying that '... research that produces nothing but books will not suffice'. He describes action research as '... research leading to social action' using 'a spiral of steps, each of which is composed of a circle of planning, action, and fact-finding about the result of the action' (see Figure 6.3). The basic idea is of a continual refinement of your thinking, built upon a foundation of reflection about the problem and ways of going about solving it. The process could be shown as Figure 6.4.

Figure 6.2   Kurt Lewin

action   critical reflection

Figure 6.3   The basis of action research

So action research is a bit like a coil or spring, where you are continually moving forward up the coil by reflecting on action and changes that you have made.

Action cycle 2 (etc.)

6. Have a revised idea
7. Examine and gather information about the (revised) idea or problem
8. Plan action
9. Take action
10. Reflect on the consequences …

Action cycle 1

1. Have an idea or see a problem
2. Examine the idea or problem and gather information about it
3. Plan action
4. Take action
5. Reflect on the consequences

Figure 6.4   Action research: a spiral of steps

Much has been written about action research over the years and there are many different ideas about the way that it should or should not be done. My own view is that there are four basic ideas at the core of action research: that it …

1. is research done by practitioners, at their own behest – not someone else's;
2. is primarily about developing practice and empowering practitioners;
3. involves a commitment to change and to action based on reflection;
4. involves moving forward, always building on what you are discovering, using the process of planning, reflection and re-planning (shown in Figure 6.4).

Beyond this, it can take almost any form that you wish it to take. Indeed, Jean McNiff and her colleagues (McNiff et al., 2003) suggest that action research is more of a 'form of dialogue' than a technique, and that it is about practitioners thinking for themselves and making their own choices, asking themselves what they should do and accepting the consequences of their actions.

For me, this sums up the spirit of action research. Beyond this, it may take shape in almost any form. For example, you may wish to do a small experiment within an action research frame. It may involve a case study. Or you may undertake action research that involves some kind of evaluation.

Example 6.1
Emily is a newly qualified teacher of history in an inner London secondary school. One of her Year 9 students, Rashid, is surly, disengaged and withdrawn, but when challenged can be aggressive and even physically violent to other students or to

(Continued)

(Continued)

Table 6.1   A circle of steps

Action research steps	Questions/issues/actions (in brief)
Define the problem	The incidence of confrontational behaviour from students and one student in particular.
Examine the idea or problem and gather information about it	Is it a problem just for Emily? How far is it a problem of her making? Is it the school's problem or the student's problem? Read around the area of challenging behaviour; ask colleagues what they have done in similar circumstances with Rashid and others.
Plan action	Define what you mean by 'challenging behaviour'; keep a record and a diary of incidents of challenging behaviour; when does challenging behaviour occur, in what circumstances; plan ways of developing relationships with the students (challenging and unchallenging); list action to be taken if it occurs.
Take action	Take the action planned in Step 3.
Reflect on the consequences	Examine records and diary. Consider the effects of the action taken. What was effective? What wasn't? Discuss with colleagues, advisor, consultant and/or tutor. Move to the next action cycle.

staff. At the end of last term he had refused to hand in a pen at the end of the session and when confronted pushed Emily out of the way to exit the classroom. For this he was temporarily excluded from school.

In working with her local university for a postgraduate qualification, Emily decided to do an action research project based not only on Rashid but also on challenging behaviour from other students. The action research framework involved trying to develop her practice in such a way that confrontational incidents would occur less often. The plan is shown in Table 6.1.

A number of issues arose for Emily in doing this; for example, with regard to point 2, some rethinking was necessary about the nature and causes of challenging behaviour. In point 3, some innovative ideas came from separate discussions with her head of year and her university tutor. The latter suggested trying to make a special relationship in some way with Rashid and, capitalising on a brief moment when Rashid had shown an interest in one of her lessons on evacuated children in the Second World War, Emily asked her uncle, who had been an evacuee, if he would email Rashid about his experiences – which he was glad to do, sparking up an unlikely web friendship. Still on point 3, her head of year helped Emily to devise a list of appropriate and inappropriate behaviours to take when physically challenged by a child.

Having completed this 'circle of steps' and reflected on the consequences in the final step, Emily was then able to move on to the next circle of steps, having seen what worked and what didn't work. Rashid certainly responded to the efforts Emily had made on his behalf and began to act, if not with enthusiasm, with more courtesy, respect and a new-found gentleness. She considered a number of possible actions having completed the first circle of steps: she considered, for example, how far the action she had taken with Rashid was relevant and generalisable to other students in her class. She therefore decided to run a number of small focus groups with three or four of her students in each, and various focus materials comprising newspaper and magazine articles for discussion. With these, she would try to do with the others what she had done with Rashid – find something of interest and use this to help develop a relationship with the students.

Part of her reflection was also to realise that the special relationship she was nurturing with Rashid as part of the research was extra-special, even with the focus groups she had subsequently planned. Given that this might create additional difficulties with other students in the class, she included as her move to the next circle of steps some special activities also with other children in the class – for example taking a group of the quieter and more able children to a local museum at the end of term.

Case study

A case study involves in-depth research into one case or a small set of cases. The case may be a child, a teacher, a class, a school, a social services department … the list could go on. The aim is to gain a rich, detailed understanding of the case by examining aspects of it in detail. The data you collect can be from different facets of the question you are examining, and these data – perhaps from numbers or from interviews or informal observations – may be combined to tell your finished story.

There is no intimation in the case study that you will be generalising from this case to others. How could you? It's one case. In other words, you are not studying this case in order to understand others. You are studying it in order to understand it in itself. For the research methodologist Martyn Hammersley (1992) this choice of one case (or a small number) is made with a trade-off in mind. You are choosing this very restricted sample in order to be able to gain greater detail, but at the expense of being able to make useful generalisations to a broader population.

How do you choose your case? Robert Stake (1995: ix) suggests the following advice:

> A case study is expected to catch the complexity of a single case. A single leaf, even a single toothpick, has unique complexities – but rarely will we care enough to submit it to case study.

In other words, you don't study a particular case just for the sake of studying it. There have to be particular circumstances surrounding the case that make it of special interest. Stake proceeds:

We study a case when it itself is of very special interest. We look for the detail of the interaction with its contexts. Case study is the study of the particularity and complexity of a single case, coming to understand its activity within important circumstances.

As he goes on to suggest, the choice made of the case may be no 'choice' at all, because we have some kind of intrinsic interest in that case, whether it be a child with particular difficulty or the involvement in some programme of innovation at, say, a school or in a social services department. This is what he calls an 'intrinsic study'. Or it may be what he calls an 'instrumental study' – in other words, undertaken for the purpose of helping to understand or to illustrate something in relation to a research question.

It depends what you want to find out. The tradition of case study has come to be associated with 'naturalistic' inquiry, but it should not be seen like this. Case study can include a range of as many different methods and procedures as necessary for understanding what is going on in a particular situation. It's like an umbrella, covering a whole range of inquiry-activity.

A word of warning about case study – the social systems analyst Geoffrey Vickers in his highly influential book *The Art of Judgement* puts it this way:

> Case histories are a laborious approach to understanding. For situations are so varied that even a large number of cases may be a misleading sample, whilst each is so complex that even a detailed description may be too summary; and none is comprehensible outside the historical sequence in which it grew. (Vickers, 1965: 173)

Vickers's reservations are meant about big case studies undertaken by professional researchers and intended to inform institutional change. On the smaller scale, undertaken in a classroom, say, and intended to inform personal understanding, the concerns about being 'laborious' are not evident. However, the general points he makes are worth remembering: generalisation is not possible; detail and contextual understanding are essential. It is the rich picture with 'thick description' (see p. 202) that we need.

Example 6.2
Robin is in his second year of teaching as a Year 6 teacher in a primary school. Last year, in the run-up to the SATs, he noticed some disturbing signs of unease and anxiety among his pupils: more absence and illness and a general sense of disquiet that he couldn't put his finger on. For his project as part of a university course, he decided during the next round of SATs to undertake a case study of his class, focusing in a detailed way on the attitudes and responses of pupils and teachers

to these assessments. Starting with the notion of a link between these changes in behaviour and the national testing programme, he knew that his case study would relate the one to the other.

Since the government's regime of testing affected him most directly in Y6 (since this is age at which the SATs are given), Robin knew that of all the teachers in the school it was his own views on the impact of the assessments that were most relevant and important. He was particularly concerned about the emotional impact on the children, so in the six weeks leading up to the SATs he kept a diary of his impressions of the behaviour of the children and his own feelings over that time. He committed to spending 15 minutes at the end of each day writing the diary, which would produce 30 diary entries (6 weeks × 5 days) for subsequent analysis. He also committed to focusing on five children in his class, whose work and demeanour he would monitor closely but informally over the same period. He would for specified periods observe the children informally. He would take notes about the children's work, their attendance and their punctuality and he would make a point of talking to each of them briefly at least once a week, asking about their work and about how they were feeling. He would then keep an audio diary of his impressions of these encounters and the children's comments.

Although the SATs affected his class most directly, Robin had a suspicion that the culture of assessment made its effects felt through the age range, so he decided to interview all of the other teachers in the school for their opinions on the influence that SATs had made, even if only informally, on their own work and the attitude of children to learning.

Robin's analysis concentrated on drawing themes from the data, for example about anxiety in the children and the formalisation of style of teaching by himself and other teachers. He related these themes to the form in which expectations about success in the SATs were communicated to teachers by government departments and their agencies, and the implicit or explicit messages that accompanied these expectations.

Possible questions for Robin in the case study:

- How would he choose the five children?
- What ethical and access issues would arise?

Classic examples of case study are in Stephen Ball's (1982) *Beachside Comprehensive* and Colin Lacey's (1970) *Hightown Grammar*, which each give a detailed analysis of what goes on in one school over a period of time, and James Patrick's (1973) *A Glasgow Gang Observed*, giving a detailed narrative of what went on in the gang from the point of view of a young man infiltrating it (I discuss Patrick's work more on p. 77). These were doctoral studies and most dissertation work will not be expected to go into any way near such detail as these authors did in their work. However, they are enormously useful to read – in the work of both Ball and Lacey for examples of the kind of data-gathering that can be done and the way that case study work can be linked intelligently to national policy, and in Patrick's work for the style of involvement and reporting discourse that he uses, which is as good as reading a novel.

Ethnography

If you do an ethnography you are working right in the middle lane of interpretative research (see pp. 75–8). This is as interpretative as it gets. Confusingly, this design frame may be called 'case study method' but as we have just seen, case study can cover a much larger range of study methods than merely this one.

Ethnographers study a situation from within. They try to become part of the situation they are studying, to understand it like the other 'players'.

The term 'ethnography' comes from a field of social research that emerged in the early part of the twentieth century as a branch of anthropology, the study of humankind and its cultures. Ethnography evolved as a response to what was considered to be an inappropriate way of studying other cultures or communities, which had before the 1920s been treated almost as scientific objects of study by anthropologists. Writing was often judgemental, wearing the moral spectacles of the Western viewer. And if you are interested, look at Stephen Jay Gould's (1996) *The Mismeasure of Man* to see how some anthropological 'scientists' used to do their work by comparing the size and shape of the skulls of different races. Displacing this style of work, the new ethnography aimed to get to the heart of people's understandings of life through fieldwork *with* people rather than supposedly objective study *on* them. James P. Spradley, a great exponent of ethnography in the middle of the twentieth century, put it thus:

> Field work ... involves the disciplined study of what the world is like to people who have learned to see, hear, speak, think, and act in ways that are different. Rather than *studying people*, ethnography means *learning from people* ... Instead of collecting 'data' about people, the ethnographer seeks to ... be taught by them. Spradley (1979: 3)

Spradley draws on the example of a young American ethnographer, Elizabeth Marshall, who, interested in the culture of the Kalahari Bushmen, went to the Kalahari with her family in the 1950s. Marshall describes her meeting with a young woman:

> Presently she smiled, pressed her hand to her chest, and said: 'Tsetchwe.' It was her name.
>
> 'Elizabeth,' I said, pointing to myself.
>
> 'Nisabe,' she answered, pronouncing after me and inclining her head graciously. She looked me over carefully without really staring, which to Bushmen is rude. Then having surely suspected that I was a woman, she put her hand on my breast gravely, and, finding that I was, she gravely touched her own breast ...
>
> 'Tsau si' (women), she said. (Cited in Spradley, 19: 3–4)

You can glean from this brief example of Marshall's writing that the purpose of the ethnographer was to understand from within, treating the people with whom she is working with respect, as different but equal. It is typical of the style of reporting of ethnographers, who work through *fieldwork*, which Spradley describes as '... asking questions, eating strange foods, learning a new language, watching ceremonies, taking field notes, washing clothes, writing letters home, tracing out genealogies, observing play, interviewing informants, and hundreds of other things' (ibid.: 3). (Note, though, that 'fieldwork' now means something much more general, i.e. any empirical work of any nature.)

He goes on to note that for Tsetchwe to turn the tables and go to a small Wisconsin town to try to understand its culture would involve her doing everything that Elizabeth had to do, which first and foremost would mean ditching a belief in *naive realism*, which is to say the belief that '*love, rain, marriage, worship, trees, death, food*, and hundreds of other things have essentially the same meaning to all human beings' (ibid.: 4, original emphasis).

Ethnographers have to try to forget the meanings that these phenomena have for themselves in order to understand their significance in the other culture. This is hard of course and it means, usually, a long immersion in the cultures they are studying – learning new languages and learning about unfamiliar customs and practices – to try to understand how sense is made out of these and how meaning is invested in them. In order to make this sense, ethnographers have to use their own resources as people: as Bob Burgess (1982: 1) puts it, 'The main instrument of social investigation is the researcher'. As an ethnographer, there is no attempt to deny your own personal knowledge or to put it to one side, though you might be expected to take an entirely new perspective on the scene that confronts you. In the sense that the person of the researcher is central to the process of research (and you are not in any way attempting to be 'objective'), you must *use* your knowledge of people, social systems and structures and how they relate rather than rejecting this knowledge, but use it in a way that enables you to 'see outside yourself'. You can do this by, for example, using Geertz's thick description (discussed on p. 202). In other words, look to see what turns the twitch into a wink or the parody of a wink. Use your understanding of people to understand this situation that you are focusing on, and tell the reader how you are doing it.

Another facet of the positioning of *yourself* as an instrument of investigation is that you are a participant in the situation that you are observing and studying, which is why the term *participant observation* is often associated with this kind of research. You are not, in other words, trying to be detached or invisible, but rather engaged, fully involved, and gaining insights from this engagement. Participant observation is not limited to observation, pure and simple, though. It consists of watching, certainly, but also conducting interviews, listening to conversations, keeping a diary, taking notes and much more – anything that will help you to record and understand what is going on.

For an interesting (and short) example of the ethnographic genre, see Clifford Geertz's *Deep Play: Notes on the Balinese Cockfight,* to which an Internet link is given under Further Reading at the end of the chapter.

Ethnography is now a well accepted way of doing certain kinds of applied social research. In fact, some of the most influential research in education has been ethnographic in character. However, doing a small ethnographic project presents some major differences from the classic studies of which I have given examples. For a start, unlike the professional anthropologists cited here, you are unlikely to be entering a culture which is *unfamiliar* to you. Rather, you are likely to be entering a very familiar situation; in fact, the situation in which you are interested may be one with which you are intimately connected, perhaps as an employee or a regular visitor. Second, you will not have the time for the deep immersion of the professional anthropologists – but this may not be as necessary because of the familiarity you already have. This in itself has pluses and minuses: you may know the 'stage' and be an accepted 'actor' on it, but this means that you have to work extra hard to see it in a fresh light.

Though your immersion in the world of your study will be different in these important respects from the immersion of the 'classic' anthropology, beyond this the rationale behind ethnographic work is the same, and is about participation, engagement, thick description and understanding.

Example 6.3

Qualifying as a teacher three years ago, Amy is now head of maths in a large inner-city comprehensive school, but she wishes eventually to move into learning support. As part of a Master's degree in education she decides to do her dissertation research on the way that support works in the school. She wishes to understand how students see support, and what support can offer them. In particular, she asks whether there are any ways that the support department in the school can enhance its offer to its students.

She decides that her research project will be an ethnography of support: how it works and how it is viewed and understood by students and staff. She negotiates with the Head of Learning Support to use some of her regular non-contact time to work as an assistant in the learning support department. She asks to be treated as a teaching assistant for these periods, and ensures that she will be working only with classes with whom she has no dealings in her maths teaching. Her sessions of involvement with the department will include attendance at meetings and work with two classes per week as a participant observer: one science class and one languages class.

She prepares for this by planning carefully to observe each of the environments into which she goes. She decides not to take notes as she does this, as this will affect the way that the students and staff react to her during the sessions. However, she will write a diary immediately (or as soon as possible) after every session. She will also conduct unstructured interviews with both teacher members of the learning support staff as well as two of the teaching assistants associated with the department. The interviews will give free rein to these staff to express their views about the operation of support. On top of this, she will interview four students – two from each of the classes that she is working with. Further, on her movements around school, she will keep an eye and an ear open for comments or actions that in any way give clues as to the way in which learning support is viewed in the school. Is it seen genuinely as a way of including all students, or merely as a way of dealing with students who are seen to be 'special needs'?

An excerpt from Amy's diary is as follows:

I make my way to Xanthe's class again, a little late, having been talking to the head of support. I haven't spoken in detail to Xanthe yet about the team teaching idea. Last week's meeting with her was too tense to broach the topic. When I come in this week the situation seems rather similar. Xanthe is taking the class from the front and the children are messing around as they were last week. Xanthe holds up a small glass tank with a funnel upside down over something (a small plant, I think) and compares it with another similar set of objects. The children have to compare the two sets and say how they are different:

CHILD: There's more water in that one.

CHILD: One's all dirty – yeugh.

The session is to show that carbon dioxide is taken up by plants:

CHILD: That dirt's carbon dioxide!

Explanations are again punctuated with inconsequential intrusions:

CHILD: Anyone got a rubber!

These become so intrusive that Xanthe eventually loses her temper and raises her voice. This has some effect on the students, who temporarily quieten down. She capitalises on this by saying:

TEACHER: Right we'll have two minutes of complete silence – not a word.

The children respond to this: they are now clear about the rules and what is expected of them. Again I feel redundant – not only redundant, but worse that I am compounding the situation by my presence, and perhaps that Pauline the teaching assistant is in a similar position. She must feel some degree of inhibition about doing what comes naturally to her to quell the sorts of problems that she is experiencing. Again, there is no way that I feel I can intervene in the immediate situation without making things worse …

Amy analyses her findings using a variety of methods (some of which are described in Chapter 9). Her main aim in the analysis is to understand how learning support is viewed and understood in the school, so she is careful to try to see through the eyes of her informants, with that view moderated and influenced by her own reflections as recorded in the diary. Each element, though discrete, goes to inform each of the others and in her discussion she integrates and synthesises the analysis from each.

Possible question for Amy in undertaking the ethnography:

- How will she be able to use this diary when it makes comments that are implicitly critical of a colleague?

Figure 6.5   Evaluation research (from Pawson, 2006)

Evaluation

Evaluation research is probably the most common kind of research done by professional researchers in education and the social sciences, being undertaken to assess how effective a programme of activity has been. When done by professional researchers it is often carried out as a form of what is sometimes called 'contract research': a university researcher is contracted and paid to provide an independent assessment of some new initiative. A government department, for example, may pay a university research team to look at how effective the policy of employing greater numbers of teaching assistants has been.

The pattern is given by Pawson (2006) and corresponds roughly to Figure 6.5.

As you can see from Figure 6.5, evaluation research is different from action research, since there is – in the usual form of evaluation – no assumption that what is being studied feeds back in any systematic way to the activity, intervention or initiative being evaluated. (In action research, remember, there is the assumption that what is being discovered during the research actively feeds back and contributes to the development of the programme of change.) Only after the evaluation has been completed may the person contracting the evaluation decide to continue with the programme, modify it in some way or completely 'pull the plug' on the innovation – depending on the findings of the evaluation. Ultimately, it may be the case that enough pieces of evaluation are conducted in different places and in different circumstances and by different teams for there to emerge a body of research about the particular kind of innovation or programme in question. This body of work can then be drawn together and examined in a systematic review that will inform the development of future practice, but this is a blunter process of feedback than that used in action research.

You will appreciate from this discussion that evaluation research is often large in scale. While this is the case, it is quite possible to set up evaluation on a smaller scale for an undergraduate or postgraduate research project. Here you will be looking to assess the impact, effectiveness or other consequences of some newly introduced programme, usually within the frame of an institution's set of policies or of some initiative that you or colleagues have personally introduced. The change is introduced and the evaluation examines the consequences.

Ideally, an evaluation will look at what happens (1) *before*, (2) *during* and (3) *after* an innovation is introduced, with as long a period of examination as possible in each of these three phases. In practice (and certainly this is the case for student project work), evaluation may begin only during the period of implementation, or even after this, though this is of course not ideal.

Given that an evaluation focuses on before-and-after elements there may be a temptation to think that it has to collect data relating to pre-specified variables – things that you can count – so that it is possible to tell whether there has been a measurable increase or decrease due to the intervention. Certainly this may be the case – for example, reading ages could be taken before and after introducing a new system of reading in groups, and if the evaluation took place over a long enough period it may be possible to draw some conclusions about the effectiveness of that new system. However, an evaluation may collect almost any kind of data that those who are involved in the implementation find acceptable as indices of effectiveness.

Example 6.4

Gemma is studying for a BA in Education and English and is on a placement in a primary school – a placement which her university expects to provide Gemma with information for a double-module research project. Knowing that the school is implementing a new policy for playground supervision she decides to make the implementation of the policy the subject of her research. The school is completing the policy and just preparing for implementation as Gemma is able to start her research.

After negotiating with her class teacher and the head teacher, she decides to undertake a three-part evaluation. *First*, at the beginning of term she will collect some data about playground behaviour before the implementation of the policy. *Second*, she will examine the implementation of the policy itself. *Third*, at the end of term she will collect data about playground behaviour again, subsequent to the completion of the formal process of implementation.

Several constraints from the 'real world' could have affected the data that Gemma could have collected here, but she capitalised on the fact that she was just in time to collect some 'before' data before looking at the process of implementation.

Gemma devised a checklist for observing in the playground which she used in the first and third phases (in other words, in the before and after phases). The checklist, which she would complete at set times during two weeks of observation before and after, included recording observed incidents of physical aggression from child to child, incidents of verbal abuse and other incidents of teasing or aggression. She would record the circumstances of these. At the same time she would record the circumstances surrounding these incidents and briefly interview staff on duty during each of the periods of intervention, asking also for reflections on the effects of the policy on the circumstances in question. She would emerge with data about 'critical incidents' backed up with (or 'triangulated with') informed comment from staff.

(Continued)

(Continued)

For the assessment of the implementation (i.e. the second stage) Gemma undertook interviews with staff – three teachers, three teaching assistants and three midday assistants – about how they felt about the policy, how they had been involved in devising it, how easy it had been to conduct it in practice and how optimistic they were about change. She interviewed six children – one from each year group – asking some basic questions about the policy (to find out how much they knew about it) and whether they felt it was altering playground behaviour.

Her analysis focused on bringing together the different kinds of data in each of the three phases, and then trying to understand how the implementation had happened in the context of the total evaluation. In other words, understanding how and why there was a fall in the incidence of difficult and bullying behaviour at playtimes but not at dinnertime. Her conclusion – properly tempered with caveats about the limitations of the data – was that the policy worked better when implemented by teachers and teaching assistants than it did when implemented by midday assistants, who had not been involved in the writing of the policy.

Possible questions for Gemma after the evaluation:

- Were there enough participants involved in the research to find out what was going on?
- How could play-fighting be distinguished from aggression in the observation?
- Were there enough 'data points' to be sure that the evaluation was reliable?
- Should the evaluation have taken place over longer periods before and after the implementation?

Experiment

As we noted in Chapter 1, one important branch of research is that which seeks to find out whether, or to what extent, one thing causes another to happen. This is in fact often the aim in social research – in other words, trying to see if *x* causes *y* – but the different design frames are differently suited to answering such questions. Experiment is taken by some to be the most reliable way of determining that such causation is occurring.

In everyday parlance, 'to experiment' can just mean to try something out, and 'an experiment' can simply mean an investigation of some kind. In science it means something more precise: it means a test done under controlled conditions to prove or falsify an idea, a conjecture. However, in social research it means something even *more* specific:

- it is about demonstrating cause and effect;
- it concerns the extent to which we have to control the conditions in the situation of interest to demonstrate that cause–effect relationship.

The reason it is difficult to say that *x* causes *y* in social research is that there are a very large number of factors and issues at play in any social situation. If you change one of these factors and claim that the change you have

Table 6.2   The classic experiment

	Pre-test	Treatment	Post-test
Experiment group	Take first measure	✓ give treatment	Take second measure
Control group	Take first measure	✗ no treatment	Take second measure

made has been responsible for the improvement (or deterioration) in another factor you are likely to be challenged by someone saying 'How do you know that it wasn't *a, b* or *c* (and not *x*) that caused *y* to change?' Using the same example I gave earlier, if a teacher introduces a new scheme of reading and she can show that the reading age of the children in her class rises following the introduction of the new scheme, how can she know that it is the reading scheme that has caused the improvement in reading? Couldn't it perhaps be that the children would have improved anyway – even with the old reading scheme? And if the improvement looks dramatic so that the teacher says 'This extraordinary improvement can only be put down to the new scheme', couldn't the improvement perhaps be attributed to the new energy that the teacher is giving to her teaching, given the stimulus to her interest provided by the new scheme?

Experiment seeks to rule out the possibility that factors such as this (and many others) could be responsible for the change. In its simplest form it seeks to isolate two variables – the one that you assume may cause change (e.g. the reading scheme), and the one that you are assuming may have change effected on it (the reading age in the example that we have been using) – from the myriad variables that might be at play in a situation. In sciences such as physics or chemistry an experimenter holds everything else – every other variable – constant in order to be able to say that any change made to the first variable has *caused* any measured change in the second.

But in social science we can't be sure that *x* has caused *y*, because the thing we are interested in measuring (e.g. reading age) has an annoying habit of changing anyway, irrespective of what is being done to it. This is why, in social scientific experimental research, we have to do something such as bringing in an extra group, as alike as possible to the first group, and giving them everything that the first group had so that we can eliminate sources of variation – every source of variation, that is, except the one we are deliberately varying. So, an experiment in a social science situation usually involves two or more groups being treated in exactly the same way, save one, namely the manipulation of the first variable. Any difference that then exists between the two groups after the manipulation is made to happen by the experimenter is taken to exist because of the experimental treatment. This classic form of the experiment is usually shown as in Table 6.2.

A lot can go wrong in all of this (see the discussion of experimental validity on p. 107), not least due to the effect of the myriad confounding variables that might affect

A control group serves as a basis of comparison in a piece of research. The control group receives no experimental manipulation.

the result of an experiment. These confounding variables include the galaxy of minor and major things of everyday life that cannot be factored into any social situation: power failures, the colour of the paint on the walls, the morning's argument with the spouse, and so on. The philosopher Alasdair MacIntyre (1985: 99), in his devastating critique of social science, puts it this way: 'There is at the outset no determinate, enumerable set of factors, the totality of which comprise the situation.' He suggests that social science will always either be ignorant of the potential effects of the indeterminate set of factors or will fail to notice the most important of them. He gives the example of the potential importance of the length of someone's nose. He noted that an historian had suggested …

> … that the cause of the foundation of the Roman Empire was the length of Cleopatra's nose: had her features not been perfectly proportioned, Mark Antony would not have been entranced; had he not been entranced he would not have allied himself with Egypt against Octavian; had he not made that alliance, the battle of Actium would not have been fought – and so on. (MacIntyre, 1985: 99)

But keeping these caveats about validity in mind, what are the practicalities?

The way that an experimenter states the expected outcome of manipulating the first variable is via a hypothesis. An example of a hypothesis is: 'Raising children's self-esteem in Year 5 will raise their attainment in English'. You can measure self-esteem with tests, and you can measure attainment in English with tests, and when you have completed your experimental study you can see whether your hypothesis is true. (You may come across the term 'null hypothesis', particularly in psychological studies, but I feel there is no need to complicate things with this, which seems to me to be an example of social scientists making things more complicated than necessary.)

It's important to understand some jargon about experiment, and I've been trying my hardest to avoid it until now, but you will need it if you decide to do an experiment and read any further about this design frame. This is given in Table 6.3.

Figure 6.6 is a greatly simplified representation of the process of an experiment, and experimenters have to set up experiments very carefully (ensuring, for example, that the groups are as alike as possible) to maximise the probability that the conclusions they draw about x causing y are correct. There are many opportunities for going wrong in all of this – in the setting up of an experiment or in interpreting its conclusions statistically. Going wrong can mean that you may assume your hypothesis is correct when it is not, or that you assume your hypothesis is false when in fact it is correct. These errors are usually summed up in some more jargon: Type I and II errors:

Table 6.3   Experiment jargon

Independent variable	*which means*	the variable you change (e.g. the reading scheme)
Dependent variable	*which means*	the variable you are examining (e.g. reading age) to assess the effect of changing the independent variable
Experimental error	*which means*	uncontrolled sources of variation that occur during an experiment

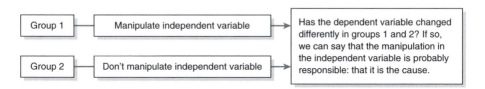

Figure 6.6   What an experiment consists of

- Type I Error: this is when you accept your hypothesis as true, but in fact it is false.
- Type II Error: this is when you reject your hypothesis as false, but in fact it is true.

We'll examine some of the ways in which the results from an experiment might be analysed and interpreted in Chapter 9.

There are many different sub-frames to the experiment as a design frame (to the extent that there is a whole branch of methodology called 'experimental design'), and it is beyond the scope of this book to examine them. One distinction that is worth making is that between 'true' experiments and 'quasi' experiments. The former include the random allocation to groups of the research participants, whereas the latter do not do this – perhaps using 'natural' groupings, such as those provided by local authority education groupings. If you wish to take this further, look at the Further Reading at the end of the chapter.

Example 6.5
Karen completed a PGCE last year after doing a first degree in psychology and is now studying for a Master's in Teaching and Learning. The major part of this comprises a research project that will be written up into a 20,000 word dissertation. Her topic for this will be the organisation of the adults in her class of Year 5 children. She has one teaching assistant permanently and two parent volunteers every morning. Management and organisation of this kind of assistance was not part of her PGCE curriculum, so Karen reads the literature and finds that there are a number of ways

(Continued)

(Continued)

of thinking about how extra assistance of this kind can be deployed. One method of organisation called **room management** (see Cremin et al., 2005) involves giving each adult a set of very specific tasks to do (such as predominantly helping individuals or predominantly helping groups), wherein those tasks constitute a named role. The roles can be changed from session to session; the main thing is that each individual knows which role they are supposed to be fulfilling.

Karen thinks that this new method of organisation holds some promise, and hopes that it will provide some structure for her work with other adults in her class. Rather than simply trying it out and proceeding on a gut feeling about whether the new system of organisation seems to be working, she does a small experiment. This involves a particular kind of experimental design, where instead of using two groups (an experimental and a control group), there is one group (Karen's class) examined under two circumstances, or **conditions**, where the only change is to the system of organisation in her class. This particular kind of experimental design is called a **repeated measures design** and is particularly suited to small-scale study. In the first condition she and the other adults are working normally; in the second condition the only change is that they are using the 'room management' system of organisation. To assess the effect of this change Karen decides to use the children's engagement with their work – in other words, looking to see whether they are doing what they are supposed to be doing: certain behaviours, such as sitting and writing, will count as 'on task', while others such as wandering around the class, will count as 'off task'. By drawing up a list of on-task and off-task behaviours and observing for these systematically Karen can keep a count of what is happening in the class under the two conditions.

The experiment requires organisation that will take many features of the situation into consideration. Karen first has to plan when the observations will take place under the two conditions. Because the two conditions must be identical apart from the change in the system of organisation, she has to ensure that the same kind of work is being done by the children and the same people are there with her class in both periods of observation. They have to be at the same time of day and even, if possible, on the same days of the week, for these are also sources of variation which could plausibly make a difference. Then she has to train the assistant and parents in the room management system and schedule the sessions. She also has to arrange for observation to happen to test the effect of the system on the dependent variable, children's engagement or 'on-taskness': she organises this by asking another parent who regularly assists in the classroom to video the sessions and she subsequently goes through the video with a checklist looking at each child in turn for a set period to work out an on-task percentage figure for each.

Each child's overall engagement (or 'on-taskness') is then plotted for the two occasions, producing the chart shown in Figure 6.7. Using some simple statistics, Karen is able to show that the differences between the two occasions are statistically significant (this is discussed further in Chapter 9). Simple 'eyeballing' of the chart (i.e. just looking at it intelligently) also shows a number of interesting things. Because Karen ranked the children's engagement from lowest to highest in the first condition, she can see how those who are at the lower end of the scale – that is to say those children who find most difficulty attending – are affected by the introduction of room management. The chart clearly shows that most of these see their engagement improve markedly over the two conditions.

(This example is loosely based on Cremin et al. (2005).)

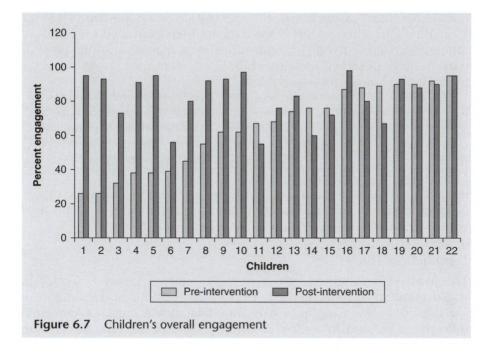

Figure 6.7 Children's overall engagement

You'll realise from all of this that an experiment, done well, requires the tight control of variables. One of the things we need to be aware of with experiment in social situations is that these situations are frail and unstable and difficult to control exactly. The American psychologist Jacob Kounin (1970) wrote a classic text about this instability, and it has profoundly influenced our understanding of what happens in classrooms. The insights it has offered are as relevant today as they were when his book was written. Kounin's breakthrough was to see the classroom as an environment with an ecology, rather in the way that a habitat for plants and animals is an ecology. An ecology is a dynamic environment: if foxes are blighted, rabbits do well. Or, to put it more prosaically, if you squeeze an environment in one place it bulges somewhere else. Seeing the classroom in this way – as an ecology – Kounin said, helps us to understand why we cannot simplistically expect to be able to impose changes without there being some unexpected consequence. We should always be aware of this when we try to manipulate social situations as tightly as is necessary for the running of an experiment.

Longitudinal and cross-sectional studies – and surveys

Both *longitudinal* and *cross-sectional studies* make use of data relating to large numbers of individuals or groups. Unlike researchers undertaking experiments, researchers in these studies do not attempt to manipulate any variables. They simply collect data relating to the variables: the longitudinal study at different points in time in relation to the same set of individuals; the cross-sectional study for subsets of a population all at the same time – in a 'snapshot'. These data are then examined for trends or differences relating to one or more variables, perhaps examining possible reasons for observed relationships between and among these variables.

The *survey* is an important method *within* the longitudinal and cross-sectional design frames and for this reason I am giving it special attention in this section. In fact, the survey is rather more than a method, and rather

Longitudinal and cross-sectional studies make use of data relating to large numbers of individuals or groups. The survey is an important method that they use.

less than a design. It is not a design frame in itself, but there are clearly defined methods such as questionnaires and interviews that are used within the survey. I shall examine these issues in a moment.

Longitudinal study

This involves the study of a group of individuals or cases *over an extended period*, regularly examining them for the effect of time on the variable or variables of interest. Because it is time that is the crucial factor, it is unlikely to be used in a short research project of the type done in an undergraduate dissertation – there simply isn't enough time for you to collect data at datapoints sufficiently far apart in time for any meaningful difference to be detected. However, for certain topics, a Master's degree and certainly a doctoral degree may provide sufficient time to sample enough points in time to provide meaningful data.

One of the decisions to be made in a longitudinal study is how far apart the data collection points should be. If changes and developments are happening quickly, frequent data collection is necessary, and vice versa.

You may come across the terms *cohort study* and *panel study* in relation to longitudinal research. A cohort is a group of people who share some characteristic or experience. These people can then be followed up at regular points in time. A panel study is similar to a cohort study and the terms are sometimes used interchangeably, though a panel study usually refers to a smaller group wherein individuals can be picked out for further questioning if necessary.

Because longitudinal studies by definition take place over a long period of time, one of the problems associated with them is attrition, or the loss of members from the group being studied. This attrition may be important in some cases as those who drop out – for example, those who move away or become

Skew: Occurs when the data being collected in your sample varies in a particular way from the data that actually exists in the complete population. This may happen because, for example, you are only questioning people who are easy to question. These people may form a particular sub-group, with views very different from the general population.

untraceable – may share particular characteristics of interest to the research, and the data may become skewed for this reason.

A major example of a longitudinal study is in the Millennium Cohort Study, which is examining all 20,000 children born in the UK in 2000–1, looking at the health and well-being of children and parents in the context of a broad range of socio-economic data. The children and their families are observed at regular intervals, illuminating 'links between the sociological and biological aspects of human development' (see www.cls.ioe.ac.uk/studies.asp?section=000100020001).

Example 6.6

Graeme is a social worker who has a particular responsibility for counselling and supporting the parents of children who are born with inherited illness or disability or the risk of these in later life. With a view ultimately to furthering his qualifications in this area, for the past three years he has been gathering data in a structured way from his own work and that of colleagues in different parts of the country. He enrols as a part-time MPhil student on a two-year university course entitled 'Psychosocial Aspects of Genetic Healthcare', explaining to his tutors that he intends for his dissertation to use the data he has already collected relating to 127 families, adding to it and eventually analysing it over the two-year progress of the course. These 127 families will form the *panel* for this study: the children are at different ages and with different inherited conditions but share the feature of inherited illness, and the group is small enough for subsets of it to be asked supplementary questions as the data emerges and themes begin to develop.

Through his professional organisation, the British Association for Social Workers, Graeme has secured a small amount of funding for the research for the purpose of helping to involve the colleagues who are assisting him in collecting data. He promises to involve them in the analysis of the research and to run an invited seminar at the conclusion of the data collection but prior to its analysis. He believes that the seminar will give him insights into how the data should be analysed.

From questionnaires he and his colleagues ask the families to complete, Graeme will eventually have data about the inherited condition, disability, illness and school circumstances of the children, and will have records on the family circumstances of the 127 families, though he expects some attrition as time passes.

Longitudinal research undertaken by professional researchers tends to involve large numbers as well as extended periods of time. The relatively small number involved in Graeme's research means (in a reverse of the case study situation) that there will be some trade-off involved in having only the limited cohort. Yet the number is small enough that it is possible to go into great depth in each situation and treat each as a case study. Nevertheless, as a panel study, some follow-up is expected with particular subsets of the group.

Graeme decides given the practical circumstances – both in terms of what can practicably be done and in terms of the ways that it can be analysed – that he will focus in his research on the stresses in the family created by inherited conditions. Because it is a longitudinal study and not a snapshot his focus is on the changes and developments to these stresses that happen over time. His data collection instruments therefore have to be constructed in such a way that they will be sensitive to stress and the ways in which it might change as time unfolds. They should

(Continued)

(Continued)

also seek to garner information about the ways in which stress is ameliorated or lessened over time – or the ways in which it increases – and what sorts of influences contribute to the lessening or the increase in stress for families.

To pilot: Means to conduct a much smaller study (a pilot study) to prepare for a larger one. It is done to refine or modify research methods or to test out research techniques.

Graeme's questionnaire, which he pilots with three families he knows well, asks about family stress (self-rated) and reasons for it, with questions about income, professional support for the family, availability of help from friends, family and community, the presence of siblings and their ages, and similar issues. As would be expected, what seems to emerge most clearly from the data is that level of stress seems to be connected most prominently to the seriousness of the inherited condition. It did not show a clearly observable trend over time in Graeme's sample, but this was because data was collected on individuals at different stages since their diagnosis. Because the data is being collected at identical points in time (September to October in 2007, 2008, 2009 and 2010), for some of the children it was collected soon after diagnosis and then at points thereafter, while for others (with whom Graeme and his colleagues had been involved over a longer period) it was collected well into their involvement with the family and some time after diagnosis. In order for trends to be discerned it was necessary to 'disaggregate' the data – to 'pull it apart' – so that it was possible to put individuals into four separate bands, grouped by time since diagnosis. By doing this it was possible to see that stress started at a high level and fell off rapidly with the input initially of high levels of support but that stress gradually rose again over intervening months and years as supporters seemed to lose interest. Looking at the panel as a whole the level of stress appeared in its ongoing nature and severity to be ameliorated most significantly by the existence of strong family support rather than professional support, and this latter observation gave Graeme and his colleagues much food for thought at their seminar at the close of the project.

As this longitudinal study is not an experiment, and the array of variables is not being held constant with only one manipulated (as would be the case in an experiment), it is not possible to say what causal relationship may or may not be involved in any of the observed relationships. All Graeme can do is to make intelligent guesses as to the meaning of the observations he makes about these relationships, and this is a perfectly legitimate thing to do.

Questions for Graeme:

- What are the ethical issues arising from this kind of study?
  Graeme considered the ethical justification in adding to the stress of already stressed families by regularly asking them questions (about stress!), but concluded from his pilot study that it was probably the case that most families valued the interest being expressed in them. Nevertheless, he was keen to avoid adding additional pressure and ensured that each family 'opted in' to the research, and could 'opt out' at any time if they wished.
- Were there enough datapoints at which data were taken?

Cross-sectional study

Here a group or groups are studied at the same time – as a snapshot. One variable may be looked at, providing a descriptive picture, or two or more variables offering the possibility of seeing a relationship among them. Alternatively, you might *at one moment in time* study equivalent groups – for example, of children at different ages. The key thing is that the observations are all made at the same moment in time, with a group whose members share some characteristic.

An example of a cross-sectional study was the report from Ofsted (Office for Standards in Education) *Leading to Excellence* (http://leadingto excellence.ofsted.gov.uk/). This looked at 84,000 early years and childcare providers, examining the quality of childcare provision made by each alongside the local authority within which that childcare was provided. It found that in the 30 most deprived local authorities, 53 per cent of child-minders provided good or better childcare compared with 60 per cent in the rest of England, with some stark comparisons between best and worst: in Hackney (East London), 29 per cent of childminders were judged to be good or better, compared to Wokingham in Berkshire where the proportion was 81 per cent. What can this tell us? Clearly the local authority is not the *cause* of these differences (even if some politicians will try strenuously to make that case), though it may be the case that in more deprived areas the pool of well educated people available to work in childcare is smaller than that in a more prosperous region. In this case the grouping provided by the local authority is perhaps misleading since it implies an association between qual-ity of childcare and the administrative authorities themselves, rather than the more amorphous geographical regions in which they are situated.

Example 6.7

Working as a nurse, Sangheeta is a part-time MSc student in healthcare. She is interested in the effects of smoking on young women who are still at school, and as part of her work decides to conduct a cross-sectional study of all the girls in Year 10 in schools of the small unitary local authority (LA) area, Gotham City, within which the hospital at which she works is situated. Having gained the agree-ment of the Gotham City LA to approach the schools in the city, and having in turn secured the agreement of nearly all the secondary schools to involvement in her research, she visits each to administer a survey to Y10 girls asking about smok-ing habits and other features of their health and their behaviour. In the question-naire she devised, she asked, for example, for the girls' own self-assessment of how fit they thought they were, including questions on breathlessness and coughing, and on how well they thought that they were doing in their school-work compared to the rest of the girls in the year group. She also asked them for their opinions on when girls usually have their first baby.

This provides Sangheeta with descriptive data (e.g. numbers of cigarettes smoked per day for each girl, a self-rating out of 7 on fitness, a self-rating on coughing, etc.).

(Continued)

(Continued)

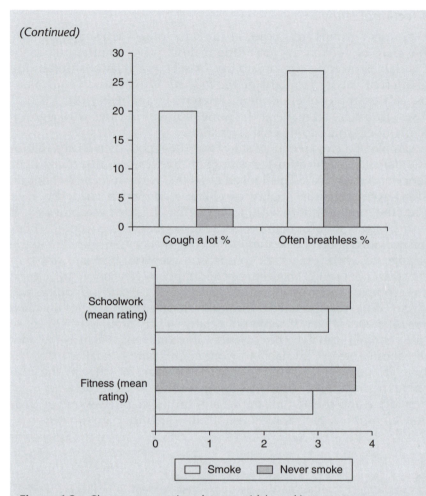

Figure 6.8   Charts representing data on girls' smoking

She is able to present graphically the data she receives from the 860 girls to whom she has given questionnaires. The self-ratings about coughing and breathlessness and the self-rating data on fitness and attainment in schoolwork she gives in the graph shown in Figure 6.8.

She finds that among girls who smoke the average age they expect a woman to have her first child is 25, while for those who never smoke it is 27. She presents this in prose form, since a table or graph is unnecessary.

The population being studied here was intended to be the entire population of Y10 girls in Gotham City, and to all intents and purposes that aim was fulfilled, though two schools did not take part in the study and some girls were absent on the day of the questionnaire. Sangheeta argued that this population was probably representative of the wider national population, and in that sense acted as a sample for this wider population to whom she argued her conclusions could apply. She argued that any relationships that were noted, while they may vary in extent in the wider population, would be unlikely to occur only in the Gotham City sample.

Some simple statistics (examined further in Chapter 9) showed significant differences between the smoking and non-smoking groups. In reporting these, however, Sangheeta had to make sure that she made no over-ambitious claims for her analysis. It is not possible to impute causation from the associations found in a cross-sectional study – or indeed from any associations. It would not be possible, in other words, to say that smoking had *caused* the greater breathlessness, lower perceived attainment, etc. The associations that were discovered could be due to entirely different factors. For example, there may be personality differences between smoking and non-smoking groups which have their consequences both in a tendency to smoke (or, perhaps, just to *say* that they smoke) and in a tendency to answer more 'daringly' in questionnaires. Or there may be differences in parental income levels between smoking and non-smoking teenagers, with associated differences in housing conditions, family size, level of parental supervision, and so on. Any combination of these and other confounding factors are quite plausibly the factors responsible for the differences that Sangheeta discovered.

What she could do, though, was to speculate intelligently about her findings and the differences that she found and to look at the levels of difference and what these might mean when looked at, one next to the other. The very large differences in coughing and breathlessness could almost certainly be attributed to smoking (though even here a confounding factor could be responsible, such as the fact that teenagers who smoke are more likely to have parents who smoke, and their coughing could be the effect of being brought up in smoky households). On the other hand, the differences in the girls' expectations regarding the age of a woman when she has her first child, and the differences concerning perceived achievement at school perhaps are more reflective of the class and social conditions that are associated more closely with girls who smoke. Sangheeta was able to discuss these possibilities and this discussion formed the basis for the next element of her work, which involved some in-depth case studies with individual girls.

Survey

As I noted at the beginning of this chapter, the survey cannot really be thought of as a design frame in itself because it exists in different design forms (principally the longitudinal study and the cross-sectional study), and yet it holds within it various different methods for collecting data (such as the interview and the questionnaire). So it is rather more than a method, but rather less than a design frame. What are its characteristics?

In a survey you are collecting data from a varied number of respondents (i.e. people who are responding). They may be responding in a questionnaire or in an interview, or they may be completing some kind of diary entry (we shall look at these in Chapter 8). The data can be many and varied. As I have noted in discussing longitudinal and cross-sectional design frames, these data are collected to describe some feature of the social situation in which they exist, and these features of the situation are not manipulated, as they would be in an experiment. Once these descriptive data have been collected they can be examined for the existence of relationships between and among them.

Example 6.8

As is the case in any design frame, the methods used to collect data in a survey will affect the findings that are made. A good example of different methods in collecting survey data involved arose in an argument over the size of the audience for **Coronation Street**. The Broadcasters Audience Research Board (BARB) has a panel (see p. 130) from

Figure 6.9   BARB and Carat came up with 14 million and 11 million respectively as the audience for *Coronation Street*

whom it finds out what programmes people are watching on TV. The method BARB uses to do this is a 'peoplemeter', which is a device given to all 5,300 households in the panel, who press buttons on the meter to tell BARB what they have been watching. The 5,300 TV sets in the panel are a sample of the 20 million or so in the country, and on the basis of the button-pressing, BARB is able to estimate how many people watched particular programmes. One January 25th, BARB estimated that 11.2 million people had watched an episode of **Coronation Street**. However, another organisation, Carat, undertook a telephone survey of a sample of viewers and estimated the audience for the same episode to be 14.5 million (see http://news.bbc.co.uk/1/hi/entertainment/tv_and_radio/1793556.stm for the full details).

Questions that might be asked about the difference and why it existed are many, and include:

* Was Carat contracted by anyone to undertake the survey?
* Might BARB's figures eliminate those who recorded the show to watch later?

Because the panel used in this survey provided both a snapshot and an ongoing picture of TV-watching over time, it could be called either a cross-sectional study (at a particular time, as in this **Coronation Street** case), or a longitudinal study, providing a developmental picture of TV audiences over time (see www.barb.co.uk).

Comparative study

Usually, the term 'comparative study' refers to the comparison of a social situation in one country with another. In the broader social sciences it can be used to mean any kind of comparison but in applied social science and education it nearly always refers to international comparison, and that is the way that I shall discuss it here. Comparative study deserves a special mention as a design frame because it faces particular challenges and it meets these with a particular range of methods used with a well developed set of considerations.

For the purposes of applied social research, then, comparative study is about cross-national, cross-societal and/or cross-cultural comparison. Clearly, a range of issues arise when such contrasts are made because differences in language, customs, value systems, lifestyles and institutions exist across these comparisons. Partly, the existence of these issues creates the need for special attention and the need for a special design grouping.

Comparative research will examine issues such as:

- contrasting patterns of development across different societies;
- how specific or how general forms of social and institutional structures are between different societies – how they are the same and how they are different;
- cultural determinants of difference across societies.

> In social research, *comparative study* refers to cross-national comparisons with the aim of gaining insights from the comparisons.

Often this kind of research is very large scale, with cooperation between and among countries, using large research teams and involving high levels of coordination and cooperation. Combinations of methods will be used involving survey, secondary analysis of national datasets, interviews and expert knowledge.

But comparative research is also quite feasible on a small scale, such as that found in your own project, particularly if the researcher has intimate knowledge of both the cultures concerned. The problem that arises on the small scale is that often the research undertaken is of two national or cultural situations, where the researcher – using a participant observation approach and relying on insider knowledge of the two situations – has, in fact, insider knowledge of only one of the cultures involved. If this is the case, it is not possible to make the rich comparisons that would be expected, depending on a fine-grained understanding of what is happening in each. There may be a richly textured understanding of one situation but far less understanding of the other.

Actually, although I note that potential problem, on a small scale a comparative study is sometimes less beset with problems than is the large-scale study. For example, where a large study is seeking to make comparisons across countries in, say, levels of attainment, the only sure way of ensuring comparability is to use the same measuring instruments in different places. But to do this, these instruments (tests or whatever) will be have to be translated from one language to another and cultural references in some way also translated. These translations are fraught with problems. The administration of these tests then has to be coordinated across two or more countries, and this is of course a very expensive business. Where identical measures are not used, the measures that are used for comparison will have been devised locally with different purposes in mind, and with different coding and standardisation procedures. The data may not have been collected in any way systematically. These issues can render meaningless any comparison between national datasets or even the comparison of data from simultaneously given but different assessment instruments.

Small or large scale, what should a comparative study be aware of?

- *Equivalence of the comparison situations.* How far is it possible, for example, to make valid comparisons between Ruritania and Lilliput in their moves to inclusive education? Certainly, the study is focusing on these differences, but maybe the differences and the parameters for them are of such proportions that a comparison is meaningless. Ruritania may be well on the path to an inclusive education system, having turned all of its special schools into inclusion services, while Lilliput has never even had any special schools and its primary schools routinely have classes of 60 or more students. To attempt to effect any comparison here would be meaningless (though that hasn't stopped people from trying to do it).
- *Equivalence of measuring instruments.* How, for example, can we ensure equivalence in the framing and interpretation of questionnaire items?
- *Language.* Differences in language may invalidate even seemingly straightforward comparisons. For example, the Swedish words which seem to be nearest to the English word 'community' (*lokalsamhälle* or *närsamhälle*) do not capture the sense of *identity* meant in the English word 'community' (when the word is used in a social science context). They mean 'local society' or something closer to 'neighbourhood'. Even the same word in two English-speaking countries means something different: in the UK education context 'integration' means the teaching of children with special needs in the mainstream school, whereas in the US it means something much more general and does not have the UK meaning at all.
- *The integrity or 'realness' of the geographical unit being studied.* Is it possible to say that you can validly compare the whole of Ruritania and the whole of Lilliput when these countries contain great regional differences? Researchers should be aware of what exactly it is they are comparing, finessing out and making explicit cultural, religious, historical and individual differences that may exist regionally.

Why are comparative studies useful?

- New insights can be obtained. Educational and social thought can develop in an insular way in particular environments and the recognition that another country or region does things differently can offer new avenues for ideas and for development.
- Potential explanations may occur for the existence of particular developments in behaviour, in understanding or even in institutional growth or decline in a particular place, based perhaps on historical or cultural differences.
- They give us a window on our own unspoken and unquestioned cultural expectations, when these are seen against the backdrop of the expectations and practices of others.
- The problematic differences that occur during analysis of different cultural situations can themselves provide insights. For example, using the

example of the meanings of the word 'community' in different languages, can this provide clues also to the growth of cultural practices and traditions? For example, might the words for 'community' in English, Swedish and French mean something different because of the different ways in which industrialisation and urbanisation happened in those countries?

Example 6.9

Hakan is from Turkey and is studying on a government scholarship for a Master's degree in social inclusion at a UK university. Impressed by Robert Putnam's book *Bowling Alone* (in which he reads that in Scandinavia someone finding a wallet in the street is far more likely to return it than someone who finds a wallet in England), he decides to compare notions of social capital and altruism in England and in his native Turkey. He chooses to focus the research project for his dissertation around altruism and its relationship to social capital and the existence of professionalised support systems in the two countries. How far can the existence of altruism be related to the kind of social capital spoken of by Putnam (1995: 73), who suggests that social capital is the connectedness among people in a society, the '... social networks and the norms of reciprocity and trustworthiness that arise from them'. Reviewing research about social capital in 35 countries, Putnam had noted that across those nations, social trust and civic engagement – from voting in elections to trusting people on the street – were strongly correlated, with a general trend to decline in such phenomena over the years, especially in the US.

Hakan's starting point is a prima facie question about whether professionalised support in different societies may serve to distance people from the natural ties that exist for them with others in their communities. Do highly funded social and healthcare services in which professionals take on the role of the supporter enable community members to withdraw from processes of engaging with others? There is some suggestion in the literature that Putnam reviews for his book that this may be the case, and if it *were* the case it would go some way to explaining the comparatively low levels of social capital noted in the UK vis-à-vis certain other European countries.

Hakan realises that he cannot realistically set up any large-scale comparison involving questionnaires and interviews, though he may be able to compare existing datasets relating to the two countries if they exist in a form that would enable meaningful comparison. His main empirical work, however, would be illuminative. He would make observations and record interviews in two situations – doctors' surgeries and school playgrounds – in the two countries. In the doctors' surgeries he has a feeling, based on some preliminary informal discussions with friends, relatives and colleagues in the UK, that a strong and highly specialised system of state-funded healthcare, existing in a long tradition since the set-up of the National Health Service, may have enabled an abdication from personal interest and responsibility among some of those who work in that system. There may have developed a sense of 'the system will provide', enabling a feeling that personal responsibility for helping others can be allowed to take a back seat. Following careful discussions with the relevant people, he decides to focus on health centre receptionists and observes them at their work in one surgery at the same time as conducting some interviews with patients in the waiting room. He does the same in his home town in Turkey.

(Continued)

(Continued)

He also does comparative case studies of children's behaviour in the playground in the two countries, not as an indicator of professional influence on altruism, but rather as a triangulation on the general issue – to provide a backdrop on issues of social capital and how it is felt and expressed in the two cultures. Again, he is careful to ensure the full understanding and agreement of the schools where he will do the work in England and Turkey and he observes in one school in each country for incidents of altruism (where altruism is defined in advance). He would record the full social circumstances of each incident in each situation and then conduct interviews with the children involved to ask about their feelings, motivations and expectations in each situation. How far, for example, were children motivated by feelings that they 'ought to' help another child in distress? Did they consider any danger to themselves if, for example, they went to the aid of a child being bullied? How did they cope with or otherwise reconcile such feelings?

Because this is a series of short case studies, albeit in a comparative context, the same considerations apply to Hakan in the conduct and interpretation of his work as would obtain in the conduct of any case study (see the section above on the case study). Briefly, this means that he cannot draw any hard and fast generalisable conclusions from his work, nor can he make any solid imputations about causation. What he can do is to look at each situation he encounters with an intelligent eye, asking questions and interpreting as he proceeds on the basis of those answers. Do his observations seem to be confirming the assumptions that were made in the prima facie research question, and if this is the case how should interviews proceed on the basis of this? Being a comparative study, the analysis will always pivot around the social, historical, religious and other cultural differences between the two countries – their institutions and their beliefs, and how these frame both the emergence of healthcare services and how these operate.

A useful resource for comparative research is the World Health Organisation (WHO) statistics, which can be found at www.who.int/whosis/whostat/EN_WHS08_Full.pdf.

Can I mix design frames and methods?

Yes, it's absolutely fine to mix design frames and methods. In fact, it is to be applauded. There is absolutely nothing wrong in using, say, a survey, an experiment and a case study all in the same research project (though you wouldn't physically be able to fit them all in to the time you have available for your project). As I keep pointing out, in doing your research it's horses for courses: different elements of your research, related to different questions, will almost certainly need different methodological responses from you. Some people talk about using a 'mixed method design' as if this were some daring, imaginative innovation; but to me it seems the most obvious thing in the world to mix methods. To go back to the example of the police officers at the murder scene, it would be very odd if they said 'No, sorry, we have made a policy decision only to collect interview data. We will *not* be collecting DNA under any circumstances.' The Chief Superintendent would be up before the Home Secretary pretty sharpish. It would be expected that every shred of evidence and every conceivable analytical tool should be used in the investigation, with appropriate caveats about the strength and weakness of various kinds of evidence and the ways that pieces of the story meshed together. It would then be for the jury to decide how convincing a case had been made. It is the same for your research and your dissertation, though the jury in this case comprises your readers and markers.

It is *not* all right, though, to mix the assumptions for one kind of design frame with another. You cannot, for example, use the assumptions behind the construction of an interpretative case study for the construction of an experiment. These design frames stem from different paradigms: one is about interpretation and illumination, while the other is about description and inference, usually involving quantification of information. Unfortunately, the failure fully to realise this causes many student researchers (and some professional ones) to follow methodological paths that are not only unnecessary but also misleading, as I have tried to show in the discussion of sampling, reliability and validity, above. (Also see: Hammersley, 1996; Bryman, 1998; Pring, 2000; Gorard and Taylor, 2004.)

Postmodernism

You may find the word *postmodernism* raised in discussions of research methodology. Postmodernism is neither a design frame nor a method. Rather, it is an approach to knowledge and inquiry, and it has relevance both for the 'Can I mix methods?' and the 'But is it science?' questions.

Postmodernism has different meanings across the arts and humanities. In the social sciences it refers to the view that there is no *one* way of understanding things, and no *one* way of doing inquiry. 'No one has the one right answer', is the motto of postmodernists. They're sceptics, and proud of it. Postmodernism is essentially a critique of the arrogance and confidence of modernism – the latter being nothing but a set of post-Renaissance delusions, postmodernists would say. The delusions emerge from a misplaced belief in the certainties promulgated by rationalism and scientific progress, combined with what is sometimes called a 'Whig view of history' (Butterfield, 1931/1973). The latter is an optimistic view of progress-upon-progress in human affairs. It's a view that can be summarised in Frank Spencer's famous assertion 'Every day in every way, I am getting better and better!'

Well, the postmodernists – despite, incidentally, all being avid followers of *Some Mothers Do 'Ave 'Em'* – would disagree with poor Frank in his endorsement of the Whig view (www.youtube.com/watch?v=qlw QVElQcIk). Behind the postmodern critique is the view that the systems of thought that have evolved in the modern world – categories for thinking in psychology, sociology, history, philosophy and elsewhere carry with them no necessarily right way of organising our inquiries. These frameworks for our thought are hopelessly ambitious, postmodernists would say, and fail to acknowledge the intricacies, complexities and sheer contingency of the social world. True, false: who knows? The social world is indeterminate and unpredictable and it is intellectually dishonest to pretend that we can explain it in terms of 'meta-narratives' – the grand explanatory schemes and theories of modernism.

For the social sciences a number of philosophers have shaped the postmodern critique. Heidegger challenged the distinction between the objective and the subjective. Wittgenstein came to the view that language cannot be dissected and analysed – meaning is in the context of what we say, not the actual words. Kuhn and Feyerabend challenged the notion that there are 'correct' (rather than just useful) scientific theories. Foucault explained how knowledge and power are interrelated and how certain forms of explanation (or 'discourses') are simply those that are convenient to people who hold power. Rorty notes that all explanation, even scientific explanation, is merely a kind of convincing and for the time being useful narrative.

People claim to be postmodernists or, just as likely, vehemently reject postmodernism, but I find this slipping into camps rather too simple. We are all postmodernists now, to the extent that we are all far more sceptical than we would have been fifty years ago about the truth claims promoted by certain kinds of inquiry. You'll notice in my ten-second review of postmodernists just now that the lines of thought that they have set off have had quite an influence on the way that we go about inquiry today. The mood now is of caution and criticality. This does not, however, mean that we have to go to extremes and deny that obvious things can be true: I am sure that I am sitting at a table, even if I can't prove it to the satisfaction of an irritable philosopher. We shouldn't disappear critically into our own navels.

If you are persuaded by the postmodern critique, how does this affect the way that you do research? I think in the real world it means that you fail to be impressed by complex explanatory theories that seek to explain too much. It means that you are ultra-cautious about the claims of method to offer answers to complex social questions or questions about individual motivation and psychology. An interesting idea related to a postmodern perspective comes from the sociologist Claude Lévi-Strauss (1962/1966). He suggested that we should in social inquiry forget the idea that there are right or wrong ways of going about it. Rather we should use *bricolage*, which is the French word meaning something akin to 'do-it-yourself'. If we use *bricolage*, we are *bricoleurs*, or DIYers. The intimation behind this is that we should reject the assumption that highly ordered methods get us somewhere in education and social scientific inquiry. We should be less self-conscious about our methods and use what seems best for answering our research questions: there are no right or wrong methods. Derrida (1978: 285), who is often thought of as a postmodernist, discusses Lévi-Strauss's *bricolage* as follows:

The *bricoleur*, says Lévi-Strauss, is someone who uses the 'means at hand', that is, the instruments he finds at his disposition around him, those which are already there, which had not been especially conceived with an eye to the operation for which they are to be used and to which one tries by trial and error to adapt them, not hesitating to change them whenever it appears necessary, or to try several of them at once ...

The first practical step is retrospective: a *bricoleur* will, Lévi-Strauss says,

... turn back to an already existent set made up of tools and materials, to consider or reconsider what it contains and, finally and above all, to engage in a sort of dialogue with it and, before choosing between them, to index the possible answers which the whole set can offer to his problem. (Lévi-Strauss, 1962/1966: 19)

The sociologist Howard Becker (1998) suggests something similar (though I don't think he would readily call himself a postmodernist) and he calls these different ways of proceeding *tricks*. A trick is, in short, a device for solving a problem and offering ways around existing discourses of explanation. He divides his tricks into those of *imagery*, *sampling*, *concepts* and *logic*. While Becker's book is not one for the novice researcher, it is certainly a refreshing antidote to recipe-driven research. It is all about using your intelligence. It's about throwing away the textbooks (but not this one, obviously) and *thinking*; it's about training yourself to think and using your own resources. While I doubt if Becker is an avid follower of *Star Wars*, I am sure he would endorse Obi Wan Kenobi's advice: 'Go with the Force, Luke'.

The key for those persuaded by the scepticism of the postmodern critique is to 'think outside the box' when it comes to inquiry. Think laterally, and beyond the confines of the existing categories of research. In my book *Education and Theory* (Thomas, 2007) I give some examples, such as 'thought experiments' or the kinds of dialogue that Plato used for his Socratic dialogues. A useful example in education is to be found in Jones and Brown's (2001) 'reading' of a nursery classroom.

Overview

The design frame is a superstructure that governs the way that your research proceeds. There are a number of such superstructures available, and each is associated with particular purposes, particular kinds of question and sometimes particular approaches to knowledge. Again, different design frames can be used in a research study, and each can complement the others. A number of considerations, such as sampling strategy, generalisation and triangulation need to be considered when using the different design frames, and it is important to recognise which of these considerations go with each of the design frames.

The design frames themselves – action research, case study, comparative study, ethnography, evaluation, experiment, longitudinal study and cross-sectional study – are not incompatible. They may nest inside each other or sit alongside each other. But each has its own way of proceeding and its own procedural ground rules, and it is important to understand why these exist and how they influence the structure of your inquiry.

Further Reading

General issues in design

Bryman, A. (2001) *Social research methods.* Oxford: Oxford University Press.

Gorard, S. and Taylor, C. (2004) What is triangulation? *Building Research Capacity, 7, 7–9*

Research methods knowledge base:
http://www.socialresearchmethods.net/kb/sampprob.php

Action research

Carr, W. and Kemmis, S. (1986) *Becoming critical: education, knowledge and action research.* London: Routledge.

McNiff, J., Lomax, P. and Whitehead, J. (2003) *You and your action research project* (2nd edition) London: Routledge.

Case study

Stark, S. and Torrance, H. Case study. In B. Somekh and C. Lewin (eds) *Research methods in the social sciences.* London: SAGE.

Hammersley, M. (1992) *What's wrong with ethnography.* London: Routledge.

Ragin, C. C. and Becker, H. S. (eds) (1992) *What is a case? Exploring the foundations of social inquiry.* Cambridge: Cambridge University Press.

Stake, R. E. (1995) *The art of case study research.* Thousand Oaks, CA: SAGE.

Ethnography

Becker, H.S., Geer, B., Hughes, E.C. and Strauss, A. (1961) *Boys in white: student culture in a medical school.* Chicago IL: University of Chicago Press.
A study, mainly by participant observation, of a class of new undergraduates as they progress through medical school.

Geertz, C. (1973) Deep play: notes on the Balinese cockfight. In C. Geertz *The interpretation of cultures*. New York: Basic Books. Available at http://www.si.umich.edu/~rfrost/courses/MatCult/content/Geertz.pdf accessed 7th September 2008.

Evaluation

Pawson, R. and Tilley, N. (1997) *Realistic evaluation*. London: SAGE.

Experiment

For an example of a small-scale experiment
Cremin, H., Thomas, G. and Vincett, K. (2005) Working with teaching assistants: three models evaluated. *Research Papers in Education*, 20, 4, 413–32.

Research methods knowledge base: experimental design. At http://www.social-researchmethods.net/kb/desexper.php

Longitudinal and cross-sectional studies

Ruspini, E. (2002) *An Introduction to Longitudinal Research*. London: Routledge.

Comparative research

Bray, M. Adamson, B. and Mason, M. (eds) (2007) *Comparative Education Research: Approaches and Methods: Approaches and Methods*. Hong Kong: Springer.

See also journals such as *Compare* and *Comparative Education* http://www.informaworld.com/smpp/title~content=t713410984~db=all
http://www.informaworld.com/smpp/title~content=t713410081~db=all

Mixing methods

Gorard, S., with Taylor, C. (2004) *Combining methods in educational and social research*. Buckingham: Open University Press.

Postmodernism

Stronach, I and Maclure, M. (1997) *Educational research undone*. Maidenhead: Open University Press.
See especially the first chapter for a discussion of what it is all about.

7

Practical matters

Introduction	
Literature review	**Your research can only proceed if you can gain access to the people and situations you are interested in, and if you can conduct your work respecting your participants' interests and wishes. This chapter considers:**
Methodology	
Fieldwork and findings	• ethics, and establishing participants' consent; • access: getting hold of the information you need.
Analysis and discussion	
Conclusion	

You are here in your project

Ethics

I have started with 'ethics' under practical matters because university procedures now make it one, but being ethical is really much more than just a practical matter. Although there are important practical matters that stem from ethical concerns, ethics is about the conduct of your work: it is about how you think about inquiry, how you think about this research project; it is about your respect for others. To put these concerns into a box called 'ethics', as university procedures are sometimes apt to encourage us to do, is to minimise considerations about conduct and respect, so I shall leave the practical matters for a moment and discuss first the wider issues about inquiry and how we go about it.

A university is a place where inquiry is put to the fore. Inquiry is taken to be not just a necessity, but almost a thing of beauty – and, as such, universities give special privileges to academics to inquire and research without constraint, summed up in the term 'academic freedom'. This is a cherished freedom and it is one that is accompanied by important responsibilities.

Our freedoms in the academic world – freedom of inquiry and freedom to disseminate the findings of that inquiry – have at their centre expectations about the importance of the freedom, the *need* even, to challenge conventional wisdom, thoughts and ideas without fear of censorship or interference. A century and a half ago John Henry Newman put it this way in his seminal paper *The Idea of a University*:

> A university is a place ... in which the intellect may safely range and speculate, sure to find its equal in some antagonistic activity and its judge in the tribunal of truth. It is a place where inquiry is pushed forward, and discoveries verified and proved, and rashness rendered innocuous, and error exposed, by the collision of mind with mind and knowledge with knowledge. (Newman, 1852/1960: 15–16)

A university is a place where ideas are challenged. It is a community of inquiry where it is expected that there will be not just critical reflection, but controversy, gloves-off critique and argument – the 'collision of mind with mind'. As a member of a university – and this includes students as well as staff – you are part of this community of critical inquiry, and by being part of it you have conferred upon you some important privileges. Those privileges, though, are balanced with responsibilities and it is in the balancing of the one with the other that ethics come in.

Ethics are principles of conduct about what is right and wrong. When applied to research, ethical principles encompass some decisions and dilemmas that pit not just right against wrong, but balance one right action against another right action, taking into account the possibly conflicting interests of the parties involved. What is right for me may not be right for you. What is right for the researcher may not be right for the participant. Or they may force us to examine what is potentially wrong, hidden dangers – force us to look at the nature of what we are doing in the name of furthering knowledge.

Clearly, we want to do what is right and avoid what is wrong. The matter seems simple, yet there are many examples in social research where a questionable action may have been taken in the name of doing right. In other words, researchers have had as the purpose for doing their research the idea that they are promoting knowledge or alleviating suffering or helping humankind in some other way and have used this as a reason for employing intrusive or distressing procedures in their research.

One of the most celebrated examples of the ethical dilemmas that emerge in social research happened in the 1960s in experiments about the power of personal authority. Stanley Milgram, a social psychologist working at Yale University, was concerned about the effects of authority on people's good judgement. If people were told to do something by someone in authority, even if went against their better judgement, would they do it? He invited ordinary people off the street to take part in an experiment about learning. They were told to give increasingly severe shocks to another person, using a dial marked from 'Slight Shock' to 'Danger: Severe Shock'. The person to whom the shocks were being given was actually an actor, and the 'electric shocks' were not real. As the 'shocks' increased in intensity, screams for mercy could be heard coming from the room where the 'victim' was situated. If the subject showed reluctance in continuing to increase the shocks, the researcher would first say 'Please continue'. If reluctance was still shown the experimenter would say 'The experiment requires that you continue', then 'It is absolutely essential that you continue' followed by 'You have no other choice, you *must* go on'. How far would these ordinary folk proceed with these electric shocks before refusing to comply with the researcher's instructions? Two-thirds of them administered the highest level of 'shocks'. This is from the abstract of the experiment ('S' refers to 'Subject'):

> 26 Ss obeyed the experimental commands fully, and administered the highest shock on the generator. 14 Ss broke off the experiment at some point after the victim protested and refused to provide further answers. The procedure created extreme levels of nervous tension in some Ss. Profuse sweating, trembling, and stuttering were typical expressions of this emotional disturbance. One unexpected sign of tension – yet to be explained – was the regular occurrence of nervous laughter, which in some Ss developed into uncontrollable seizures. The variety of interesting behavioral dynamics observed in the experiment, the reality of the situation for the S, and the possibility of parametric variation within the framework of the procedure, point to the fruitfulness of further study. (Milgram, 1963: 371)

One of the interesting things about this paper is that several major journals rejected it on ethical grounds. Yet ultimately the work was awarded the annual Socio-Psychological Award of the American Association for the Advancement of Science. It is interesting to read Milgram's (1981) reflections on the experiments, on ethics and on the process of peer review and his ultimate award at www.garfield.library.upenn.edu/classics1981/A1981LC33300001.pdf.

Clearly opinions differ as to the ethics of the experiment here, and there is a whole branch of academic study into ethical issues of the kind that it presents. In the case of this experiment and many others the issue is, in short, 'Does the end justify the means?' The end purpose was the better understanding of obedience to authority. Coming quite soon after the Second World War, when many had justified their actions in perpetrating appalling crimes by saying that they were only obeying orders, the experiment could be said to be defensible. It was warranted if it helped an understanding of why it seems to be so easy for people to do this to others in the name of obeying authority.

But deception was used and people were distressed, some of them quite seriously, by the experience. Was *this* justifiable ethically, even if it advanced knowledge about obedience to authority? Could this knowledge have been found any other way than by deception? It is unlikely: if we were asked what we would do hypothetically in such a situation, how many of us would be able to be honest, even with ourselves?

You are most unlikely to be contemplating anything quite as dramatic as the Milgram experiments. However, there may be ethical issues lurking of which you were not aware or which you had not considered. Many of these will present questions of the kind that confront us now looking back at Milgram, albeit on a smaller scale. Who is the research benefiting? Do you have the right to take up people's time and energy? Is there any possible discomfort that participants will have to experience? Are you invading their privacy? Is it justifiable to have a control group, if you feel that the experimental group is getting something worthwhile?

There may be more mundane motivation than promoting the good of humankind for using procedures that do not fully respect the wishes, the privacy or the integrity of the people with whom you are working. You may be in a hurry; you may think it is obvious that participants would not mind taking part in your research. But there are many reasons participants may mind: they may be embarrassed; they may, if they are children, not want to lose respect amongst their peers; they may, if they are professionals, not want to be seen taking part in a project that has the endorsement of management or, conversely, not want to be seen to be critical of management, and so on. The potential reasons for not wanting to participate in a research project are legion, and you should be aware of this. And they may feel pressurised, just by being asked, however nice, however gentle you are in your request for participation.

Most research in the social sciences involves some kind of direct or indirect involvement with people, and will need some kind of ethical consideration. Whether your involvement with those people is direct, for example through interviews, questionnaires or direct observation, or indirect through interviews about someone else or looking at documentary records, you will need to consider the ethics of what you are doing. However, ethics will not be a matter of concern if you are looking at matters that do not involve individual people – such as policy issues or data that is in the public domain.

Consent

Because of the harm that might be caused during research involving people, an important concept when considering the ethics of research is that of consent. Consent is about the agreement of people to take part in the study. More than simple agreement, however, is needed, given the issues noted above. *Informed consent* is needed. In other words, potential participants should understand what they are agreeing to. Informed consent is centred around the points in Table 7.1.

Table 7.1   Informed consent

(a)	The information participants need to know; this will include:

- – the nature and purpose of the study, including its methods
- – expected benefits of the study
- – possible harm that may come from the study
- – information about confidentiality, anonymity, how data will be kept and for how long, with details of when data will be destroyed
- – ethics procedures being followed and appeals
- – your full name and full contact details

(b)	The presentation of (a) in a meaningful and understandable way, explaining any unusual terms simply, in non-technical language
(c)	The option for a potential participant to choose to take part or not

Opting in versus implied consent

An important distinction exists between *opted in* consent and *implied* consent:

- With *opting-in* participants have to make an active choice about becoming involved and signal their willingness to take part in the research. You would have to offer an invitation to participants to become involved, preferably in writing, requesting that they return a form indicating willingness to participate. This could be done directly and orally if written communication is not possible. Alternatively, some other *active* choice of the participant would have to be involved, as would be the case in returning a question-naire. It must be made clear that consent (from the participant) may be withdrawn at any time and that if this is the case there will be no further collection of additional data, no further analysis of data initially collected and removal of existing data from your records.
- With *implied* consent, you tell participants about the research and assume that they give their consent unless they tell you other-wise. Information about the research can be distributed by a range of means, for example by a letter from the school to all children who would be personally involved. The letter would include the information in Table 7.1 above, but would be accompanied by a phrase such as 'I am assuming that unless I hear from you, you have no objections to Ellie's participation ...' Depending on the degree of risk assumed to be involved, information might also be communicated by announcements or leaflets, as long as it can reasonably be assumed that the intended recipients will receive the information. There should, of course, in every case be a clear explanation of the provisions for opting out and people should be

given the easiest possible way of doing so – by letter, telephone or email, or personally to you.

There are pros and cons to opting-in versus implied consent. If there is any degree of significant risk, then opting-in procedures are clearly to be preferred. Opting-in involves more work for the researcher than does opting out. However, there is some evidence also that samples may be skewed by the use of opting-in procedures (because only really willing people opt in, and this may exclude important subsections of the population). Junghans et al. (2005), working in a medical context, therefore suggest that 'The opt-out approach should be the default recruitment strategy for studies that pose a low risk to patients.' The key phrase here is 'a low risk' and what constitutes low risk is a matter of judgement. This can be discussed with your supervisor and your local ethics representative if necessary.

Issues of consent are particularly important with children. There is an unequal power relationship between any adult and any child and your position as a researcher heightens the perception of authority held by the child. Good discussions of the ethics of working with children are provided in Lewis and Lindsay (2000), Alderson (2004) and Kellett (2005).

Ethics procedures and forms

The use of formal procedures by universities for ensuring ethical practice in social science research projects is relatively recent and still regarded by many researchers, both student and professional, as a bit of a chore. This is particularly so when universities seem to be overzealous in their scrutiny procedures. Certainly, when a 15-page ethics form was introduced by one of the universities I have worked for, this was my own reaction, for it seemed to me that the motivation of the university in question was principally to protect *itself* from litigation: its procedures seemed to be more about self-protection than protection of research participants.

However, this is not the right attitude, and it stems – I speak only for myself – from a less than self-critical belief that I could not possibly be doing anything that would harm anyone with whom I researched. It stems from a belief that my own judgement about the balance of rights and wrongs is naturally the best judgement and that it is an attack on my integrity to question this. But the passage of time and experience has shown me how delicately balanced these matters can be and how necessary it is to have ethical concerns explicitly articulated and systematically checked. In fact, the systematic checking of these concerns with another person often will add insights beyond ethics to the design and conduct of the research.

The passage of time seems to be bringing with it more considered and streamlined procedures from universities, with protocols that are more fit-for-purpose. There is now usually a two- or three-part process that may include a self-assessment form at the first stage with no need to proceed to the next stage if any risks are felt to be minimal. Beyond this, it may be possible to have a decision made at a local level (i.e. within your own department) by a person or group who have been given authority by the university to make decisions about small projects. Only if the risk is considered to be in some way significant will the application have to undergo more searching scrutiny, perhaps from a central university committee. Usually, this will not be the case, but you should be aware that it may be necessary and build time into your schedule to allow for it. If it is the case that full scrutiny is felt to be necessary the risks of your proposed project will be assessed against the potential benefits: the scholarly merit. How far will your project promote understanding and knowledge in your field? Do the potential benefits outweigh the potential risks to participants?

Potential risks include:

- causing psychological or physical harm to participants or others;
- damaging the standing or reputation of participants or others;
- infringing the privacy of participants or others;
- breaking the law;
- harming a community in some way (for example, by drawing attention to differences within it).

If there is considered to be any significant risk concerning any of these matters you should consider its extent and duration. You may need to consider also the extent to which any risk can be 'undone', either naturally or through steps taken by you. Benefits or scholarly merit may include particular advantages to participants or others or any potential advance in knowledge. You should be prepared to expand on all of these and make a good case for your research. I give an abridged version of one university's ethics form in Figure 7.1, and you can see how many of the matters discussed here are tackled in the form.

Your university will have a code of conduct for research, and it will have a helpful webpage outlining procedure. As an example, my own university's is at www.rcs.bham.ac.uk/staff/researchers/pi-howto.shtml. The relevant professional organisations also have policies and guidelines on ethical research. Those for the British Educational Research Association (BERA) are at www.bera.ac.uk/publications/pdfs/ETHICA1.PDF.

The key thing to remember in looking at any of these protocols is that it is the consideration of ethics that is important – not the protocols themselves, helpful though these can be. A reflection on ethics should be integral, and not seen as a bolt-on or a chore to be squeezed into your timeframe.

Project details

- Title
- Duration including dates for data collection
- Short description
- Aims and justification
- Proposed method
- How will findings be disseminated and how will participants be informed?
- On university site or off-site?
- Are other institutions involved and has their permission been sought?
- Is another ethics committee being consulted?

Participant details

Will you be recruiting:

- students from this university?
- adults over 16 and competent to give consent?
- children/legal minors (anyone under 16)?
- people from non-English speaking backgrounds?
- anyone with a physical disability?
- patients or clients of professionals?
- anyone in custody, custodial care, or for whom a court has responsibility?

Number age range and source of participants

Means by which participants are to be recruited

Will any part of the project be carried out by others?

Are any of the participants in a dependent relationship with any of the investigators?

Will there be any payments or incentives for participants?

Risk management

Does the research involve:

- questionnaires?
- interviews?
- participant observation?
- observation of participants without their knowledge?
- voice or picture recording?
- access to personal or confidential data?
- administration of any questions or procedures that may cause mental or physical discomfort during or after the research?
- performance of any acts that might diminish self-esteem or cause embarrassment?

- involvement of participants in any illegal activity?
- procedures that involve the deception of participants?
- administration of any substance or agent?
- use of non-treatment or placebo control conditions?
- collection of body tissues or fluids?
- administration of any radiation?

Potential risks and benefits

- In the light of the above, what risks (physical, psychological, social, legal or economic) may be associated with the research? What arrangements to manage that risk or those risks have been put in place?
- Are there likely to be any immediate benefits to participants?
- Are there any specific risks to researchers?
- Explain how potential benefits to participants outweigh any risks.
- Have you put in place any arrangements for support after the study?

Consent, confidentiality and feedback

- Will you be obtaining consent in writing from participants? If not, explain how informed consent will be documented.
- Consent form should include:
  - title of project and name(s) of researcher;
  - confirmation that the project is for research;
  - confirmation that involvement in the project is voluntary and that participants are free to withdraw at any time and/or withdraw data supplied;
  - confirmation about requirements of participants, e.g. whether audio or visual recording will be involved;
  - if the sample size is small, any implications for anonymity;
  - arrangements for debriefing and feedback.

Figure 7.1   An abridged example of a university ethics form

Access

Access is about getting hold of the data that you want, and where people are providing the information that you need this can present some dilemmas. Whether you are conducting a set of interviews or questionnaires or making some formal or informal observations, you will need to identify those people, contact them (and often their colleagues) and secure their agreement, attending to all of the issues we have just discussed about informed consent. Table 7.2 lists some possible forms of contact, with some considerations of which to be aware.

Table 7.2   Possible forms of contact

Through personal contact, or that of a colleague	You will be an insider in the organisation. This has advantages and disadvantages. You have easy access to people. Your knowledge gives you insights about the culture and the politics of the place. But on the downside, others in the organisation or system have expectations of you that may affect their opinions or reports to you. This may or may not matter. If you are working as an interpretative researcher, these expectations are part of your place and context (see *positionality* above), but if you are expecting to achieve any sort of objectivity, you must examine your questions to see how your position may affect the answers you get from others.
Through the knowledge of a friend or relative	For undergraduates, this is often the best 'way in' to an organisation. However, it does not mean that you can avoid getting the permission of those in authority and other key stakeholders in the organisation. If in a school, for example, it is essential to involve the head teacher (or their delegated deputy) – and not just to get an 'OK', but also if possible to achieve their active support. You should therefore go through points (a) to (c) in Table 7.1 under 'Consent', explaining the project as clearly as possible.
From your supervisor's lead	Your supervisor may well know of an organisation or group or individual that would provide a suitable base. However, you cannot expect your supervisor to do any more than give you the initial contact. Beyond this, the liaison and everything that comes after is your own work.
Random or other forms of sampling	You may simply be picking names from a hat – for example, a group of physiotherapists who work in a particular region to whom you send a postal questionnaire. Or your sample may be more purposive – you may know the individuals that you need to contact. (See 'Sampling' on p. 101 for the various forms of sampling.)

Overview

While you are thinking about the shape of your inquiry you must think about the ethical dimensions of what you intend to do and how you are going to get access to the people you intend to involve in the research. These issues, if not addressed at the planning stage, can easily derail the best strategy. It's important to think about them not just for practical reasons but because they raise questions about the nature of your inquiry, why you are doing it and whom it is going to benefit.

Further Reading

Ethics

Alderson, P. (2004) *Ethics, Social research and consulting with children and young people.* 2nd edn. London: Barnardo's.

Farrell, A. (2005) *Ethical research with children.* Maidenhead: Open University Press.

Gorard, S. (2002) Ethics and equity: pursuing the perspective of non-participants, *Social Research Update,* 39, 1–4

Apart from the codes already referred to:
American Sociological Association Code of Ethics
http://www.asanet.org/cs/root/leftnav/ethics/code_of_ethics_table_of_contents

The British Psychological Society (BPS) code of ethics has a ridiculously long URL, so just Google *BPS code of ethics.*

The Right Tools for the Job: Data Gathering

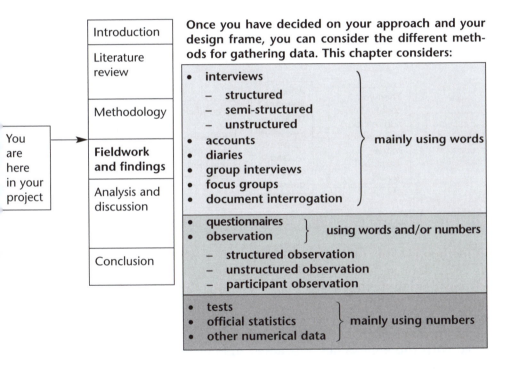

Introduction	Once you have decided on your approach and your design frame, you can consider the different methods for gathering data. This chapter considers:
Literature review	
Methodology	

You
are
here
in your
project

**Fieldwork
and findings**

Analysis and
discussion

Conclusion

- interviews
    - structured
    - semi-structured
    - unstructured
- accounts
- diaries
- group interviews
- focus groups
- document interrogation

mainly using words

- questionnaires
- observation

using words and/or numbers

    - structured observation
    - unstructured observation
    - participant observation

- tests
- official statistics
- other numerical data

mainly using numbers

Tools and methods

I have been talking about design up to now. Design itself is not much use without a construction to follow it. A chair *designed* by Thomas Chippendale would be nothing without the subsequent *construction* of the chair, and for this Mr Chippendale needed *tools*: saws, hammers, chisels, screwdrivers, scissors, lathes and so on.

It's the same with research design. Once you have decided how you are going to approach your question and the broad design frame that you will be using you can make up your mind about how you are going to collect your data – make up your mind about the tools that you will use: the instruments and techniques with which you will gather information. It shouldn't be the other way round. You shouldn't, in other words, come up with a tool first and then try and find a way of using it. The psychologist Abraham Maslow (1966: 15–16) said: 'I suppose it is tempting, if the only tool you have is a hammer, to treat everything as if it were a nail' and his cautionary words should be heeded: we shouldn't let our methods dominate. They shouldn't have precedence over our questions, or we end up in a world where research tells us only certain kinds of things, and our understanding can be correspondingly distorted.

Let's have a recap on how the research process has progressed …

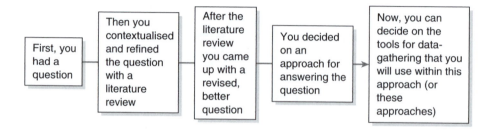

A method is a way of doing something, often with an intimation that it is being done systematically. In this chapter I shall outline a number of data-gathering methods which are ways of getting hold of data systematically. By 'systematic' I don't mean rigidly and formally, with tight, standardised procedures (though this *may* be the case). Rather, I mean done in a considered, thought-through way. These methods may be used with the approaches and design frames explained in Chapters 5 and 6. Some of these methods collect data mainly comprising words; some convert information into numbers; some collect both words and numbers.

Just a note about vocabulary: already in this chapter I have talked about tools, methods, techniques and instruments, using the terms almost interchangeably. This is a little confusing, I realise, especially as textbooks sometimes conjoin these terms also with the terms of research design. I'll try to explain by extending the metaphor I used before. Screwdrivers, chisels and hammers are undeniably tools – not methods. But they have to be used with a method: watching an inexperienced person wield a saw is an almost painful experience. You need to understand how to use the saw – find a good sturdy base, hold the wood on it with your foot, gently make a starting groove holding the wood firm, push down hard with the saw, and pull back lightly. Until you have learned this, the saw is as good as useless. So, tool and method go together. This is even more the case with social research: tool and method are almost bonded together, to such an extent that it is sometimes difficult to separate them out – the method *is* almost the tool in itself. This is why the terms are sometimes used together. So, you can think of this chapter being about tools, or methods, or techniques, or instruments.

Be creative

Right at the beginning I must say that you should not feel constrained by the tools that I am going to outline in this chapter. There is room for your creativity and imagination in the techniques that you adopt to collect data. The ones outlined under the subheadings below are some of the most commonly used methods for gathering data, but the list is neither definitive nor exhaustive. I spoke to a student recently who had been really creative in the way that he had thought about collecting data. He was collecting life histories from veterans of special schooling – people who had attended special schools in the 1930s and 1940s – to ask how they thought special schooling had affected their lives. Apart from the conventional method of interviewing these people, he also drew timelines on two pieces of A4 paper glued together lengthways (see Figure 8.1) on which he drew important historical events relevant to this lifespan which he could talk through with his research participants.

Figure 8.1   A timeline for stimulating memories

The events on the timeline would serve to jog memories and help put things in the right place. He could leave these long pieces of paper with the participants for them to look at on their own and to discuss with friends and relatives. Though I know this method for gathering 'data' is not unique to my student, it will not be found in any of the general text-books (or none that I have seen, anyway). This doesn't stop it from being a first-rate, home-made technique for both stimulating the production of information, and for helping to ensure its veracity.

So, in gathering the data you can be as imaginative as you want, and you should not feel constricted by the tools outlined in the subsections that follow. Many of the considerations raised in these, though, are rel-evant for any research involving people, and it is worth reading through the general advice accompanying each of these for pointers on the con-duct of work with people. The watchword is imagination concerning the tools that you use, and you can get help here from friends and relatives: ask them for their ideas, or have a brainstorming session (see p. 13). Check the ideas with which you emerge with your tutor.

Data-gathering tools – mainly for use with words

Interviews

An interview is a discussion with someone in which you try to get infor-mation from them. The information may be facts or opinions or attitudes, or any combination of these. There are three basic sub-types of interview: structured interviews, unstructured interviews and semi-structured inter-views. Each involves the interviewer in face-to-face contact or telephone contact with another person, namely the interviewee. (Incidentally, 'respondent' and 'informant' are words that are sometimes used instead of 'interviewee'.)

A great deal is provided by this personal contact: you are another human being (I'm just guessing here), and interviewees will respond to you, in bod-ily presence, in an entirely different way from the way that they would have reacted to questionnaires that came through their letterboxes or to emails. This is a ready-made support for you: most people want to help and give their opinions (as long as the topic is not in some way sensitive for them-selves, their colleagues, friends or family), and they will usually be energised to help by your physical presence. If you take the trouble to schedule a visit you can be more or less guaranteed of a response. Most importantly, though, you will be able to relate to interviewees while you are talking to them; you will be able to hear and understand what they are saying and use gesture or words to encourage them to say more (or less). You will be able to watch and listen for nuances of their behaviour which will give you important clues about how they feel about a topic. Because of the primacy of the personal contact, your appearance, demeanour and tone are important – how do you want to be seen? As 'one of us' (i.e. like the interviewee)? As a person in authority? As a neutral observer? … Or what? Your decision should influ-ence the way that you look, sound and behave.

However you decide to present yourself, it is good practice of course to try to put the interviewee at ease before the interview proper begins – to talk about the weather, about your journey, about anything inconsequential that will break the ice. This is sometimes called 'establishing rapport'. Its nature, of course, varies with the nature of the interviewees and your relationship with them. Remember, though, that establishing rapport is not simply a mechanical process to be gone through; it is a process of actually making contact – of proving that you are human – and this can be far more difficult in some cases than others. With children it can be particularly difficult and because of this interviews with children are often best avoided unless you know them well. I can remember doing a piece of research for a government department in which I conducted a series of interviews with half a dozen or so 13-year-olds in a special school for children with behaviour difficulties. From memory, I think the most extended response I received was 'Dunno', despite my heroic attempts at rapport establishment.

With the element of personal contact being so important, you will have to ask yourself before the interviews begin what it is that you are trying to get from your interviewees and how the personal contact will help. Does your design (i.e. your purposes, questions, approach and design frame) mean that you will be interpreting what your respondents say for illumination of the research scene? Or does it lead you to want straightforward 'facts'? If the former, you will be trying far harder to 'read' your interviewees' behaviour – their mannerisms, gestures, hesitations, glances away – and you will be recording these (in your head or on a notepad) as carefully as their words. You will be using these clues to make informed guesses about what interviewees might really mean beyond the actual words that they are using.

'When I use a word,' Humpty Dumpty said in rather a scornful tone, 'it means just what I choose it to mean – neither more nor less.' (Lewis Carroll, *Alice Through the Looking-Glass*)

… and he was right: words do change their meaning, depending on context – and meaning goes *beyond* the words, so that we can often 'read' what another person means, irrespective of the words they use. So, sometimes when I say 'Yes' I mean 'No' and I guess that those around me can tell I mean 'No' by my manner and my demeanour: I may say it sarcastically or hesitantly; I may be lying and avoid eye contact (not that I lie often, obviously). When I answer open-ended questions I may seem to be skirting around or fudging the issue. This is where being in a face-to-face interview is invaluable, in divining these quite subtle behavioural or linguistic giveaways to the meanings people might really hold.

> **Transcript** or **transcription:** A *written* form of something that was originally in *spoken* words. So, if you have interviewed someone and have recorded the interview on tape or MP3, then played it back to yourself and typed it all out, the typed out form is called the 'transcript'.

In recording what people are saying, you have a choice: you can take notes there and then (or very soon afterwards), or you can electronically audio-record for subsequent transcription. It depends on how faithfully you feel you need to record every word that is said, though of course audio recording doesn't pick up the behavioural cues that I have just noted, so an accompanying set of notes can be useful as well. It can be very helpful to have an accurate record of an interview, especially if you are doing interpretative research, and if you feel this will be necessary then ensure that you are set up for electronic recording (and practise at home first, because it is easy to get things wrong). Whatever methods you use to record, you will need to explain these methods briefly to the interviewee and what is being done with the data – how it is being stored, analysed and subsequently destroyed (see the discussion of ethics in Chapter 7).

Telephone interviews are bounded by the same considerations as face-to-face interviews, but you miss the contextual and behavioural detail, not to mention the commitment of your respondents.

Structured interviews

A structured interview is a meeting with another person in which you ask a predetermined set of questions. Beyond this set of questions there is very little scope for further following-up – little scope for pursuing an interesting comment from the interviewee. The idea behind the structure is that there is a degree of uniformity provided across the different interviewees you meet. The interviewees' responses will be recorded on a form that will probably mix different kinds of response, both open-ended and closed.

Open-ended and closed questions

An open-ended question is one that allows respondents to reply in whatever way they wish. For example, you may ask interviewees 'What are your feelings about the National Lottery?' and they can give vent to whatever opinions or prejudices they wish, taking as long as they like. It is your job then to record this information as accurately as you can (or need to) ready for subsequent analysis. Closed questions are those that demand a particular response, such as 'Do you approve of the National Lottery? Yes or No', or 'How comfortable are you with the idea of the government raising money by the National Lottery? Very comfortable, comfortable, no opinion, not comfortable, very uncomfortable'. Respondents have to respond in the way that the closed question format demands. They can't say 'Well, it depends what you mean by "comfortable"' or 'I have mixed opinions'.

A structured interview has a limited number of strengths. First, compared with other kinds of interview, it can be administered relatively easily and quickly. Second, interviewees' responses can be quite easily coded. Beyond this, though, the structured interview has not very much in its favour. Remember that you are interviewing in order to get something other than an assured response: you want to be reaching something that comes from the person-to-person contact that goes beyond mere ticks in boxes. The face-to-face interview is giving you an opportunity to gain an understanding of the interviewee, and this ready-made strength of the interview situation is not being used with a structured interview. You may as well be giving a questionnaire if you are using a structured interview. While you can note the respondent's general demeanour in response to your questions, you don't have an opportunity to follow up these signals with further questions if you limit yourself to the format of a structured interview.

Because there is no great advantage in the structured interview to giving it in a face-to-face manner, it may as well be given in written form – in other words in a questionnaire (see p. 173).

Unstructured interviews

An unstructured interview is like a conversation. There is no predetermined format to the interview beyond your general interest in the topic. You don't meet your interviewee with a pre-specified list of questions. The idea behind the unstructured interview is that interviewees should be allowed to set the agenda. *They* should be the ones who are determining the important issues to be covered. This is of course what is wanted in interpretative research: in this kind of research you are looking for your respondents to set the scene and let *them* tell *you* what the issues are. You, the researcher, go in with an open mind and it is important that the 'frame' set for the research allows the interviewee scope to do this.

Beyond this desire to let the interviewee lead the way, there are variations on a theme of just how unstructured the interview should be. If your respondent goes completely off the topic then you would wish to bring them back to it in some way. However, this would need to be done sensitively, since it may be the case that this is the way that they talk – going 'off message' for a while before they return to the topic. Or they might like to tell a story when they are talking, and the unstructured interview gives them a chance to do this. Sometimes an interviewee will use the opportunity of a 'sympathetic ear' to ventilate about something or to use you almost as an unpaid counsellor. Within reason, you should try to be understanding here. Not only has this person given you their time but they may be offering you something of great relevance in doing this. If it seems the case in this sort of circumstance that something of a delicate or sensitive nature is being disclosed you should clear with your interviewee after the interview that they are happy for the specific information to be used and in what kind of disguise – you could reveal it only as a general comment, perhaps, or it may be acceptable to your interviewee to quote from them in an anonymous way on which you can agree.

How should you prompt the interviewee without setting the agenda yourself? There are degrees of strength of prompt: you may simply say

'Can you tell me more about that?' or offer something stronger such as 'How did that make you feel?' or 'What happened next?' However, if you really are interested in what the interviewee has to say you would avoid a question such as 'Does that make you feel angry?' This really would be putting words into the interviewee's mouth.

Semi-structured interviews

The semi-structured interview provides the best of both worlds as far as interviewing is concerned, combining the structure of a list of issues to be covered together with the freedom to follow up points as necessary. Because of this combination it is the most common arrangement in most small-scale research. However, this does not mean that it is always the best, given your purposes and your design frame: one of the other arrangements may be better suited to your needs. If, for example, you really are interested in interpreting your interviewees' comments and if you are a participant observer in the situation that you are researching, an *unstructured* interview would be a better choice. I say this because too many students (in my opinion) opt for the semi-structured interview as the most straightforward and seemingly obvious choice, where in fact it can lead them to do a different kind of research from that which they set out to do. If you really do intend to do an ethnographic piece of research, entering your research environment as a participant observer, you are trying to understand how the 'players' in that research are play- ing their roles – depending on the meanings that they construct within that environment. If this is the case, if this is what you want to do, then the semi-structured interview is too rigid a tool to be working with. It's like asking your respondent to be an artist and giving them a painting- by-numbers kit with which to do it.

In order to get the best of both worlds afforded by the semi-structured interview, you will need an *interview schedule*, which is a list of issues which you want to cover. These issues don't have to be in the form of questions; rather, they provide merely an aide-mémoire of the important points for discussion. However, you are not forced by the procedure to go through these points in order, or to keep in any way formally to a set format for the interview. Rather, they are a reminder of what you intend to cover.

If, for example, you find that your interviewee has provided a response to your second point while addressing your first issue, there is no need subsequently raise this as a specific question, unless you feel that there is more you wish to know. In fact this is the hallmark of the semi-structured interview: if you wish to know more, then you ask about it. Prolong the discussion on that point.

Your interview schedule, drawn up prior to the interview, is a framework of issues, leading to possible questions, leading to possible follow-up ques- tions, leading to 'probes'. Probes are encouragements to interviewees to proceed with aspects of their answers; these may be verbal – for example 'Go on …' – or non-verbal, in a tilt of the head or a nod or a raising of the eyebrows (but preferably not all three at once).

Issue/topic	Possible questions	Possible follow up questions	Probes
Conflict with authority	Can you tell me about a time when you have been treated differently because of your race or colour? What sort of things do people do? Do they look at you differently, or speak to you differently, or what? Can you tell me about a time when you have been stopped by the police?	What was your reaction? How did that make you feel?	Tell me more about that. And then?
Reactions when spoken to	Can you tell me about a time when you have been treated badly?	What did you do? What happened then?	And ...? Can you tell me more?
Perception of racial element	Do you think the police treat you differently because you are Asian/black? Are some people better or worse than others?	How do you know that? In what way? What kinds of things do they do to show this?	Go on.
Attitudes of parents	Do you tell your parents if you feel you have been treated badly?	How do they react?	Really?

Figure 8.2   The beginnings of an interview schedule

Let's take an example of how that might be done. Supposing you were a probation officer studying for a Master's degree in forensic psychology and were interested in perceptions of victimisation among young offenders from black and minority ethnic groups. You decide to conduct interviews with young men in a young offender institution which you occasionally visit. The questions you choose are based around experiences of dealings with the police, with teachers and with others such as shopkeepers and how far there is a perception among your interviewees of victimisation because of race. You begin by asking questions about the situations in which conflict has occurred, about the young men's reactions when spoken to, the attitudes of their parents to the police. Your schedule looks like the one in Figure 8.2.

This schedule of issues, questions and probes is just a guide from which you can deviate as necessary: it's a structure to help you conduct the interview; it is not a straitjacket. In other words, you should feel free to ask different questions or supplementary questions as the need arises.

You may find that one particular element of the interview is yielding particularly interesting comments and if this is the case you may wish to spend nearly all of the interview in this area. This is the essence of a semi-structured interview – namely that the structure reminds you of your aims and themes, but it does not constrict you.

Accounts

Accounts are really the products of unstructured interviews but without the expectation that these will have been collected via an interview. The account could, for example, depending on your informant, have been provided in the form of a long, written piece of prose like an essay, or it could be a similar account kept in audio form for subsequent transcription. An account will be handled in the same way as the data from an unstructured interview.

Diaries

In everyday use, a diary is a regular, usually day-by-day, record of thoughts or occurrences, or it may be a record of forthcoming and past appointments, activities and events. A diary is an invaluable data-gathering tool for the researcher undertaking a small project. It may involve you, or a participant in your research, making a record of thoughts, feelings, actions, responses, conversations, etc. Or it may involve a more structured record being taken of specific activities. If you are asking an informant to complete a diary there are advantages with some informants that are conferred by the personal and private nature of the process: some people will be more fulsome in accounts in a private disclosure of this kind than they would be in a face-to-face interview. This is often the case with children and young people, as long as they have the writing skills. You will probably write up your diary immediately after your session in the field, recording an assortment of facts, opinions, views, interpretations, snatches of remembered conversation and so on. You can keep it in written form or in audio recording to be transcribed subsequently.

You may even wish to keep a video diary, though always ask yourself what is added by the use of a particular method. Are you really adding anything special with the adoption of video that could not be provided with audio? Video is certainly a wonderful way of recording information for research, but ask yourself whether, in the case of a *diary*, it is actually offering any extra value. Are there expressions, gestures, sighs, grimaces, frowns, tears even, that would be missed in a written or audio diary and which you could subsequently draw on in your analysis? If you think that this is the case, then a video diary is worth the extra effort.

Below is a section from a diary I took for a piece of (eventually abortive, probably wisely) research I was doing on the role of the governor in school. Being on the governing body myself, I could be a participant observer.

Wed. 21 March. Full governors' meeting. Arrived on time and sat next to JJ, near the front and near the chair and the head teacher. Sit and get my papers out while things are settling down. People are arriving. We eventually get going about 5 minutes late. Go through papers for accuracy and matters arising at the same time. Nothing very interesting arises. Onto the reports of the subcommittees. We get through them faster than usual. I give mine – I'm chair of the pastoral and curriculum sub-committee and race through mine, which contains nothing that we needed to discuss: school minibuses: who should drive them – a management decision – nothing to do with us; daily worship – should we continue to condone the breaking of the law by not insisting on daily worship. Of course, in my opinion: silly law, but no one can say this for fear of being taken to court. Reviewing whole school policies: do we want to? Even the reports of the premises committee is quick; MB usually reads his minutes out verbatim, embellishing them with interminable comments about the lintel over G block main entrance. Today, inexplicably, he is remarkably quick. Perhaps he wants to get home early.

The head teacher's report is a model of boredom, covering nothing that could remotely be said to have anything to do with the strategy or the direction of the school. There's something on some exchange students from Germany (who are 'very attractive' according to head teacher – seems an odd way to describe the students), something on staff, something on drugs with a cut-out from the local paper saying that drugs are a problem, as if we didn't know they were a problem – and as if we needed a cutting from the paper to tell us. Nothing about the strategy of the school. Just something to keep the head teacher talking for 20 minutes. We listen politely. No: more than politely. Everyone here seems to acquiesce in this, as though that's what they're here for – a bunch of people who have been put on the planet for the purpose of listening to the head spout forth about mundane happenings at the school. They seem to think that they are here as a hybrid of guardian and trustee – to make sure that good is done and no one on the staff gets up to any mischief, and I suppose there's some justice in this. This is perhaps what the original purpose of the governors was. The irony was that (as I distantly remembered it) old fashioned governors – fierce old ladies and retired colonels – probably did serve something of this function. This new breed, though, has had its remit changed to that of strategic arrowhead and holder of the legal responsibility. But this doesn't quite seem to have got through to your common-and-garden governor who still sees herself (or more likely, himself) as guardian/trustee. But the problem in this new mixed-mode governor is that they are not remote like the old fierce ladies and the colonels. They have gone native. They're there, wanting to be liked by the head teacher and the deputies, wanting to get invited to the opening of the new building, wanting to be wanted, as we all do. Maslow was right; it's the fundamental human need and is almost crushingly overpowering. Because the need to be wanted is so powerful, no one says to the head teacher 'Shut up you boring fart; this is not only irrelevant, it's also incompetently presented and incoherent. Please desist immediately.' No – instead we all listen, all 20 of us in complete silence apart from the occasional polite titter at the bad jokes, and at the end the chair says 'Thank you P for that very full and informative report.' Me too. I want to be liked too. So I nod my head weakly and smile in the direction of the head teacher when he finishes and hope he notices me.

You will see from this diary that it is more than simply a record of this happened, then that happened, then that happened, etc. Rather, it is a record not only of events but also of my interpretations. In line with the expectations of ethnography it is a set of my own interpretations of events – interpretations concerning the roles of governors and how they constructed their own identities in the committee meeting and on the board generally. Why did they think they were there? What did they think they were doing? What did the head think he was doing, and how did he construct ideas about the roles of governors (if indeed he had any ideas at all – about anything)? *Not* to make these interpretations (and you don't have to be as cruel as I have been here) is one of the most common weaknesses of the research diary or its analysis. Taken as part of an ethnography, a diary is not simply a record of events.

Alternatively, a diary can be more structured, collecting data about specific events or activities. In a small study I undertook as part of my PhD, I asked 100 primary school teachers to keep a diary in the format of a timetable. It was about the people who worked alongside them in the classroom, how long they worked for and what they were doing. I had done a questionnaire previously asking about the general categories of person who might be working, which turned out to be parents, teaching assistants, 6th form students, volunteers, etc. I also wanted to find out about the type of activity, the group size being worked with and the length of time these people were working in the classroom. This was a lot of information to collect and it was an important consideration that information about the associations among these people and their activities be preserved without in so doing generating a form that would be intimidatingly complex and time-consuming for busy teachers to unravel. I decided on a diary for each of my informants, with the familiarity of a timetable format used as a means to gaining the maximum possible information in the minimum possible time for the teachers. As it worked out, they seemed to like the familiarity of the format, which made it simple to complete, and I obtained a 60 per cent return rate (which is very good for a request for involvement of this kind sent by post). In fact, simplicity is the watchword for any request of this kind: if it looks hard to complete, the bin beckons.

The diaries were completed for one week of the winter term. Teachers coded the type of people working with them in the classroom (6 options), the type of activity (15 options), the group size being worked with (5 options) and the length of time worked. They were asked to put the initials of the participants alongside the codes and using these it was possible to determine the number of times a particular individual within a category worked during the week. Most of the data were handled in terms of sessions of help, a session being an uninterrupted session or consecutive sessions (i.e. only interrupted by break or lunch) undertaken by one individual. The diary would return to me in the form of a timetable like that in Figure 8.3. Teachers would also add codes representing the kind of activities

Mon	MT all mornings (TA)		Mrs B (support se...)	ZS all pms (TA)
Tue				
Wed		Mrs V (parent)		
Thu				
Fri		Mrs I (parent		

Figure 8.3   Diary kept in the form of a timetable

undertaken. On the reverse side they could add day-by-day comments of their own choosing – thoughts, feelings, ideas, regrets, missed opportunities, etc.

So, like any data collection method, a diary can take a number of forms, with the emphasis on the *regular* collection of data.

Group interviews and focus groups

Group interviews warrant a discussion separate from individual interviews since a particular way of behaving overcomes a group and you need to be aware of this if you are interviewing more than one person at the same time (and, yes, for these purposes two people constitute a group). People behave differently in groups: particular individuals may become more talkative or less talkative; some people take the lead, while others follow; some will tend to be 'stroppy', others helpful. And there are particular ways a whole group will behave, differently from individuals. So, for example, there is an inclination for a group to display what is called a 'risky shift phenomenon', a tendency well established in social psychology. This is the likelihood that a group will make a riskier decision than an individual. If you asked a set of groups a question such as 'Would you have a person with a criminal record to stay in your house?' and then asked an equivalent number of people but as individuals, you would probably find a riskier decision (i.e. more likelihood of saying 'yes') in the groups. There's safety in numbers, and this maxim applies even if decisions are being made about wholly imaginary happenings.

So before you set up the group interview you need to establish why you are doing a group interview rather than a set of individual interviews. Is it to save time? If it is, then you must be aware that you will be getting different responses from those you would have obtained from the same people interviewed individually. Aside from any tendency to 'risky shift' and other phenomena associated with groups, the group may be dominated by one or two voices and these may not be at all representative of the general opinion. There are, of course, legitimate reasons for wanting to interview a group, and these will concern the group psychology itself. Do you want to find how a group (i.e. *as* a group) will behave or move in response to an imaginary event? Do you want to *compare* the group attitude with a set of individually assessed attitudes within the group, perhaps to judge the impact of the power or influence of one or two group members? It is factors such as these for which you can legitimately use a group interview.

The term *focus group* has come to be used interchangeably with *group interview*, but the two kinds of group are different in important respects. In group interviews the emphasis is on the researcher taking a lead role, asking questions and being in control of the discussion – rather in the way that an interviewer is leading the discussion in a structured or semi-structured interview. So the researcher asks questions and respondents answer. But in focus groups (which emerged, incidentally, as a technique from marketing research), the researcher plays the role of *facilitator* or *moderator*. If you are running a focus group your aim is to facilitate or moderate discussion *among participants*, not between yourself and the participants. The idea is that you take a marginal rather than a pivotal role.

In the focus group, participants, usually eight or so, who have a relevant characteristic or feature of their lives in common will be brought together in an informal setting to discuss the topic in question. As in an unstructured interview with an individual, the idea is to get at the understandings, beliefs and values of the participants. And in the same way that in an individual unstructured interview the aim is to let the *individual* take the lead in setting the direction of the discussion, so in the focus group the aim is to let the *group* take the lead. As facilitator, your role is to stimulate discussion, and you may do this with your comments or you may prepare a range of *focus materials* for the group to discuss. These are materials – for example, objects, artefacts, photographs, drawings, newspaper clippings, short videos, audio recordings – that help the group focus on the topic of interest. If, say, you were interested in the views of parents on testing, you might collect some examination papers, some photographs of young people in a hall sitting an examination or a video of a news programme showing students' reactions on the day that 'A' level results are published. You might set off discussion following such a video with the starter: 'Reactions?'

Given that you need your wits about you to facilitate effectively in a group such as this, it is common practice in professionally conducted research to use an observer to record information about context, environment and participants' behaviour. In small-scale research it will not usually be possible to get help in this way, so it may be helpful to record proceedings using audio and/or video.

Document interrogation

Gathering data from documents represents an entirely different proposition from gathering data from people. Essentially, the knack is to find the right documents, read them and think about them.

All documents – and all documentary interrogation – is different, so it is difficult to give general advice. I can, however, give an example from a piece of research that I did for a government department (Tarr and Thomas, 1997). In this, I was asked to look at schools' special educational needs policy documents, which schools were obliged to produce by law, to see how far the documents met the expectations of statutory guidance. The research involved obtaining the policy documents from a representative sample of schools, examining what was in them and cross-checking these against the government's guidance on the contents of a schools policy document of this kind. So, there were two forms of documentary interrogation involved here:

- interrogation of the schools' policy documents
- interrogation of government advice, published in different documents

… and my job was to check one against the other to see how schools were meeting expectations.

My colleague and I first read the government documents to garner information that we considered would be important for writing a school policy on special needs. There were two such documents containing such information: (1) the Education (Special Educational Needs) (Information) Regulations, and (2) the Code of Practice on special educational needs. Our main task was to distil from these documents a list of issues that a policy had to cover. This was a difficult task, because the criteria to be met appeared in different forms in these two documents. We were eventually able to group the criteria under 15 main headings, each of which had several subheadings. The main headings are given in Table 8.1.

Table 8.1   A checklist derived from government guidance: main categories which should appear in each SEN policy

1.	Principles and objectives held by the school
2.	SENCO's name and role
3.	Strategic management and target setting
4.	Admissions
5.	Specialisms
6.	Resource allocation
7.	Identification, assessment and review procedures
8.	Curriculum: strategies to include all children
9.	Integration strategies
10.	Complaints: how parents can complain and how complaints are dealt with
11.	INSET and staff development: plans for teachers and assistants
12.	External support: sources and LA agreements
13.	External relations: liaison arrangements
14.	Parents: how a working partnership is ensured
15.	Transition: between schools/to adult life; SEN register; LA pro-formas

We then had the job of looking at schools' policies. We asked the head teachers of 252 schools from 9 local authorities (with a stratified sample of secondary, primary and special schools) for a copy of their SEN policies. Of those approached 181 obliged, providing a 72 per cent return. Each policy received was examined against the criteria in the checklist. First, did each policy cover every point in the checklist? There was no magic way of finding this information other than through stapling a checklist to each policy, reading each one from cover to cover, and ticking (or not ticking) the checklist point by point as we judged that criteria were (or were not) covered.

While we were doing this we also had to judge *how well* each policy addressed each of the criteria in Table 8.1. Again, this was a question of intelligently reading the policies. Did they merely mention (or fail to mention) each point on the list? Did they elaborate on the issue? Or did they explicate fully? The answers were a matter of judgement, and while it may have been possible to make these judgements more objectively (e.g. by counting the number of words given over to an issue), we decided against this course of action, believing that it would provide a less valuable picture than our own assessment from reading. (It might be possible for one school to say more in 25 words than another said in 250.) Essentially, there was no substitute for reading and thinking.

From the overall sample of schools, 18 policies were then selected (two from each local authority) for detailed examination. The more detailed examination involved comparing the policies with the corresponding local authority policies (which also had to be read), assessing readability, accessibility and length. To assess readability, the documents were scanned using optical character recognition software. They were saved into Word, which we then asked for readability statistics.

You will note from this example that there were few technical tricks or special procedures available for interrogating the documents. Given the ease with which documents can now be downloaded (particularly government and other policy documents), a key shortcut is in some basic document interrogation using computer software. This is easy if the document is in Word, but a bit trickier if it is in pdf. If the latter, you can, after checking copyright, copy the whole thing and then paste it into Word. (*Tip*: To copy the whole lot in a pdf file, press Ctrl A, which selects the whole document; then Ctrl C, which copies it, then switch to a blank Word document and paste it into that with Ctrl V.) If you are not able to download the relevant document in word-processing or pdf format, the one technical trick that is widely available now is through electronic scanning. Most scanners now are provided with optical character recognition (OCR) software which will do the 'reading' (but sadly not the thinking or understanding) for you. When you scan your text your software should give you the option of enabling the text to be 'read' as text (as distinct from simply taking a picture of the text). It will then save this into a word-processing file, and once this is done there are a number of ways in which your computer can help you to analyse the text, and these forms of analysis are covered in Chapter 9. Unfortunately, though, there is no substitute for intelligent reading in the interrogation of documents.

Documents occur in many and varied shapes and forms and we can be creative in their location and interrogation. Again, there is no sense to be had in a separation of types of inquiry into 'scientific' and 'non-scientific' here – it's a question of 'Where can I find the information, and how can I use it intelligently to come up with answers to my questions?' Science, whether it is astronomy or social science, is eclectic in its attitude to evidence – and documents, whatever their provenance, are invaluable. The great astronomer and scientist Edmund Halley back in the eighteenth century used documents to predict the return of his comet. Coady (1994: 13) notes that Halley relied …

> … upon earlier testimony in identifying his famous comet and predicting its return at seventy-five-year intervals. It was while Halley was studying the comet of 1682 that he noticed the similarities between it and two other bright comets reported by earlier astronomers in 1531 and 1607. Noting the intervals of approximately seventy-five years he predicted the return of the comet in 1758 – which proved correct.

Seek documents relevant to your research topic on the Internet. As I write, it has been announced that court records are to be published online in order to make more transparent the sentencing of law-breakers. Such records will be invaluable to the social scientist. A useful website is Teachernet's document bank, at www.teachernet.gov.uk/docbank/index.cfm?id=9502.

If you are contacting schools for documents, a useful website is www.edubase.gov.uk/, which is a database of all educational establishments across England and Wales, and it will find for you, for example, all primary schools in Swindon (or Swansea, Scunthorpe or Stalybridge).

Data-gathering tools – for use with words and/or numbers

The data-gathering tools I have outlined so far are used mainly with words. In this section, I am describing tools that will collect words or numbers or both – or they may commonly convert the words into numbers in some way.

Questionnaires

The defining characteristic of a questionnaire is that it is a *written* form of questioning. Beyond this, that is to say beyond being in written form, the questions may be open or closed (see the box on p. 162). You may be collecting facts (for example, 'How many cups of tea have you drunk today?')

or attitudes (for example, 'Do you think parents should be stopped from smacking their children?'), or you may use a questionnaire as part of an assessment procedure to assess something such as personality. To extend the analogy of data-gathering instruments as tools, the questionnaire is a versatile tool and is used in a number of different kinds of research design. It can be tightly structured, but can also allow the opportunity for a more open and discursive response if required. Questionnaires may be read out by interviewers (either face-to-face or by phone) or sent to respondents for them to complete themselves; they may be sent by post or email or may be presented online.

There are some basic considerations in constructing a questionnaire:

1. Keep everything short. If possible, limit your questionnaire to one side of A4. The number of people who respond to a questionnaire will decrease in proportion with its length. Also, keep the questions short.
2. Be clear about what you are asking. Only ask for one piece of information at a time. I made the silly mistake recently in a short questionnaire of asking for two pieces of information in one sentence. This confused the respondents, who latched onto the first part of the question and ignored the second.
3. Be precise. Because the only source of clarification is on the piece of paper in front of your respondents, you have to be clear about what you are asking. So, instead of asking, for example, 'How often do you read academic journals?' you would be better to ask 'Do you read academic journals …' and then give a choice of options, such as 'more than once a month, once a month … [etc.]'.
4. Collect all necessary details. It is frustrating to look at a returned set of questionnaires and say to yourself, 'Oh, I wish I'd asked about …' For example, it may be useful to have information about gender on the form, or years of experience in the profession. Sometimes, these factors, while they may not have seemed important at the outset, become important after your 'eyeballing' of your data (see Chapter 9). They can add an additional dimension for very little extra work, particularly if you are analysing your responses statistically.
5. Be aware of 'prestige bias'. Most people want to look good: to appear clever, nice, rich (or, in the case of students, poor), educated, ethical, and so on. The phenomenon that makes us want to appear any or all of these things can lead to 'prestige bias' in the responses to questionnaires. Be aware of this in the way that you pose questions and interpret the responses.

This kind of bias can occur in a different form if your respondent assumes any kind of 'right answer'. If you were to ask university students, for example, about their use of the library they might well feel that it would be helpful to them in some manner (even if the questionnaire is anonymous) to answer in a way that would indicate more frequent rather than less frequent use. When I ask students to complete an evaluation questionnaire at the end of a term's teaching, for example, I am aware (because they tell me) that students think that I look for similarities between handwriting on the evaluation and handwriting on other samples of work. Slim as they must realise the possibility is that I pore for hours over their written responses looking for this kind of similarity, it clearly nevertheless is something that occurs to them, and probably has an effect on their responses. You should be aware of the possibility of this kind of bias when you construct your questions and in the way that you distribute and manage the collection of responses. Don't just tell people that it is anonymous, but make it clear how anonymity will be achieved and respected.

Kinds of question and kinds of response

I have already noted the difference between open and closed questions (see the box on p. 162). You can think of *open questions* in a questionnaire in the same way that you think about unstructured interviews, diaries and accounts. They are bounded by the same considerations, in that you are aiming to get at the central concerns of an issue as your respondents see them. In a written questionnaire, though, where there is little in the way of stimulus (as there would be in an interview), you will have to give more of a prod to jog the mind of your respondent. It will be no good asking 'Is there anything else you would like to say?' as an open question at the end of a questionnaire, since a good proportion of your respondents will be overcome with the well known syndrome of mind-emptying – certainly familiar to me in many and varied situations from the doctor's surgery to the job interview, where my memory is suddenly and inexplicably flushed clean of all those desperately important matters that I had been anxious to discuss.

Open questions may be simply a question such as 'How would you describe your manager's management style, in two or three sentences?' Or you may structure them differently, for example:

- If I had to sum up the culture at my place of work in a word or phrase, it would be …
- I am/am not enjoying my work because …

Closed questions can be organised in a number of ways …

Dichotomous questions

'Dichotomous' means 'two-way', and the dichotomy is usually 'yes' or 'no'. For example:

Have you ever applied for a post of responsibility?   Yes   ☐
                                                        No   ☐

These can often be screening questions. In other words, you may use the question to separate respondents into groups, who can then be questioned separately. If they haven't applied for a post of responsibility (in this example), why not? Your subsequent questions to this group will pursue this theme. And if they have applied, what happened? A separate route of questioning can be used for this sub-set.

Multiple-choice questions

These contain two or more answers where respondents can be told either to tick one box or to tick as many boxes as needed. For example:

> In an emergency, which of the following would you feel confident in teaching to a Year 7 class (tick as many as you like):
>
> | | |
> |---|---|
> | Maths | ☐ |
> | English | ☐ |
> | A modern language | ☐ |
> | Science | ☐ |
> | History | ☐ |
> | Geography | ☐ |
> | Other | ☐   Please specify _____ |

Depending on the purpose, the form of the multiple-choice question will change, of course. If you were interested in respondents' knowledge rather than their beliefs and there was only one right answer, you would restrict the number of choices to one.

Be aware that this kind of question can be useful where it relates to a fact, such as the years of experience of a respondent in the profession. Rather than simply asking for a bald figure, by putting figures into bands it can obviate the respondent spending unnecessary time working out exact figures (in which you probably are not interested anyway) and the bands (for example, less than 7 years, 7–19 years, 20 years or more) provide a useful grouping for any subsequent analysis.

Rank order questions

Here, respondents have to rank items (i.e. put them in order) on a list according to some criterion – for example best to worst, most able to least able, degree of difficulty, and so on. Within this ranking, you can either ask for a limited number of choices (e.g. first, second and third), or require respondents to rank the whole list. For example, you may be interested in asking recently retired teachers about the postwar development of educational systems in relation to the prevailing political climate and the degree of leadership provided by the Secretary of State for Education. Your interest may centre on the impact of such leadership as they felt it in the classroom. As part of this you ask them to rank Secretaries of State between 1980 and 2008:

> Please rank these Secretaries of State for the degree of their influence (positive *or* negative) on educational practice 'at the chalk face' as you saw it during your time as a teacher. Please rank them in order of significance, with 1 for the most influential, and 9 for the least influential.

Kenneth Clarke   □
John Patten   □
Gillian Shephard   □
David Blunkett   □
Estelle Morris   □
Charles Clarke   □
Ruth Kelly   □
Alan Johnson   □
Ed Balls   □

Rating scale questions

These require the respondent to rate some experience, attribute, attitude, etc. along a continuum. You may for example wish to ask adults about their experience of testing and assessment when they were at school:

> Remembering back to when you were at school, would you say that your experiences of formal assessment and testing were

Very positive   □
Positive   □
Neutral   □
Negative   □
Very negative   □

The respondent will tick only one of these boxes.

Constant sum method

The constant sum method requires the respondent to distribute 'points', usually 100, to a set of answers. It's as if you give respondents 100 counters to pile up in any of the category boxes as they deem fit. For example, suppose you were interested in parents' perceptions of a good teacher. You might come up with a taxonomy (i.e. an arrangement of ideas) that contains a number of features which might be associated with good teaching: kind, thoughtful, generous, etc. Using the constant sum method, you ask your respondents to divide their points among these features:

> What for you are the important characteristics of a good teacher? You have 100 points to distribute among the characteristics outlined below. You can distribute the points entirely as you wish, but the points must add up to 100:

Kind   □
Thoughtful   □
Generous   □
Good communicator □
Good listener   □
Well organised   □
Caring   □
Considerate   □

The constant sum method is best done with you, the researcher, present.

One of the advantages of this method is the attribution of a 'strength of feeling' weighting to various answers, revealing the relative importance attributed to the different options, so you may be able to see, for example, that 'Kind' is felt to be twice as important as 'Well organised'. This allows some statistical manipulations of the data that would not be possible with other questionnaire data collection methods.

Matrix or grid questions

Matrices (grids) provide a series of questions, which all have the same answer scale. For example, if you were interested in canvassing parents on what constitutes a good teacher, you might ask them to suggest how important each of these criteria were, all on the same scale of 1 to 5.

	Importance →
	1 2 3 4 5
Caring	☐ ☐ ☐ ☐ ☐
Efficient	☐ ☐ ☐ ☐ ☐
Reliable	☐ ☐ ☐ ☐ ☐
Kind	☐ ☐ ☐ ☐ ☐
Understandable	☐ ☐ ☐ ☐ ☐
Helpful	☐ ☐ ☐ ☐ ☐

It is necessary to make clear to respondents the 'direction of travel' of the numbers being used in this kind of scale. I have used an arrow in this example, but you may wish to make this doubly clear by, for example, adding words such as 'high' or 'low' at each end, or adding a graphic such as a smiley. *Tip*: Smileys and other useful graphics such as ✐ and ✓ can be found in Word under the Wingdings font. Click 'Insert', Click 'Symbol', scroll down under 'Font' to Wingdings, scroll through the pictures, click on the one you want, and press Insert. ☺

Scales

Scales, that is to say sets of items and responses, appear in some of the question formats above. However, there are a couple of kinds of well-known scale that are worth mentioning as easily used tools: the Likert Scale and the semantic differential scale.

The Likert Scale

The Likert Scale was thought up by the psychologist Rensis Likert primarily for measuring attitudes: respondents indicate their levels of agreement to statements provided by the researcher relating to that attitude, belief or characteristic. The respondent, rather as in rating scale questions, responds to each item on a five-point scale, usually with answers from strongly agree, agree, neither agree nor disagree, disagree, strongly disagree. To remove the tendency for some people to over-choose the middle option, this middle option is sometimes removed, making a four point scale. The latter is used in the Rosenberg Self-Esteem Scale, where the first three items are:

	Strongly agree	Agree	Disagree	Strongly disagree
1. On the whole I am satisfied with myself.				
2. At times I think that I am no good at all.				
3. I feel that I have a number of good qualities.				

Here is part of a questionnaire using a Likert Scale that colleagues and I (Vincett et al., 2005) used as part of a larger piece of research with children in Essex schools:

	Yes ☺	A bit 😐	No ☹
My teacher likes to listen to my ideas			
My teacher helps me with my work			
I think my teacher's classroom rules are fair			
If I have a problem I can tell my teacher			
Sometimes my teacher lets me choose what work to do			
My teacher tells me when I have done something well			

A Likert Scale can be used in any situation where belief or attitude is to be measured. The important thing to remember is that you are asking for agreement or disagreement with a *statement* that you provide. (The Rosenberg and other scales can be accessed via http://eib.emcdda.europa.eu/html.cfm/index3676EN.html.)

The semantic differential scale

Using opposite-meaning adjectives such as *'kind/cruel'* or *'exciting/boring'*, the semantic differential scale requires the respondent to rate something on a seven-point scale in relation to those adjectives. You may be interested in the assertion that rap music encourages sexism and violence among young people. Rather than simply asking 'Do you think that rap music encourages sexism and violence among your age group?', you could use the semantic differential scale to draw a more 'textured' picture of respondents' thinking and look at interesting differences where they occur between sub-groups within your sample. For example:

> Thinking of [name of rap singer's] music and its lyrics how would you rank it along these criteria? Put a tick in the appropriate box on each row.

Because the semantic differential is a little out of the ordinary for many respondents it is probably best done in a questionnaire format with you present. If you did not intend to be present, at the very least you would need to give an example of an already-completed (but irrelevant) one to explain what needs to be done.

Exciting								Boring
Kind								Cruel
Generous								Tight
Selfish								Altruistic
Active								Passive
Racist								Non-racist
Fair								Unfair

Questionnaire structure

Give some thought to how to arrange the questions. For example, don't start with difficult questions, or open-ended questions: leave these until the end, since they require thought and may put off a respondent from bothering. Remember that you are dependent entirely on their good-will. Start with something easy such as a 'How far do you agree with ...' question. This will ease them into the questionnaire and whet their appetite to carry on. Most people, after all, do like to give their opinions: you just have to make it easy for them to do it.

Remember that not all of your questions will be relevant to all of your respondents, so make sure that you include *filters* if necessary, for example: 'Have you ever written for a professional journal? Yes ☐ No ☐. If Yes, please go to Q 5. If No, please go to Q 9'. You can use arrows and boxes to make it clear to respondents where they should go next.

		Create a link to send in your own email message or to place on a webpage
		The simplest and fastest way to collect responses. We generate a link for your survey that you can just copy and paste.
		Upload your own emails and have us send a survey invitation
		You can upload your emails, and we will send a survey invitation on your behalf. You can customize the message that is sent, and track who responds in your list.
		Create a popup invitation for your webpage
		We give you the code to generate a popup invitation on your own webpage.

Figure 8.4   SurveyMonkey's offer for 'posting' your survey

Especially if the questionnaire is sent by post it is a good idea to include a personalised covering letter or some kind of introductory page explaining briefly the purpose of the research and why it is important. This should include information about confidentiality, publication and ethics (see p. 146), and who is responsible for the research. Don't forget to thank the respondent profusely at the end of the questionnaire.

Because a questionnaire is out of your control once it is sent out, it is important that it should be foolproof in its interpretation. To make sure that you get things right you should always pilot a draft questionnaire on a small group of people who can give you feedback.

Questionnaires online

If you want to conduct a survey online there are a number of web-based services available. One of the best known is SurveyMonkey at www.surveymonkey.com. This lets you construct your own questionnaire free for a survey of up to 100 respondents. It guides you very helpfully through the questionnaire construction process and then offers you a way of 'posting' your survey, as shown in Figure 8.4. The whole process is easy and presents your respondents with a professional-looking interface. Do test out a pilot survey first, though, with two or three friends.

If you want anything more complex than a basic questionnaire or if you want to send it to more than 100 people you will need to pay for the SurveyMonkey service or for another one like it. The one that my university department uses is the Bristol Online Survey (BOS). This provides, as they describe it, 'a fully integrated Web environment for the design, delivery and analysis of online surveys'. It doesn't require any technical knowledge and will give you instant feedback on the survey as it progresses. Data can be downloaded into Excel, and you can set up your supervisor, your colleagues or fellow students to view results. There is also 'free' support provided. The downside is that it comes at a price (£500), but your university will almost certainly subscribe to a service of this kind, and if yours does you should have free access: ask your supervisor. If, in the unlikely event of your university department or faculty not subscribing to such a service, BOS will consider on a case-by-case basis appeals from individuals for a reduced-cost provision.

	Yes	No	Not sure	Further comment
a. We intend to discontinue the Editorial as a feature of each issue of BERJ. Do you agree that this is an appropriate change?	☐	☐	☐	

Figure 8.5   Example question on BOS

Figure 8.5 is an example of a question from a survey that I put together on BOS. It was to members of the British Educational Research Association about their views on the Association's journal. You'll note that the questionnaire provides 'buttons' for users to click on. If the people you wish to survey have access to the Internet, then this really is the preferred method of questionnaire distribution, saving a great deal of time in distribution, collection and analysis. It should help also in boosting response rate, obviating the need for envelopes, stamps and other paraphernalia. Figure 8.6 is an example of the output, ready-organised for you.

To contact BOS go to www.survey.bris.ac.uk and if your institution does not subscribe you can direct it to: www.survey.bris.ac.uk/support/sign-up-instructions. There is also a facility for a demo account.

1.a. We intend to discontinue the Editorial as a feature of each issue of BERJ. Do you agree that this is an appropriate change?			
Yes:		38.7%	120
No:		23.5%	73
Not sure:		37.7%	117
1.a.i. We intend to discontinue the Editorial as a feature of each issue of BERJ. Do you agree that this is an appropriate change? -- Further comment			
There are too many responses to display on this page and so all the responses to this question are available on a separate page.			

Figure 8.6   BOS output

Observation

Observation is one of the most important ways of collecting data in social research. Observing means watching carefully, and you can do this careful watching in some very different ways, depending on the approach to research that you have decided to take (see p. 69). For our purposes here, the basic difference is between a kind of observation in which you systematically look for particular kinds of behaviour and one in which – remembering back to Chapter 5 – you watch as a spy or a witness, informally (but methodically) recording important facets of the stage on which you observe.

The first kind of observation, where you watch for particular kinds of behaviour, is called *structured observation*. The second kind, where you get on the stage, take part, record from the stage and watch from there, is called *unstructured observation*.

Structured observation

In structured observation you are making assumptions that the social world is viewable through a prism that enables the breakdown of social activity into quantifiable elements – bits that you can count. Like a prism breaks white light into its separate colours, so the prism of the structured observer breaks the social situation down into separate bits.

The first thing that the observer has to do is to define what these bits are to be. They may be individual pieces of action or language, such as a child physically touching another child or a teacher using a particular kind of question. The next thing that a structured observer has to do is to devise some way of counting these elements. This is done in a number of ways.

Duration recording
The observer measures the overall time that a target behaviour (such as 'child out of seat') occurs. You will end up with an overall time, e.g. 27 minutes in a session of 60 minutes.

Frequency count recording
The observer records each time the target behaviour (e.g. the teacher's use of praise to the whole class) occurs. You will end up with an overall number, e.g. 4 times in a session.

Interval recording
You decide on:

- an interval (3 seconds, 10 seconds, 20 seconds, or whatever – depending on the complexity of what you are looking for);
- target individual(s); and
- categories of behaviour (e.g. on-task, off-task).

You will end up with data which can be processed in a number of ways. The most usual way of processing it is to count up the number of times that the target individual has scored in, say, the behaviour category of interest and then to express this as a percentage of the total number of possible observations.

For example, if your interval is 10 seconds, it means that you are going to be making 6 observations a minute and therefore 360 per hour. Out of these 360 possible observations you may have only seen the child being on task on 36 occasions – if this were the case then you could express this as $36/360 \times 100 = 10\%$ on task.

> **Nature of structured observation:** Defining, counting – characterised by non-participant observation.
>
> **Data gathering:** Various methods of recording particular behaviours: duration, frequency, interval recording.
>
> **Instruments:** Various checklists (e.g. Flanders Interaction Analysis).

Time sampling

You may come across the term 'time sampling'. This simply refers to the fact that you are selecting intervals out of the total time available for observation and then only observing during the selected periods (e.g. the first half hour of the morning, over a period of five days). It is not therefore a data collection method in itself but may be used with any of the methods listed above.

Figure 8.7 is an example of an actual piece of recording undertaken by teachers in their classes in a piece of research I undertook with colleagues into classroom organisation, where the various kinds of organisation were called 'learning zones' (Vincett et al., 2005).

There are some well tried and tested schedules for structured gathering of classroom activity. One of these is the classic but still widely used Flanders Interaction Analysis (see Flanders, 2004). It is about classroom talk and consists of a schedule of categories which a researcher will use to examine how language is being used in the classroom:

A **Teacher Talk**

  1. Clarify feeling constructively
  2. Praise or encourage
  3. Clarify, develop or make use of ideas suggested by students   } *Response*
  4. Ask questions
  5. Lecture
  6. Give directions
  7. Criticise   } *Initiation*

B **Student talk**

  8. Student talk in response to the teacher   –   *Response*
  9. Student talk initiated by the student   –   *Initiation*

C **Silence**

  10. Silence or confusion

EVALUATING LEARNING ZONES: PUPIL ENGAGEMENT
Collecting data

Engagement refers to the extent that pupils are 'on task' during any teaching period. It provides a useful measure of how well organised and industrious the class is. One reason for this choice in our research is that this measure has been successfully used in other research into room management and zoning procedures. It proves to be a robust and useful measure of classroom activity. There is research to show that engagement rates relate solidly to achievement.

If using this method to evaluate an intervention such as Learning Zones, a baseline measurement would be used prior to beginning to use these models, and then again once the models have been used for several weeks. If the intervention is successful, there should be an improvement in on-task behaviour.

Instructions for collecting data

Identify ten pupils for data collection – a mixture of boy/girl, different abilities.
For a period of twenty minutes complete the pupil engagement tally for the ten pupils.
Every minute look at each pupil quickly in turn and note whether they are on or off task. Put a tick if the pupil is on task and a cross if not.
For each pupil calculate the percentage of time on task (number of ticks divided by total number of tallies x 100). For example, if a pupil obtains 16 ticks out of a possible 20, then 16/20 x 100 means the pupil was on task for 80% of the time.

Pupil	1 min	2 min	3 min	4 min	5 min	6 min	7 min	8 min	9 min	10 min

Figure 8.7   Structured observation

The researcher checks every three seconds which of the categories is relevant and marks it on a list similar to the one in Figure 8.7.

Structured observation was extensively used in a major piece of classroom research known as the ORACLE project (Galton et al., 1980). It is worth looking at this if you intend to undertake structured research.

Unstructured observation

Consistent with the tenets of interpretivism (see p. 75) unstructured observation is undertaken when you are immersing yourself in a social situation, usually as some kind of participant, in order to understand what is going on there. Ethnographers, with whom this kind of observation is usually associated, often discuss social life as if it were a stage, or a set of stages, on which we act out roles. Unstructured observation will be geared to understanding how these roles play themselves out on the stage of life.

Often this kind of observation is called *participant observation* because it is associated with researchers becoming a participant in the situations they are researching. I have already discussed participant observation on p. 119, but as Burgess (1982) points out, the term 'participant observation' is a little confusing since it connotes much more than simply observation. It entails talking to people, watching, reading documents, keeping notes and anything else that enables you to understand a situation.

A distinction is sometimes drawn between different kinds of observation that all occur within the participant observation frame. Burgess (1984), for example, outlines three types: complete participant; participant as observer and observer as participant. These represent, if you like, different 'levels' of participation. With the first, complete participant, the assumption is that you are an integral part of the situation you are studying, as with the school gover-

Nature of unstructured/ participant observation: Not breaking down the situation; becoming part of it; seeing the situation as a whole.

Data gathering: Interviews, introspection, reflection, direct observation.

Instruments: Watching, keeping a diary, interviewing, introspection, examining documents.

nor diary I described on p. 167, or as with James Patrick's (1973) 'participation' in the Glasgow gang he describes. 'Membership' is probably a better word than 'participation' in these examples. With the last, observer as participant, there is no attempt at involvement in the situation. And this is all, of course, within the ethnography fieldwork tradition.

Personally, in practice I find it difficult to disentangle where one kind of participation begins and another ends in this kind of classification and I am not going to offer a taxonomy which implies that researchers should have to slot themselves into one notional type rather than another. Rather, for me there is simply a continuum of

Figure 8.8 A continuum of observation and participation

observation (see Figure 8.8), with structured at one end and unstructured at the other, and while each extreme end tends to be associated with particular approaches to research, there are no hard and fast rules about which to adopt. As I have been at pains to point out throughout this book, the central consideration in choosing approaches, methods and tools is their quality of fit for the purposes and questions in your research. It is these that should always be at the front of your mind.

So, the continuum of types of observation and types of participation or involvement given in Figure 8.8 shows a number of potential forms of combination. You *can* do structured observation as a participant, but this would be unusual. Likewise, you *can* do unstructured observation as a non-participant, though the latter does not quite fit the frameworks of research design offered by textbooks. Nevertheless, it is a combination commonly adopted, particularly by students, who perhaps are attracted by the apparent straightforwardness of the unstructured approach to observing, but who perhaps feel that the exigencies of life will interrupt a full ethnographic involvement. At its worst, though, this sort of unstructured observation is unstructured by *anything at all* – even by a view about how we can find out and how we can know – and it can end simply as a catalogue of quotations and observations, with little in the way of cement to give it integrity, interest or meaning. So, while unstructured observation may seem to be an easier way of observing than using structured observation, in fact it requires a great deal of preparatory work and devotion to become part of the situation you are observing and it needs sensitivity, commitment and thought to analyse the findings meaningfully.

Having issued this dire warning about the unconsidered use of unstructured observation, what can I suggest should be done? I can give Figure 8.9 as an example from a piece of research that I undertook for the children's charity Barnardo's (Thomas et al., 1998). As part of this research I undertook some observations in mainstream classrooms to try to understand how well some children with physical disabilities who had formerly attended special schools were becoming included in the mainstream. My observation was unstructured though I was not a participant in the situation. I think my answer to the question that I posed just now about 'What should be

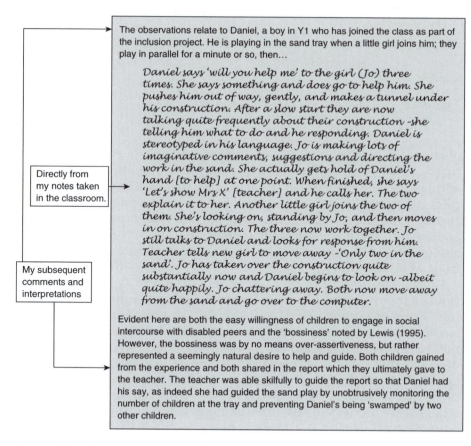

Figure 8.9 Unstructured observation

done if you can't be fully involved as an ethnographer?' is that my notes were bounded by the same considerations as the ethnographer's, even though my involvement in the activity of the class was minimal.

I hope it is clear that I have in my notes attempted 'thick description' (see p. 202), for example in my comments about the teacher's intervention. That intervention was skilfully and tactfully made to prevent the developing bond between Daniel and Jo unravelling with the intrusion of another child, who would have almost certainly have offered Jo more enticing conversation opportunities. Through my observation I was trying at the same time to interpret – using my understanding of situations like this to enable this interpretation. The subsequent comments and interpretations attempted to capitalise on and develop the notes taken in the classroom, tying in the latter with commentary I had garnered in my literature review.

Data-gathering tools – mainly for use with numbers

I said at the beginning of this book that *experience* is at the heart of empirical inquiry, with experience in this context meaning our perception of the world around us. Words and numbers are our messengers about the experience we draw on in empirical inquiry. As messengers, words and numbers do not themselves constitute direct experience. Rather, they stand in the place of experience: they *represent* experience.

I begin with this point while talking in this section about the use of numbers because there can be the tendency in social research to treat numbers as if they are in some way superior as envoys of truth – that they are in some way cleaner, more objective vehicles for the carriage of knowledge than are words. This is partly because they tend to be associated with certain approaches to research (see Chapter 5) that in the popular mind accompany the methods of the natural sciences.

But this notion of clean, simple efficiency in the transport of knowledge is misleading, for in social research numbers are only as reliable as the concepts that underlie them. I can try to explain what I am talking about here by reference to the notion of intelligence and its translation into a number in the form of an intelligence quotient (IQ). In the popular mind IQ represents a robust and stable measure of a straightforward concept: intelligence. As such, it has entered the public consciousness as an unproblematic representation of an uncomplicated mental faculty. But intelligence is now widely critiqued as a concept – it is lying in the gutter of social scientific thinking (see, for example, Gould, 1996; Devlin et al., 1997; Klein, 1997; Dickens and Flynn, 2001; White, 2006) – and if the undertaker hasn't actually been called yet, we can at least say that the last rites are about to be read any time now. However, you wouldn't guess this from looking at magazines and television programmes which are replete with IQ tests: test your own IQ, test the family's IQ, test the nation's IQ – even test the dog's IQ. This peculiar resilience is down to the allure of a simple figure which seems to carry the imprimatur of science.

The IQ story is just a brief health warning about the risks in using numbers in social research, which doesn't mean that *all* numbers are automatically suspect. Some numbers are perfectly straightforward, though of course there are always possibilities for counting things in different ways and for measurement error. Where you should be automatically wary and instinctively suspicious is in the attribution of numbers to complex ideas (as in the IQ example) and in the use of complex statistics. Again, they may represent satisfactory analyses of quantified phenomena, but we should always be aware that the more complex something is the more chance there is of something going awry or of the wool being pulled over our eyes. I shall look further at this in Chapter 9, where I shall also look at some of the features of the kinds of numbers we can use in social and educational research in preparation for a discussion of some basic ways in which these numbers can be used for analysis.

Measurements and tests

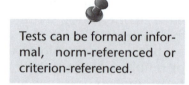

The word 'test' has a general meaning of 'check'. In using a test you are checking the extent of something, whether this be learning of some topic at school, or the level of cholesterol in the bloodstream.

Tests can be formal or informal, norm-referenced or criterion-referenced.

The results of a test will nearly always be in numerical form. In health-care, tests will nearly always be of the simple measurement form, whereas in education they take more varied forms, being formal or informal measures of some attribute, personal feature or attainment. They exist in simple, home-made measures, and also in complex and well standardised forms. Test construction and standardisation is a large and separate field of study and it is beyond the scope of this book to examine it in any detail, so I shall confine myself to some general comments about tests and how you may collect data from them.

In its simplest form, a home-made test assesses something that has been taught, or a level of pre-existing knowledge. The teacher may devise a spelling test or a tables test, and give marks out of 20, say. In the same way, for a small research project you may devise a test to assess the extent of learning.

Tests can be divided into those which are *norm-referenced* and those which are *criterion-referenced*. A norm-referenced test compares the person being tested to a sample of their peers. A criterion-referenced test simply assesses whether someone is able to meet some criterion, irrespective of how well other people perform on the test. The purposes of norm- and criterion-referenced tests differ: the norm-referenced test aims to compare individuals, one against others, while the criterion-referenced test merely says: 'Person A can do *x*'. Intelligence tests and most reading tests are examples of norm-referenced tests, since they seek to tell testers how well testees compare next to other people. A driving test is an example of a criterion-referenced test, since there is no comparison going on with the cohort of other people doing the test. It doesn't matter how many people can or can't do the three-point turn – if you can do it, then you get your box ticked: you have passed this part of the test. It is quite easy to devise a criterion-referenced test yourself.

When using norm-referenced tests, testers are more interested in differentiating among a sample – in comparing this child with others, or in comparing one group with another. In order to make accurate comparisons of this kind, a procedure known as standardisation is used in the construction of norm-referenced tests. This involves constructing the test under particular specified, repeatable conditions with large samples from a population (of, say, 11-year-olds) and, in turn, it is expected that the test will be administered and scored in practice under those same conditions. A good test is one that is reliable and valid, these words in test construction having rather more specific meanings than those they carry in research design generally. Broadly speaking, reliability refers to the test's ability to measure something consistently, while validity is a measure of how well it is assessing what it is supposed to measure. You can usually be confident that in most commercially produced tests reliability and validity will be satisfactory.

Many standardised tests – of attainment in reading, maths, non-verbal ability or a wide range of other faculties – are now available online, e.g. at www.gl-assessment.co.uk/.

Official statistics

Official statistics can form the basis of first-rate research yet are used surprisingly little in student projects. It's almost as if most student research still exists in the pre-Internet era. If you can therefore show that you have drawn relevantly from these statistics it is a bonus for you in the way that your project is viewed. There is a variety of websites from which you can easily download data of extraordinary detail and richness. This can nowadays be manipulated in your own spreadsheet remarkably simply (I'm using Excel in the examples here).

The DCSF's invaluable document *Education and Training Statistics for the United Kingdom* is available at www.dcsf.gov.uk/rsgateway/DB/VOL/v000761/index.shtml – go to 'Download formats' and download as a pdf.

To get hold of the data for your own manipulation, this is what you do, after checking for copyright. Once you have opened the pdf you can then drag your cursor over the table you are interested in, copy it (Ctrl C) and paste it (Ctrl V) into Excel for subsequent analysis. This is how you do it:

- Select the material you want (choose the cursor tool in Adobe if it does not at first appear).
- Copy it (Ctrl C).
- Open Excel.
- Make sure the top lefthand cell is selected in your Excel spreadsheet.
- Go to Edit, and click 'Paste special'.
- Click 'Unicode text' in the dialogue box that appears. Click OK.
- Put your cursor over the little clipboard sign that appears at the bottom of your pasted material. Click on the little arrow that appears to the right of it (labelled 'Paste options').

	A	B	C	D	E	F	G	H	I	J
1	Academic	years								
2			1980/81	1995/96	2000/011	2004/051	2005/061	2006/07		
3	Public	sector mainstream								
4	Nursery		1,364	1,488	3,228	3,425	3,349	3,326		
5	Primary		24,135	23,441	22,902	22,343	22,156	21,968		
6	Secondary		4,790	4,483	4,337	4,230	4,206	4,176		
7	of which									
8	Middle deemed secondary		491	400	316	260	250	248		
9	Modern		171	113	145	124	115	113		
10	Grammar		222	231	231	234	233	233		
11	Technical		3	1	3	2	2	2		
12	Comprehensive		3,696	3,509	3,443	3,427	3,424	3,398		
13		of which 6th Form colleges	118							
14	Other		207	209	199	183	182	182		
15	of which specialist schools			107	523	1,955	2,381	2,811		
16	Non-maintained mainstream		2,508	2,500	2,412	2,476	2,493	2,542		
17	of which Academies					17	27	46		
18	Special schools		1,830	1,580	1,498	1,436	1,416	1,391		
19	of which maintained			1,458	1,401	1,329	1,311	1,285		
20	of which non-maintained			104	97	107	105	106		
21	Pupil referral units			315	338	478	481	489		
22	ALL	SCHOOLS	34,627	33,755	34,715	34,300	34,101	33,982		

Here, 'years' is in the wrong place, and can be moved over to cell A1. So click on cell B1, press 'Delete'. Then, click on A1 and move to the formula bar and add the word you want (in this case 'years')

Figure 8.10   A spreadsheet of 'Number of schools, by type of school – time series' taken from official statistics (DCSF, 2007): tidying up

- Click on 'Use text import wizard'.
- Click 'Finish' (or answer each question in turn if you can make sense of them).

While Excel makes a good job of copying the table, certain cells will probably be out of place, and you will have to spend 15 minutes or so tidying up the table so that material is in the right place. For example, if a row of cells has been shifted one column to the right, drag your cursor over it so that it is selected. Then click on the heavy border around the selected material and drag it to the right position. You will end up with something like the spreadsheet in Figure 8.10. Something will inevitably still be wrong. For example, if you want to add or delete text (which may be in the wrong place), click on the cell you want to change, and go to the box at the top of the page to alter it, as in the figure.

Figure 8.10 is taken from the very first table of the DCSF's statistical bulletin, and I have just taken it as an example. I'll say some more about how this kind of data can be *analysed* in Chapter 9.

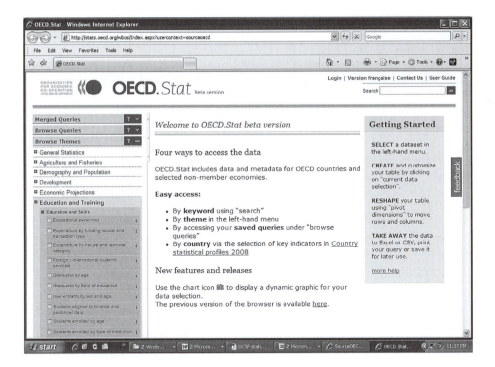

Figure 8.11   The OECD website – excellent for comparative research

However, for now, let us look at how you can transfer this to your Word document. Click over the top left cell (A1) and drag down until you reach the bottom-right one (H22). Copy (Ctrl C), move to Word, place the cursor where you want the table and paste (Ctrl V). You can then edit as you wish.

Another excellent statistics resource, particularly for those undertaking comparative research, may be found at http://stats. oecd.org/source/ or http://stats.oecd.org/wbos/Index.aspx?usercontext=sourceoecd which give a wide range of statistics gathered by the Organisation for Economic Co-operation and Development (OECD) (see Figure 8.11).

The Neighbourhood Statistics supplied by the Office for National Statistics gives a mass of information, for example about census data, which includes accommodation types, numbers of cars, country of birth, distances travelled to work – and much more – related to people and regions in the UK. It is especially useful if you wish to relate your data to general statistics for a region or nationally. It can be found at www.neighbourhood.statistics.gov.uk/ dissemination/.

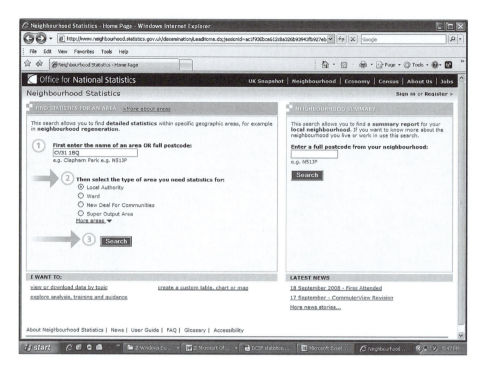

Figure 8.12 Office for National Statistics Neighbourhood Statistics

Figure 8.13 Neighbourhood statistics unpacked

Emma Smith's excellent website at www.secondarydataanalysis. com gives access to these and a broad range of other UK, US and international data websites. The US sources, for example, lead you to administrative records, archives and gateways including FedStats and public opinion research, census records, and longitudinal and cohort survey data.

Overview

I've looked at a wide range of data-gathering tools and methods, some that concern the collection of numbers, and some the collection of words. Some collect both. As Angharad's 'itinerary' on p. 96 in Chapter 5 indicates, these are tools that can be employed in a variety of ways with the design frames of Chapter 7. The techniques associated with these tools can be quite specialised but it is important not to get hypnotised by these complexities. At the end of the day, these are tools that help you to gather data associated with the design path that you have followed.

Further Reading

Interviews and accounts

Barbour, R. and Schostak, J. (2005) Interviewing and focus groups. In B. Somekh and C. Lewin (eds) *Research methods in the social sciences.* London: SAGE.

Diaries

Altricher, H and Holly, M. (2005) Research diaries. In: In B. Somekh and C. Lewin (eds) *Research methods in the social sciences.* London: SAGE.

Focus groups

Bloor, M., Frankland, J., Thomas, M., and Robson, K. (2001) *Focus Groups in Social Research.* London, SAGE.

Parker, A. and Tritter, J. (2006) Focus group method and methodology: current practice and recent debate. *International Journal of Research and Method in Education,* 29, 1, 23–37.

Questionnaires

Oppenheim, A.N. (2000) *Questionnaire design.* London: Continuum.

Observation

Structured observation
Croll, P. (1986) *Systematic classroom observation*. Lewes: Falmer Press.
A good, balanced overview.

Unstructured observation
An excellent outline of participant observation is given at www.infed.org/research/
    participant_observation.htm

Tests

http://www.gl-assessment.co.uk/
Includes access to tests and various online assessments.

Official statistics

Smith, E. (2008) *Using Secondary Data in Educational and Social Research*.
    Maidenhead: Open University Press.

How to Analyse the
Information you Gather

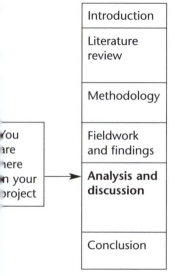

| Introduction |
| Literature review |
| Methodology |
| Fieldwork and findings |
| **Analysis and discussion** |
| Conclusion |

You are here in your project

Following the collection of your data, you need to analyse it. Your data may be in any of a variety of forms, and the methods for analysing the data will vary. This chapter considers:

- analysing words – the constant comparative method: coding, sorting and patterns;
- analysing numbers – understanding what numbers are saying and making your numbers meaningful to others: eyeballing, descriptive and inferential statistics, significance;
- understanding what your analysis tells you: discussing your findings in the context of previous research and developing theory.

You are now analysing the data that you have collected, in whatever form. There is a wide array of analytical methods for handling the data that you have gathered, and I can only look at a small sample of them here. I shall look at some of the most commonly used methods, but will also try to explain some of the principles of data analysis that underlie these and other methods.

As in every other section, I stress here the importance of the coherence of your story. Your analysis should fit the approach you have taken in your research. Or, if there are different elements to your research, each structured by a different approach, the analysis relating to each element should be appropriate.

Analysing words

When you have gathered data in words – and you don't intend in any way to convert those words into numbers – you are seeking to use those words in descriptive or illuminative analysis of the situation in which you are interested. Let's begin with illuminative analysis, adopting the assumptions of interpretivism.

Constant comparative method

The basic analytic method of the interpretative researcher is *constant comparison*. Sometimes called the 'constant comparative method', it stands behind every technique in this paradigm. The constant comparative method involves going through your data again and again (this is the *constant* bit), comparing each element – phrase, sentence or paragraph – with all of the other elements (this is the *comparative* bit). There's nothing more complicated than that, though there are different ways of going about the constant comparative method, many of which are outlined in texts such as Miles and Huberman (1994). Some of these are useful; others, in my opinion, make things appear to be more difficult than they really are.

From the constant comparison you emerge with *themes* that capture or summarise the contents of your data. The general process is shown in Figure 9.1.

These *themes* or *categories* are the essential building blocks of your analysis. Remember that the aim in using an interpretative approach is to emerge with the meanings that are being constructed by the participants (including you) in the situation.

There are various ways in which you can *map* your themes to show the *interconnections* between them. This mapping is often the weakest part of students' use of interpretative data. While the identification of themes is important, students sometimes go little beyond this and do not manage to explain how ideas are related to one another. The two methods I shall outline here for mapping of themes are *network analysis* (Bliss et al., 1983) and my own adaptation (Thomas, 1992) of *construct mapping* (Jones, 1985). I shall illustrate these methods by drawing on my own use of them.

Network analysis

In network analysis you aim to show how one idea is related to another using a network, which is a bit like a tree, with a trunk which is the basic idea and branches coming off the trunk representing constituent ideas. This is useful where there is a core theme which you consider comprises a range of sub-themes. Network analysis shows how themes are related to one another in a nested arrangement, with each branch holding a range of other ideas. In this sense it provides a hierarchical organisation of the ideas contained in your data.

One of my own uses of network analysis was in a piece of research where I was interested in the role of teaching assistants (TAs) in the classroom. How did TAs construct ideas about their role? I interviewed a

1. Read all of your data: interview transcripts, diaries, notes from unstructured observations, etc.
2. Make an electronic copy of all of your raw data. Mark it 'RAW'. You now have two copies: your raw data and your working data files. Keep them separate.
3. Read through your working files. As you are reading, underline or highlight parts that you think are important. As you proceed, you will get an impression of important ideas or subjects that are recurring. We can call these your *temporary constructs*. Make a list of these.
4. Read through the data again, using the list of temporary constructs from your first reading to check against. Draw up a grid with the temporary construct on the left, and page references to where the construct is evidenced on the right. Make notes and observations on the grid as you do this. You will get quite a long list – Table 9.1 shows an abbreviated example.
5. Eliminate any temporary constructs that do not seem to have been reinforced in the rest of the data. Don't delete that actual data itself, though – it may form an important counter-example against the general themes that are emerging. Highlight these counter examples in a different colour on your working data records, and keep a separate list of them.
6. From the second reading, come up with *second-order constructs* that seem to be making a good 'fit' with your data. These second order constructs should make a good job of summarising the important themes in your data.
7. Look through once more, refining these second-order constructs now as marker-posts for the organisation of your data. Once you are satisfied that these capture the essence of your data, label these as your *themes*.
8. Think about the themes. How do they seem to be connecting together? What matches with what? Are there any unanimous areas of agreement? Are there any contradictions or paradoxes?
9. Find ways of *mapping* your themes (see below under *network analysis* and *construct mapping*).
10. Select good quotations or sections from your work to illustrate the themes.

Figure 9.1   The constant comparative method

Table 9.1   Examples of notes and observations

Temporary construct	Page numbers and notes
Territory	Diary, p 15, 17, 19. Interviewees: Sara p 3, 4; Geoff pp 4, 6. Big issue for Geoff – got q. emotional
Threat	Diary, pp 1, 7, 9, 15. Interviewees: Sara p 7, 9; Geoff pp 5, 6

range of TAs, transcribed our interviews and then went through the procedure in Figure 9.1. This enabled me to boil down the general commentary on role to two basic themes – about pedagogy (i.e. teaching) and about affective (i.e. emotional, personal) concerns. These were the basic ways in which TAs seemed to be thinking about how their place, their value, their contribution, their sense of self-worth were constructed. I was able to break down these two basic themes into sub-themes, as in the summary diagram in Figure 9.2.

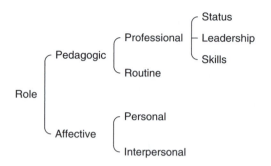

Figure 9.2   Summary network of themes and sub-themes

Having satisfied myself that this summative network of themes and sub-themes adequately summarised the data of the TA interviews, I went back to each of those interviews looking for examples of each of these themes and sub-themes in the interviewees' comments. For each interviewee, I was then able to come up with a network analysis of the interview. An example of one of these, together with my commentary, is given in Figure 9.3.

Construct mapping and theme mapping

While network analysis provides a hierarchical arrangement of ideas and themes, construct mapping puts those themes in sequential order from the interview and uses lines and arrows to make the connections between the ideas and themes. I have called it 'construct mapping' here out of respect for the person, Sue Jones, who developed the idea out of George Kelly's (1955/1991) Personal Construct Theory. Jones (1985) devised a method for drawing on Kelly's notion of bi-polar constructs governing the way that we all see the world. In fact I found this theoretical lens too complex and adapted the construct mapping for my own purposes to a method I shall call *theme mapping*.

Theme mapping begins, as does most qualitative analysis, with constant comparative method (see Figure 9.1). Once you have established your themes you go through your working data files and look for good quotations that illustrate those themes. Now, in the order that those quotations appeared in the interview, put them into boxes on the page. The page now becomes your 'map'. You may also find other quotations that in some way complement or contrast with these quotations. Put these in boxes on the 'map' too. Now, label the boxes with the names of the themes and draw dotted lines if ideas seem to be connected between themes, and solid lines with arrows where one theme (the theme towards which the arrow points) seems in some way to account for or explain the theme at the other end of the arrow.

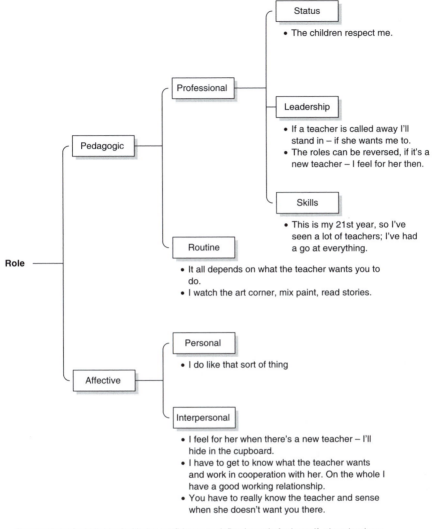

Status
- The children respect me.

Professional

Leadership
- If a teacher is called away I'll stand in – if she wants me to.
- The roles can be reversed, if it's a new teacher – I feel for her then.

Pedagogic

Skills
- This is my 21st year, so I've seen a lot of teachers; I've had a go at everything.

Routine
- It all depends on what the teacher wants you to do.
- I watch the art corner, mix paint, read stories.

Role

Personal
- I do like that sort of thing

Affective

Interpersonal
- I feel for her when there's a new teacher – I'll hide in the cupboard.
- I have to get to know what the teacher wants and work in cooperation with her. On the whole I have a good working relationship.
- You have to really know the teacher and sense when she doesn't want you there.

Commentary: An individual with the confidence to define her role for herself, given her long experience. A certain amount of conflict arises precisely because of this experience and the esteem in which she is held: professional constraints work to elevate her status, a process which she evidently has to try and minimise. Affective factors are important in helping to define the role, though she has to rely on 'sensing' that the teacher may not be at ease in her presence.

Figure 9.3   Network analysis

The example I give in Figure 9.4 is a theme map following the analysis of some interviews I conducted with support teachers for children with special educational needs. Rather than withdrawing children to work with on their own, these teachers had recently changed their way of work to be in the classroom, working alongside the class teacher. I was interested in their perceptions and feelings concerning their role in the classroom. Did they feel useful? Were there tensions, and if so, of what kind? How did the other teacher react to them? How did the children view them? And so on. From my interviews and from my own diary working as a support teacher I emerged with a number of themes relating to these questions. These were: status and self-esteem, territoriality, threat/suspicion, interpersonal factors, ideology–professional, communication, organisation, school policy and role clarity. You will see that seven of these nine themes are flagged in the interview theme map in Figure 9.4.

Aside from anything else, the theme map gives a kind of mini-representation of the interview, because the illustrative quotations are given in the order that they have appeared in the interview.

Tip: when drawing a diagram of this kind use the Text Box facility in Word. Go to the menu bar near the top of the page, right-click and a list of menus will appear. Click 'Drawing' and the drawing toolbar will appear at the bottom of the page. Run your cursor over the icons until you get to 'Text Box' and left click. Then use the cross-cursor to draw a box in which you will be able to write text. Also, by clicking on the *edge* of the box you will be able to drag it around to where you want.

Grounded theory

Many people say that they are using a grounded theory approach when what they mean is that they are using constant comparative method (see Figure 9.1). In fact, many of the assumptions behind grounded theory – for example, about grounded theory enabling prediction – seem inappropriate and outdated now, and I have explored this elsewhere (Thomas and James, 2006). Lincoln and Guba (1985: 339) make a similar criticism, suggesting that constant comparison is the kernel of grounded theory worth preserving. Indeed, the nuts and bolts of grounded theory procedures are unnecessarily complex and I advise you to avoid them. Stick to constant comparison.

What *is* nice about grounded theory is that it offers a neat encapsulation of the essence of interpretative inquiry – in that you let the ideas (the 'theory') emerge from your immersion in a situation rather than going in with fixed ideas (fixed 'theory') about what is happening. But the inventors of grounded theory (Glaser and Strauss, 1967) did not contrive this idea *de novo*: it has always been at the heart of interpretative inquiry. Some people speak about grounded theory as if it is synonymous with interpretative inquiry. It's not.

Thick description

I noted *thick description* in Chapters 5 and 6 when talking about interpretivism, case study and unstructured observation. I include thick description here, in a discussion of how to analyse, because it is, in a sense, both a form of data gathering *and* a form of analysis. When you are

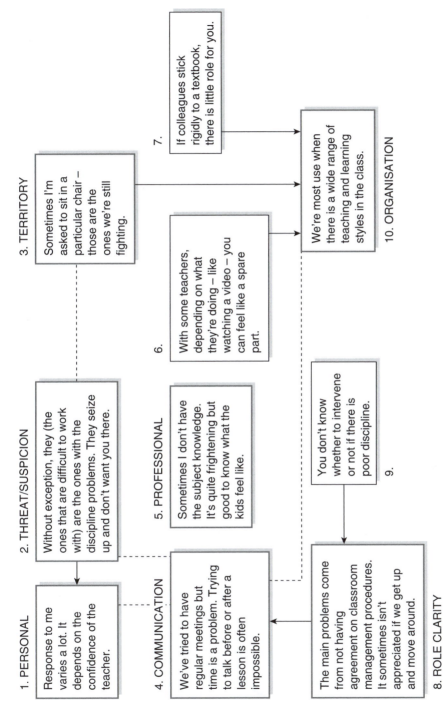

1. PERSONAL

Response to me varies a lot. It depends on the confidence of the teacher.

2. THREAT/SUSPICION

Without exception, they (the ones that are difficult to work with) are the ones with the discipline problems. They seize up and don't want you there.

3. TERRITORY

Sometimes I'm asked to sit in a particular chair – those are the ones we're still fighting.

4. COMMUNICATION

We've tried to have regular meetings but time is a problem. Trying to talk before or after a lesson is often impossible.

5. PROFESSIONAL

Sometimes I don't have the subject knowledge. It's quite frightening but good to know what the kids feel like.

6.

With some teachers, depending on what they're doing – like watching a video – you can feel like a spare part.

7.

If colleagues stick rigidly to a textbook, there is little role for you.

8. ROLE CLARITY

9.

You don't know whether to intervene or not if there is poor discipline.

The main problems come from not having agreement on classroom management procedures. It sometimes isn't appreciated if we get up and move around.

10. ORGANISATION

We're most use when there is a wide range of teaching and learning styles in the class.

Figure 9.4   Theme map of an interview with a support teacher making the description you are also doing the analysis. You are doing this by intelligently reflecting on the scene, imagining, putting yourself in another's shoes, 'seeing' what the other person is doing. You are doing this not just with the knowledge you have of people, but also of life and of the contexts that people inhabit. If you opt for doing this kind of thick description, it helps, then, to know something of the situation that you observe.

A good example of this making use of your ready-made knowledge – the knowledge of being human – is found in the great sociologist Erving Goffman's (1956) book *The Presentation of Self in Everyday Life*. In this, Goffman unpacks a storehouse of examples of how people behave in social life as if on a stage, always conveying some meaning with their behaviour. In doing this, he is employing thick description. He describes a man walking down the street who trips on a loose kerbstone. The man doing this, observes Goffman, will invariably turn round to look at the offending stone. He does this, Goffman says, not out of any profound interest in the kind of phenomena that trip people up, but in order to *convey* something to any onlooker who might have seen him trip and humiliate himself. He is saying, with the turn and the look, 'I am not the sort of fool who habitually trips over things – what kind of extraordinarily disguised danger could have led me to stumble?' In other words, the turn and the look have a meaning. It is these meanings that you have to look for in thick description.

I attempted thick description in my diary of my own time as a governor. In the passage below, you can see how I was using my knowledge not just of social situations, but also of social behaviour and of professional contexts.

Noticing of the development of a club, with 'solidarity'.	Lastly we talk about the member of staff whom the Head has been having trouble with. He says that she is now taking it to the Union. I report that the teacher governor had approached me in the car park; feel almost that I am betraying confidences, but I'm sure that it's not inappropriate to be saying this here. However, there is the warm, cosy feeling of the men's club again here in this sub-group: odd little comments reinforce the view that it's a difficult world – us against them and the feeling that if you support me I'll support you and we'll all have an easier life. I don't often think in genderist terms but there is a male–female difference here, I'm sure. The view that women are bickerers, complainers, petty is never explicitly articulated, but unless I'm being
The club is all-male.	unusually over-sensitive today I think I sense the feeling that as men we ought to have solidarity in maintaining a level headedness; in maintaining the momentum of the status quo; in preventing anyone from rocking the boat – and certainly not rocking it ourselves. But perhaps this is all delving a bit too deeply and imagining plots; if the reports of my children are anything to go by the

> | Comment on Head's weakness. | teacher in question is 'absolutely horrible' and ought to find another career rather than simply having her duties taken away. The ambivalence of management in this case, manifested by bringing the issue to governors, is probably just weakness: cock up rather than conspiracy. |

Sadly, my own thick description contains none of the creativity of Goffman's. However, what I hope that I have been able to show here is the willingness to try to understand what is going on in a social situation; to try to use my knowledge of it, and *not* to attempt to be some kind of neutral bystander.

Discourse and content analysis

Discourse analysis is the study of language in social use and, confusingly, is spoken about in different ways in different branches of the social sciences. Psychologists think of discourse as the language that goes on between people, tending to focus on small units of language such as the choice of individual words and intonations ('micro analysis'). Sociologists, by contrast, tend to think of discourses as forms of language use that define social relations, and particularly power relations between and among people ('macro analysis'). You'll understand from these very different starting points that there is no one method to discourse analysis. The term *content analysis* is sometimes used when the analysis refers to written text rather than the spoken word.

Fairclough (1995) describes what he calls a 'critical discourse analysis' which is useful for us in the applied social sciences because it combines both psychological and sociological traditions. His outline of it is shown in Figure 9.5.

Fairclough puts it this way:

> ... a piece of discourse is embedded within sociocultural practice at a number of levels; in the immediate situation, in the wider institution or organization, and at a societal level; for example, one can read an inter-action between marital partners in terms of their particular relationship, relationships between partners within the family as an institution, or gender relationships in the larger society. The method of discourse analysis includes linguistic *description* of the language text, *interpretation* of the relationship between the (productive and interpretative) discursive processes and the text, and *explanation* of the relationship between the discursive processes and the social processes. (Fairclough, 1995: 97)

For simplicity's sake, take it that the general method in 'gutting' an interview or some other sample of language use is broadly the same as in the constant comparative method (see Figure 9.1). The difference is in the focus of the discourse analyst. Rather than being at the first level on

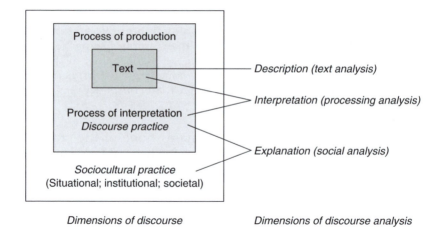

Dimensions of discourse   *Dimensions of discourse analysis*

Figure 9.5   Fairclough's 'critical discourse analysis'

ideas, it is on the use of particular words, phrases, idioms, similes, metaphors, kinds of rhetoric, and so on. How are these used to construct notions such as 'education', 'health', 'order', etc.? In each case the discourse analyst will look to see how notions are constructed by the choice of words and language forms used in a discourse, whether that be an interview transcript or a document. So, the difference of emphasis that the discourse or content analyst will put on the process outlined in Figure 9.1 is on the particular words and phrases used. Discourse analysis thus stresses the *coding* aspect of the analysis of an interview or a text, paying more attention to the choice and use of words and phrases. Given that the actual words and how they are used play more of a part than they do in an ethnographic use of constant comparison, it is more important that you are aware of your protocols for recording. A good example is given by Fairclough of a transcript of a conversation between a doctor and patient:

1. Patient: but she really has been very unfair to me . got(⌈no
   Doctor: ⌊hm
   Patient: respect for me at ⌈all and I think . that's one of the
   Doctor: ⌊hm
5. Patient: reasons why I drank so ⌈much   you ⌈know   ⌈ —
   Doctor: ⌊hm   ⌊hm   ⌊hm
   Patient: and ⌈em
   Doctor: ⌊hm   are you you back are you back on it have you
   started drinking ⌈again
10. Patient: ⌊no

                                                    (Fairclough, 1995: 98)

You'll notice a number of features of this transcript:

- The lines are numbered (every five lines) for ease of reference when referring back to the text in a subsequent analytic discussion

- There are devices used to indicate a gap or pause or discontinuity in the conversation. In this case a single dot ('.') is used. For longer pauses a dash is used.
- Brackets [are used to indicate 'overlaps' between one person and another in the conversation.

This close attention to (and recording of) the fabric of the conversation is because of the special attention that is given to the actual words being used and how they are used. It is important to be able to refer, for example, to interruptions and what they might mean. In this particular example Fairclough is able to show how the doctor is struggling with two discourses that he sees governing his professional work: the counselling discourse, which has to be non-directive ('hmmmm', 'go on', etc.), and the medical discourse in which he is expected to take the lead. This forms an interesting 'lever' on the professional role of the GP for anyone making an analysis of it.

Computers and verbal data analysis

There are a number of data analysis programmes available (sometimes called *computer-assisted qualitative data analysis software*, or CAQDAS). Whether or not you use these depends on the amount of data that you have to process. Nothing, of course, substitutes for your intelligent reading of your data, and this to my mind is the main danger of software in qualitative data analysis: it leads you to the false belief that something else is going to do the hard work for you. My one trial of CAQDAS left me disappointed and I have never used it again. It left me believing that there's no substitute for a good set of highlighters from W.H. Smith, a pen and paper, and a brain. You can also use Word for a large number of operations, such as word count (Alt T W), or the readability statistics that are provided as part of the spelling and grammar facility (press the F7 button and go to the bottom of the dialogue box, press Options, then tick the box offering readability statistics). You can also use the Find facility (Ctrl F) to find strings of text or important words that you have identified.

Although I have not been very positive about CAQDAS, it may work for you, particularly if you have a very large amount of data to analyse. Well known packages are *NVivo* and *Atlas.ti*, and your choice should depend largely on the one favoured by your institution – you should then (a) be able to draw on the institutional licence, and (b) be able to find someone who can give you support in the software's use. (You'll notice that both *NVivo* and *Atlas.ti* have silly idiosyncrasies added to their brand titles to try to make them look more technical. This is one of my main bugbears about research method and design – that people try to make it look more technical and complex than it really is. It happens both here and in statistical analysis and you should be doubly sceptical about any brand name or statistical test name that is (a) unpronounceable, or (b) makes no sense.)

Sociograms

A *sociogram* is a useful way of *mapping relationships* among children (or, less usually, adults). It involves asking them who they would like to sit next to, who they would like to work with – or the opposite: who they would *not* like to sit next to, and so on. The posh name for this is *sociometry*.

For the standard sociogram you will give each child a piece of paper on which they write their own name and the two names of their choices. You then map these to the sociogram, eventually producing a chart like that in Figure 9.6. For each choice you draw an arrow indicating the direction of choice. So, for example, Stacy on the far left chose Hannah and Lara. If a choice is returned, or *reciprocated*, the arrow becomes double ended.

Features that may emerge from the sociogram are:

- isolates: those with no choices from other individuals;
- reciprocated choices: where individuals choose each other;
- one-way choices: where someone chooses another but this choice is not reciprocated;
- cliques: tight-knit groups of three or more whose choices are all made within the group, e.g. Kylie, Alison and Ellie;
- clusters: more general groupings, for example the fairly significant one around Robbie, Simon and Ben;
- stars: individuals who have a large number of choices, for example Lara and Ben;
- power-brokers: individuals who have choices from the stars but not necessarily many others.

The sociogram given in Figure 9.6 is taken from research I undertook for Barnardo's on the inclusion of children with physical difficulties in mainstream schools. The children in one primary school class were asked to say in confidence who they would like to sit next to or play with. The included student is Luke. In each of the classes I studied it was interesting that in general an unremarkable pattern of relationships emerged for the included students. Even where the students had severe disabilities they emerged as well-integrated socially into their classes. For several of the 'included' children reciprocated choices are made. Interestingly, Luke is the only child crossing the gender barrier.

There is a basic freeware programme for drawing sociograms available at www.phenotyping.com/sociogram/. This lets you enter your names and then draw lines between them. Although you cannot draw the arrows to show direction of relationship these could be added afterwards by hand. Although a bit clunky (and you may find a better one by Googling), what the programme does offer is the chance to move people about so that you can show clusters more easily without having lots of crossing lines. You could then, once you have the clusters clear in your mind, transfer to free-hand drawing or drawing in Word (using text boxes).

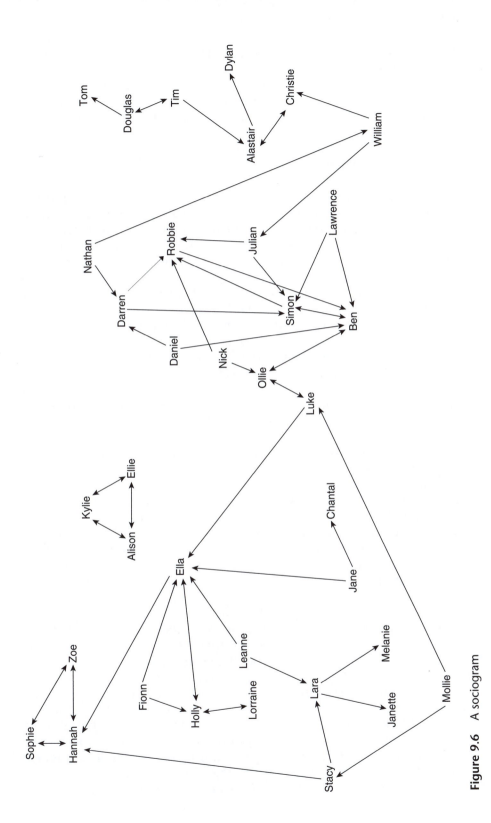

Figure 9.6 A sociogram

Sociometry involves some significant ethical issues. You should think hard about how you phrase questions and how you present the material to those participating in your project. You must assure absolute confidentiality and anonymity and take great care not to allow participants to see others' papers. Pseudonyms must of course be used in any write-up.

Analysing numbers

I'm fully aware that some people who study in the social sciences don't like numbers. After all, you came into the area – teaching, psychology, social work, nursing, medicine, dentistry, probation, or whatever – because you want to work with people. You find people interesting, and numbers somehow don't fit into the people scenario. In fact all the best clichés about people put people and numbers at the opposite ends of a continuum. If, like me, you are old enough to remember *The Prisoner* you will remember Patrick McGoohan's line, 'I am not a number: I am a person!' (For those too young to remember, see www.youtube.com/watch?v=29JewlGsYxs&feature=related.)

If you side with Patrick McGoohan on this issue, bear a few things in mind. First, statistics are not as hard as you thought. Second, they actually can be quite useful. Third, if you really can't get a grip of them it's not the end of the world, because it is research you are interested in, not statistics per se, and research is about finding out. There are many ways of finding out, and the more complex statistical ways get too good a press in the finding out stakes: they're not the only way or even the main way; they are just analytical tools. Fourth, if you really can't understand statistics (and you *will* understand most of the basic methods) don't blame yourself. Blame the statisticians for not explaining them properly.

It's rather like the phenomenon of going into a builder's merchant and the men (it's always men) behind the counter pretend slightly impatient bewilderment that you don't have any idea that what you need is called a bayonet grit-edged flange. It's the same with most statisticians: they seem almost to delight in the complexity of the names of statistical tests, which are named after letters of the Greek alphabet, like 'chi' (Why? Don't ask me) or the names of Russian statisticians like Kolmogorov-Smirnov. If the chi-square test were to have its name changed to the Cuddly Test and the Kolmogorov-Smirnov test were to have its name changed to the Fluffy Test, I'm convinced that fewer people would be put off statistics in the social sciences. And statisticians seem to feel that it is a crime only one notch down from first degree homicide to simplify their explanations: you are seldom likely to hear a statistician saying 'I'm oversimplifying, but think of it this way …' They mix a fascination with the mathematical and logical beauty of the statistic and the expectations that surround its construction with a kind of self-conscious awareness that if it is used wrongly it will be meaningless. Such self-conscious awareness is, in one way, commendable but it means that whenever they explain something the explanation has so thoroughly to explain every detail of construction and use that it becomes meaningless to anyone without a degree in statistics. What they don't accept in this honest explanation is that these statistics are only crude tools anyway: being exact about the details won't alter this.

Anyway, I digress, partly to try to put you at your ease, but this is perhaps better done by suggesting that you get a glass of wine and sit down in your best armchair and let the words flow over you in this bit of the book. If some of them float slowly enough to stick, then so much the better. You may even be tempted to use numbers.

Even if you are stats phobic, do try to have a look here because even if you don't feel confident enough to use them yourself a basic understanding will help you to interpret published research more intelligently.

Let's start with the numbers that are used in statistics. You thought you knew, roughly speaking, what numbers are, didn't you? 1 is 1 thing, 2 is one more thing than 1 thing, and 3 is … er, one more than two things. I don't want to disillusion you about this: most of the time you're fine working on this assumption. But, you know the story about physics students when they reach university having to forget all they knew about physics and starting again? It's a bit like that in the social sciences when it comes to numbers. But the good news is that the alternative is really easy – and you understand it already (honestly). It's just a question of putting what you already know into the language used by social scientists. Just think of it this way:

- There are categories of things, e.g. the categories of gender (female and male), kinds of disability, types of schools, etc. For ease of working things out in research, these categories may be given numbers (e.g. female, 1; male, 2); these numbers, because they are really just shorthand for names, are called *nominal* or *categorical*.
- Things can be put in order, e.g. top, middle, bottom; 1st, 2nd, 3rd, etc. These orderings can be given numbers: top (1), middle (2), bottom (3); 1st (1), 2nd (2), 3rd (3), 4th (4), etc. Because they are in order, these are called *ordinal* data. Although there is an order indicated here, there is no value implied beyond this. Certainly, one value is larger or faster or better than the next. If your respondent is ranking their fondness for school on a 5-point scale (1 hate; 2 dislike; 3 neutral; 4 like; 5 adore) you know only that 5 is better than 4, or 2 is better than 1; but you do not know by how much.
- There are the 'everyday' numbers that you and I usually think of when we talk about numbers – here we are talking about *interval* data, because the intervals between the numbers are always the same (unlike nominal and ordinal data). So the number of children in a class or the amount earned in pocket money in a week are interval data.

You can probably see why it is not good to mix these kinds of numbers. For example, you can't multiply nominal data. And the distance between ordered numbers is not always the same, so these can't be treated the same as other numbers. It's just a question of putting what you already know into the slots used by statisticians.

A good website which explains all of this in more detail is www.stats.gla. ac.uk/steps/glossary/presenting_data.html.

Now that we have got types of numbers clear (have we? – don't worry if you haven't; you'll still be able to manage) in statistically analysing the data you have gathered there are three principal branches of statistics that will help you deal with most of the methods that I have discussed in this book:

- one branch is about *statistics that describe* – this is very the easy one;
- the next is about *statistics that help you understand a relationship* – this is also easy;
- the last is about *statistics that enable you to deduce (or infer)* something about a large group from a small one – this is slightly harder (but still understandable).

Eyeballing

The first rule of analysing by numbers is *eyeballing*.

 Eyeballing is having a look at a range of numbers to see what the look tells you. Though it doesn't appear in the statistics textbooks, it is perhaps the most valuable statistical technique, since it forces you to think intelligently about what the numbers are saying, and it discourages you from making silly statements about a set of numbers based on an erroneously used statistic. Does a series of numbers seem to be going up or down or staying the same? Does it seem to be fluctuating wildly or is it quite stable? Are there any 'outliers' (data points that don't agree with the others) – are they interesting (in a good or bad way)? Does one set of numbers seem to vary with another set? Your most valuable tool is your eye – not the Kolmogorov-Smirnov. Use it.

> Numbers can help you to describe, to understand a relationship or to understand what may be causing what. But much depends on how the numbers are collected and analysed.

Using Excel to do your data analysis

Beyond eyeballing, you will want to do some actual calculations, and I have tried to limit all of the workings involved in the statistics that follow to Microsoft Excel, since this spreadsheet is bundled with nearly all home computers and you should have easy access to it. Where more sophisticated statistics-handling software is needed I say so in my discussion.

In the analysis of numbers that follows I am assuming a very basic working knowledge of Excel. Having said that, here are a few basic facts that I find students sometimes do not know about Excel:

1. Data entry: data are put in individual *cells*: 27 and 15 in my example here.
2. The cells have *references* (e.g. A2, D22).
3. Formulae (i.e. 'sums') are also put in cells, and the formula always must begin with an equals sign. The formula relates to the data references of the cells.
4. When you have finished the data entry and the formula, click on the *tick*. When I clicked on the tick in this example, the answer (42) appeared in the cell.

If you are a complete novice with spreadsheets, hopefully this will get you started. Play around with Excel: it's quite rewarding.

You will also find it useful to install the Excel Data Analysis ToolPak, which is not installed with the standard Excel setup. (This is not absolutely necessary for all of the examples below, but it's a helpful tool, and worth looking at.) To find the ToolPak, look in the Tools menu. If you do not have a *Data Analysis* item (usually at the bottom of the list), you will need to install the Data Analysis tools. Here are the instructions from Excel on how to do this:

On the *Tools* menu, click *Add-Ins*.

In the *Add-Ins available* list, select the *Analysis ToolPak* box, and then click OK.

Statistics that describe

Descriptive statistics are about the simplification, organisation, summary and graphical plotting of numerical data. They are easy. I know I've already said that, but they are. They are about questions such as 'How many?'; 'How often?' and will be presented in figures such as pie graphs and bar charts. There are also simple statistics such as percentages and averages (technically called 'derived statistics', because they are derived from the descriptive ones). Many dissertations are marked down because the authors make surprisingly little attempt to use these to show the figures in a way which will be immediately meaningful to the reader. If you have a list of numbers, do try to make them meaningful to the reader by using statistics. I'll give some examples and show how you can

Table 9.2   Numbers of schools in England and Wales

	1990/91	1995/96	2000/01	2004/05	2005/06	2006/07
Nursery	1,364	1,486	3,228	3,425	3,349	3,326
Primary	24,135	23,441	22,902	22,343	22,156	21,968
Secondary	4,790	4,463	4,337	4,230	4,206	4,176

Source: DCSF (2007).

translate them to a more meaningful form with Excel. *Tip*: Don't bury your tables and/or the statistical analysis of them in an appendix. Too many students do this: I have no idea why.

Let's take some numbers – a *frequency distribution* – from the DCSF statistics website (DCSF, 2007). Table 9.2 shows numbers of schools in England and Wales going back over a series of years.

You should be able to copy these numbers directly into your spreadsheet from the pdf (see p. 191 on how to do this). Once they are there and you have edited the figures for the ones you want (let's say as in the table above) paste these figures to a new sheet (see Figure 9.7). Now, here's how to turn the table into a bar graph …

1. Select the *area* of the figures (including header rows and columns) by dragging your mouse over it.
2. Click on the *chart tool* icon.
3. When the dialogue box appears, just click 'Finish' for the chart to be pasted into your worksheet, or, if you want a custom-made chart, where you have been offered the option of presenting the data as, for example, a pie chart, then press 'Next' instead of 'Finish'.
4. When the chart has appeared click on it, press Ctrl C (copy) and then paste it (Ctrl V) into your Word document.

Once you have done this, it is up to you to interpret the chart. Why have numbers of secondary and primary schools decreased, for example, while numbers of nursery schools have increased? It is up to you to offer an explanation to the reader.

Let's take another example from the DCSF statistics website (DCSF, 2007). Table 9.3 is about annual expenditure per student in a range of OECD countries.

Now, using these statistics, you can easily sort them for a very useful analysis. The one I am going to describe can even be done in Word, without recourse to Excel. I notice, from *eyeballing* that the UK's expenditure on 'early childhood education' appears high. So I can sort this table to put the countries in order by early childhood spending. Here's how in Word (you don't even need to use Excel):

1. Put your cursor anywhere in the table
2. Click 'Table' on the toolbar at the top of the page

Chart tool icon

Area

Figure 9.7   Turning a table into a bar chart

3. Click 'Sort'
4. Click the little arrow to the right of the 'Sort by' box, ~~and click 'Early~~ childhood ...'
5. On the right, click 'Descending'

... and the table you will get is shown in Table 9.4.

I find this table interesting: the UK is top in early childhood spending! Hooray! It is interesting particularly when you also look at the amount spent on each secondary pupil, which appears – on eyeballing – almost as if it might tend to go down as the expenditure on early childhood goes up. If you make a finding of this kind it is worth exploring further. You might, for example, want to do a bar chart (using the method described in Figure 9.7) of these figures to pursue any such relationship. It's easier to see such a relationship in a graph rather than a table. To take it even further you might look to see whether they statistically relate with one another (co-relate, or correlate). I describe how to do this in the next subsection.

You may want to show a *measure of central tendency* – an *average* to you and me. Averages are split into three kinds: the *mean*, the *median* and the *mode*. The different kinds of average are useful for different

Table 9.3   Annual expenditure on education per student, 2004

	Early childhood education	Primary education	Secondary education
Australia	–	5,776	8,160
Belgium	4,915	6,636	7,751
Denmark	5,323	8,081	8,849
Finland	4,282	5,581	7,441
France	4,938	5,082	8,737
Germany	5,489	4,948	7,576
Greece	–	4,595	5,213
Ireland	4,948	5,422	7,110
Italy	5,971	7,390	7,843
Japan	3,945	6,551	7,615
Luxembourg	–	13,458	17,876
Mexico	1,794	1,694	1,922
Netherlands	5,807	6,222	7,541
New Zealand	5,112	5,190	6,299
Norway	4,327	8,533	11,109
Poland	4,045	3,130	2,889
Portugal	4,461	4,681	6,168
Spain	4,617	4,965	6,701
Sweden	4,417	7,469	8,039
Switzerland	3,581	8,570	12,176
Turkey	–	1,120	1,808
UK	7,924	5,941	7,090
USA	7,896	8,805	9,938
OECD average	4,741	5,832	7,276

Source: DCSF (2007).

circumstances. The mean is the 'average' that most of us are familiar with: it's the total amount of the characteristic you are studying (e.g. children's scores on a test) divided by the total number of observations (e.g. the number of children). But sometimes a mean isn't the best way of showing the 'centre'. By eyeballing the figures you may see that the typical value is such-and-such but that this would be misleading if a mean were used. Let's take the example of ten children's scores on a test and assume that they have scored as follows:

0, 9 ,9, 9, 9, 9, 9, 9, 9, 9

Here, the *typical* value is clearly 9, though one person – who may have been asleep during the test – is going to distort the figures and bring the mean down to 8.1. So, the mean is a bit misleading as a *typical* value. Here, the *median* will be useful because it is the 'middle' figure. If the scores are arranged in order (lowest on the left, highest on the right), the median is the score which falls bang in the middle. In this case, the median is therefore 9.

Table 9.4   Information sorted by expenditure on early childhood education

	Early childhood education	Primary education	Secondary education
UK	7,924	5,941	7,090
USA	7,896	8,805	9,938
Italy	5,971	7,390	7,843
Netherlands	5,807	6,222	7,541
Germany	5,489	4,948	7,576
Denmark	5,323	8,081	8,849
New Zealand	5,112	5,190	6,299
Ireland	4,948	5,422	7,110
France	4,938	5,082	8,737
Belgium	4,915	6,636	7,751
OECD average	4,741	5,832	7,276
Spain	4,617	4,965	6,701
Portugal	4,461	4,681	6,168
Sweden	4,417	7,469	8,039
Norway	4,327	8,533	11,109
Finland	4,282	5,581	7,441
Poland	4,045	3,130	2,889
Japan	3,945	6,551	7,615
Switzerland	3,581	8,570	12,176
Mexico	1,794	1,694	1,922
Turkey	–	1,120	1,808
Luxembourg	–	13,458	17,876
Greece	–	4,595	5,213
Australia	–	5,776	8,160

The other measure of the average is the mode. This is the most frequently occurring value. So, in a list that goes: 1, 2, 3, 3, 7, 9, the mode is 3.

It is easy to find the measure of central tendency using Excel. Suppose, for example, you have a range of test scores which is: 1, 2, 3, 3, 3, 5, 6, 7, 8. Enter these numbers into separate cells on a worksheet …

In a nearby cell type
=mode(a3:a11)

You'll notice the formula appears in the formula bar as you type. Then click on the tick box, and the answer, namely 3, will appear in the place of the formula.

If you want the mean, type
=average(a3:a11)

If you want the median, type
=median(a3:a11)

You might be interested in showing how much *variation* there is in a range of numbers. For instance, our test wouldn't be much good if it produced a range of scores which looked like this: 5, 5, 5, 5, 5, 5, 5, 5, 5, 5 in ten children. (It would probably mean that five of the questions were absurdly easy, and five absurdly hard.) Here the variation between the values is zero. To measure how much variation exists, a statistic called *standard deviation* (SD) is used. Put simply, standard deviation is the average amount by which each score differs from the mean.

To calculate standard deviation in Excel, using our data from the previous example, type = **stdev(a3:a11)** and follow the same procedure. The answer in this case is 2.39.

Statistics that help you understand a relationship between two variables

You may want to look at *two* features of a situation and see whether the two are interrelated: you may be looking at children's scores on test A and test B in order to see if there is any relationship between the two sets of scores. For example, when I was an educational psychologist visiting a young offenders institution I was required to test the young men's reading. It struck me that their

> Co-variance: How things vary together – how they *co*-vary. So, in a silly example, we can show that shoe size and reading age co-vary. One goes up with the other. The example shows the caution that needs to be exercised with co-variance: just because things co-vary doesn't mean that one causes the other. The co-variance in this case is of course due to a third variable: maturity, or age. As age goes up so does reading age (in general), and so does shoe size.

reading was generally very poor, but their self-esteem was also poor, along with their verbal reasoning and other aspects of their makeup. I could have looked (I didn't actually do it, so these are imaginings) at the relationship between reading and self-esteem (the latter as measured by the Rosenberg Self-Esteem Scale, as described on p. 178). To look at the relationship and present the findings in a readily digestible form I could have used a *scatter graph*, where reading age (in months) is presented along one axis and self-esteem along the other axis.

I show my imaginary data and its translation to a scatter graph in Figure 9.8. The self-esteem scores are in column A and the reading ages (in months) in column B.

To get this scatter graph, do the following

1. Enter your data – in my example in columns A and B.
2. *Select* the data by dragging your mouse over it, from top left to bottom right.
3. Click on the *Chart Tool*.
4. At the first dialogue box, scroll down to XY (Scatter).
5. Keep clicking 'Next' until you reach finish. At each point, you will have the opportunity to customise your graph.

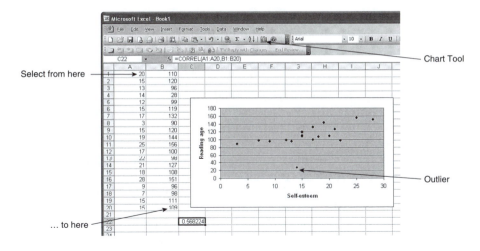

Figure 9.8 The relationship of reading and self-esteem: correlation and a scatter graph

You will see from the scatter graph that the results on self-esteem and reading tend to 'go with' one another. In other words, if self-esteem is lower for one young man, reading also tends to be lower (and vice versa). The important words here are 'tends to'. It isn't a hard and fast relationship, as you can see especially from one *outlier*, who has very low reading but reasonable self-esteem. The way we describe the extent of the connection between one variable and another is with the *correlation coefficient*. Correlation tells us the *strength* of the relationship between one variable and another.

When you ask Excel to work out the correlation figure for you, the result will be a number between −1 and +1. The nearer +1 the result is (e.g. 0.8), the closer is the relationship between the two sets of scores. If the score is 0, there is no relationship; if the score is near −1 (e.g. −0.7), the relationship is inverse, i.e. if the score on one variable is high, the score on the other will probably be low.

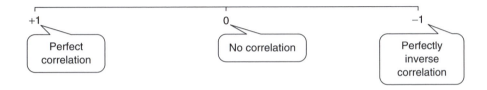

To get the correlation coefficient for the scores in the example, type in a spare cell:

          =correl(a1:a20,b1:b20)

Once you have worked out a correlation, it is possible to do two things: first you can work out the level of significance of the correlation (significance is explained in the next subsection); second, you can predict one score from another using a technique called linear regression (see the Further Reading for this chapter).

Of course, the fact that there is a relationship says nothing about the cause of the relationship or – if there *is* a causal relationship – the direction of the causation. I have found a reasonably high correlation in the example of my imaginary young offender institution data, but this does not tell me that poor reading *causes* poor self-esteem, or that poor self-esteem *causes* poor reading (though either is a possibility). More likely is the fact that we live in a world of closely interrelated social phenomena and that *all* things of this kind 'go together'.

I found it to be a depressingly consistent phenomenon with these young men that on almost any measure of social adaptation or attainment their scores were low. Why? The 'cause' is probably closer to factors to do with culture and poverty rather than any of the multitude of psychological phenomena measurable by instruments of the kind I have been outlining here. It has been realised since the 1920s and Gordon's (1923) studies of canal boat children in the UK or Wheeler's (1970) similar studies of, and findings about, 'mountain children' in the US that it was (and is) the cultural milieu rather than any psychological characteristic that determines a child's success at school. It has, in other words, been known for yonks (a technical term) that this is the case. Sadly, it is often the ideas and research methods of social science that propagate the belief that it is ability (and disability) of some kind – not poverty, difference or life experience – that is the principal force at play in determining such success or failure. The lesson? Measurement is useful in many kinds of social research, but when we look for relationships between variables we have to be very wary about imputing reasons for any relationships we discover.

Statistics that help you to deduce (or infer)

These statistics, also known as *inferential statistics*, form a large branch of analytical statistics in the social sciences. They are used particularly where we are trying to interpret the results of an experiment (see p. 124). In fact, what the tests do is to enable you to say whether the results you have obtained are extendable beyond the data you have gathered in your sample: is the difference you have noted between the experimental group and the control group one on which you can rely for this purpose of extension, or is it one that may have occurred by chance in your study?

Most of these statistics tell you something actually quite basic: whether the difference that you find between this set of numbers and that set of numbers is just down to chance or – if you have designed the study well – due to some feature of the situation in which you are interested. You will produce a figure after having completed your statistical test which will tell you the level of chance stated as a one-in-something (say, one in 20, or one in 100). This is where there is often confusion, with many people believing that once the issue of chance has been dealt with in the interpretation of a study's findings, everything else is OK. It's not: the study must have been designed properly, and this involves thinking about a whole range of design considerations from sampling to wording to control, which I mentioned in Chapter 6. When, and only when, we are sure that these design dimensions have been addressed appropriately can we go ahead and get fussed about whether the findings could have occurred by chance. I mention this only because some beginning (and some experienced) researchers treat the statistical test, well chosen and calculated, as if it is the most important guarantor of a study's worth. It most definitely is not, partly because of *the* GIGO *principle* – Garbage In, Garbage Out.

The GIGO principle is an important one to remember in any use of statistics, and particularly in inferential statistics which are used in more complex studies where there is more chance of design error. But assuming that everything has been set up properly (a big assumption), the statistic *is* a necessary part of a study which examines relationships, whether or not these involve assertions about cause. I shall run through one or two examples of how these tests are used in a moment, but before that will have to look briefly at the importance of *statistical significance*.

What does significance mean in a statistical context? Let's take a simple example: suppose you gave a maths test to 15 boys and 15 girls and you have the children's results in front of you, with a difference between them. The statistical test will then tell you how likely it is that you would find the same (or greater or lesser) difference by chance. The result is expressed in a 'probability figure', such as 'p is less than 0.05'. This means:

probability is less than 5 in 100 that this result would have been found by chance

... which in the language of statisticians becomes:

... or another way of putting it is that there is less than a 5 per cent (i.e. 1 in 20) chance that this result would be obtained by chance. Yet another way of saying it is that if you repeated the experiment again and again, only one time in 20 (i.e. 5 times in 100) would you achieve by chance a result like the one you obtained. The probability figure can be made more difficult to 'hit' by changing it to .01 (i.e. 1 in 100), or easier, by changing it to .1 (i.e. 1 in 10 that it would have been found by chance).

That's all that *significance testing* is about: these figures relating to chance. Important though it is to the interpretation of findings from certain kinds of research design, it's certainly not worth getting in a tizzy about not understanding how to calculate it. However, as is the case in much research study, it is useful to *understand* how published research uses statistics such as these and what they mean, even if you don't intend to undertake a study in which you would wish to calculate them.

I shall examine two of the most frequently used statistics of this kind here: *chi-square* (pronounced kye-square) and the *t test*. I have chosen these as examples, since they have a range of uses in the kind of research in which we are interested. It is worth noting, though, that Excel is a spreadsheet rather than a statistical package, and it is rather clumsy at calculating chi-square. If you want to do a lot of chi-squares it is probably worth investing in a student version of the well-known statistical package *SPSS* (Statistical Package for the Social Sciences), which is very easy to use yet does everything (and more) that a student or professional researcher would wish it to do. You can buy these at most university Computer Centres. Alternatively, SPSS is usually installed on pooled university machines, so you could save your analysis for times when you have access to a pooled room.

Chi-square is used to determine the likelihood that a distribution of *frequencies* would have been found by chance. Supposing we had asked a group of 99 newly recruited police officers about their attitude to stop and search procedures, with the options and findings shown in Table 9.5 then chi-square will tell you the likelihood that this range of findings would have been obtained by chance.

Table 9.5

Category of attitude	Police officers
1 Keep the law on stop and search as it is	58
2 Make the law easier for us to stop and search	32
3 Make the law more difficult for police to stop and search	9

I have worked out 'by hand' that with a chi-square statistic of 36.42, this is significant at the .01 level. Here's how I worked it out in Excel (and – tech talk for a moment for those who want it: beware that there is no formula for a one-way chi-square in Excel, though there is for a two-way, so you have to do the calculations bit by bit for this kind of finding):

First, the formula:

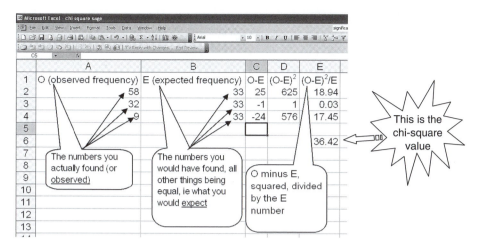

Figure 9.9   Calculation of chi-square

$$\text{Chi-square} = \Sigma \frac{(O - E)^2}{E}$$

I laid out my actual data (or 'observed frequency' 'O') in column A. Then I worked out the 'expected frequency' ('E') in column B. (This 'expected frequency' is the number of responses that 'should' be in each category, all things being equal, so in my example of 99 possible responses shared between three categories, it should be 33 in each.) Then I subtracted each column B figure from each column A figure and put the result in column C. I squared the column C figure and put it in D. For column E, I divided the column D figure by the column B figure. Then I *added* all the column E figures *together* (this is what Σ means) to give 36.42, which is the chi-square value. As Brucie says: 'That's all there is to it!' Figure 9.9 shows what it looks like in Excel.

What does the 36.42 mean? Good question. To interpret it, you have to look it up in the appropriate table (see the Appendix on page 244) together with the degrees of freedom for the data. The latter is simply the number of rows minus one. So, in the example, there are three rows, thus the degrees of freedom (df) is 2. Have a look in the table along the row for df 2. If your chi-square value is greater than any of the figures for the row (4.00, 5.99 and 9.21 in this case), then you can say that it is significant at that level. In fact it is greater than the largest of these (9.21), so it is significant at the .01 level. In other words there is less than a 1 in 100 chance that this finding would have been made by chance.

Is this worth knowing? Well, if I'm honest, I have to say that any argument I might choose to put on the basis of these data is hardly very much stronger with the significance figure added, though with a more complex range of data it may have been useful to calculate the statistic. In my opinion, the value of this kind of significance figure is more important in fields of study outside the social sciences (such as medicine), particularly where it is possible to control trials more precisely, though there are of course

Figure 9.10 Are trainees or trainers better when learning from lectures?

circumstances where it may be useful to us in applied social science. Again, it is the way in which the study is set up that is more important than this significance figure. You must always keep design issues in mind – the words that are used in the question, the people who are chosen, and so on – both when constructing your study and interpreting its findings. Moving on, and continuing to bear all of this in mind …

In chi-square, you are comparing frequencies of data and looking to see whether the numbers represented by those data are significantly different. Suppose, though, that you have a *comparison* to look at – comparing, say, the results of two groups on a test. Here, the *t test* is useful. I can give as an example a piece of research that I conducted with some trainee dentists and their field tutors. The study was to look at whether e-learning or a lecture was better for getting over some boring information about dental practice management and governance, and we were also interested in whether trainees and tutors responded the same or differently to the two methods of teaching (see Browne et al., 2004). I won't try to disentangle the full analysis here. Rather, I have extracted some of the data and performed a t test on one group of trainees' and one group of trainers' results after they had been taught by lecture. I present the Excel workings in Figure 9.10.

The t test tells you how likely it is that these two sets of results – those from the trainees and those from the trainers (in columns A and B) – would be found by chance. Eyeballing them, we can see that they *differ* (though not by very much: the mean for the trainees is 9.07 and that for the trainers is 9.69), but we are interested in the magnitude of this difference and how likely it is that the findings would have arisen by chance. Given that the difference isn't very much, I would guess that the scores are not significantly different; that is to say I would guess that this might just be a difference that could be accounted for by chance factors.

So, how did I do the t test? After entering my data in columns, as in previous examples ...

... in a spare cell on my worksheet I typed =**ttest(a2:a15,b2:b14,1,3)**

This means a 'one-tailed test'

This refers to the type of t test

These are the references for the first column...

... and the ones for the second column

Just a word about the '1' and the '3' at the end of the formula line. The '1' tells Excel that you want it to do a one-tailed as opposed to a two-tailed test. For details on what this means you will need to read one of the texts listed in the Further Reading for this chapter. The '3' tells Excel that you want it to do a comparison of unrelated groups. Again, for the details of the alternatives, consult the Further Reading or look at the Help facility for t tests in Excel. (However, the latter seems to have been written by someone without the remotest sense that people will (a) be reading it, or (b) will need to understand it. It will therefore probably make you feel suicidal, as it did me, so I don't recommend it if you are not feeling cheerful.)

Once you have clicked the tick, the result will appear where you typed the formula: 0.21

What does this 0.21 mean? It is the *actual significance figure*, not the t test statistic result, so you need go no further. Excel has done it all for you. Marvellous – no sums, no tables, no nonsense about degrees of freedom. Why isn't it in the form of p < .05, or p < .01? It's because computers work out the *exact* probability. So the exact probability of this result being made by chance is 0.21, which isn't really good enough for us, because it means, roughly, a 1 in 5 chance. You would not be satisfied with anything less than 1 in 10 (0.1). (Well, you and I might in the real world, but it's not taken to be good enough in academic social science.)

If you want to do anything much more complicated than any of these operations here you will need to consult a more specialised book and ask for help from a tutor who specialises in statistics. When you read more specialised statistics literature, be aware that in order to make my explanations here half-intelligible I have taken several shortcuts, not least in my dispensing with the use of the null hypothesis. For further reading, you will need to get your head around this. Be aware that reading explanations based on the null hypothesis is all a bit back to front, like trying to work out what 'not unhelpful' means. Good luck.

Discussing your analysis

This discussion is the completion of your research – its fruition. In it, you are coming full circle and returning to your initial questions and the context provided by your literature review. Remember the questions that you posed at the outset and the foundations provided (and the gaps left) by your literature review. The literature review provides a great basis for your thinking, but on its own it's a bit like a gin and tonic without the gin. Your research itself, all of the painstaking work that you have been doing out there in the field, is the gin that gives the kick – the element that makes the whole thing exciting.

Discussion occurs in different forms in different kinds of project write-up. It should always tie your findings and analysis with your questions and with the issues you disclosed in your literature review. And like the literature review, it is a synthesis, a narrative, a discussion – not a list.

How is the discussion that integrates these different elements of the report organised? It is in the presentation of findings, their analysis and discussion that there is perhaps the greatest room for variation between different kinds of project write-up. In the most formal social scientific research – that which follows the lead of natural science and traditional social science – there are clear delineations between these elements of a study. However, in applied social research it is often far more difficult to separate out one part from another. In an ethnographic study the findings *are*, in a way, the analysis. When you are watching and taking notes and then making a 'thick description' you *are* analysing.

And I think this ethnographic principle, in more or less diluted forms, is probably taken to apply now to a far wider range of research. It is, to a greater or lesser extent, the watchword in nearly all social research. No longer is it the case now that you can pretend that you are a dispassionate, objective observer having little or no influence on the research scene that you are observing. Or at least you can pretend, but no one will believe you. It was the assumption that this *was* indeed the case – that you could be disinterestedly separate and objective – that made supervisors once upon a time (when I did my own psychology degree in the late Middle Ages) insist on the formal separation of these elements. You had to pretend almost that you did not possess corporeal status, and this extended to the abolition of the first person singular: the word 'I' was forbidden in written work. I and my fellow students all had to pretend that we weren't actually embodied – almost as if the words had been beamed spiritually onto the page via a medium. We had to write in the passive tense, and say daft things such as 'The researcher believes ...' Did this actually make people believe it was objective? Well, it's amazing what people will believe.

And, as part of all this nonsense, it was assumed that *data gathering* could be cleanly separated from *analysis*. Now, though, there is the recognition that data gathering, in some way or another, is always infused with the person of the researcher. There is little point in pretending that this is not the case.

All research in education and the applied social sciences takes on these assumptions to some extent now: there is the acknowledgement that applied social research is complex – messy, even – often involving a knotty intertwining of ideas, facts and person. The corollary for the presentation of this chapter (about analysis and discussion) and the previous chapter (about data gathering) is that there is a continuum of kinds of organisation of your write-up. At one end, if you are doing a fairly formal study involving, say, an experiment, it is legitimate to adopt the linear approach outlined in Chapter 1: the presentation of your *findings*, with little in the way of commentary, will precede the *analysis*, which will precede the *discussion*. The discussion will take place separately, placing your statistical analysis in the context of the wider body of work that has occurred before it.

However, for a more interpretative piece of research you will not want to separate parts in this way, since all the time you will be testing out your emerging findings against your thoughts. All the time you will be validating or rejecting your findings against the body of knowledge that you already possess by virtue of your own experience and your reading. In these circumstances it is inappropriate to impose a strict line between analysis and discussion. One suffuses into the other. The difference between the different kinds of study is shown in Figure 9.11.

Formal linear study	Findings ——→ Analysis ——→ Discussion
Mixed study	Findings/analysis ←———→ Discussion
Interpretative study	Findings, analysis and discussion

Figure 9.11   Different kinds of analysis and discussion

How do you do this process of integrating the various elements of your project? It involves recursion (i.e. retracing your footsteps), summary, synthesis, putting ideas (yours and others') next to each other to see how they shape up together. You should be doing this all of the time anyway in doing your work, but it is here in the discussion that you have to bring it all together and make it meaningful to the reader. To do this, there has to be a continual revisiting of ideas and arguments to see which seem more or less valid. Some ideas may be rejected or put into abeyance. Tell readers about this: tell them about your process of acceptance, rejection and reformulation and the conclusions to which you have come. Table 9.6 gives some key words and phrases that you might use in doing this. You might also wish to look at Frank Smith's (1992) excellent book *To Think* and his list of 77 'thinking words'. Here's how Smith explains the way that the storehouse of words is used:

> Some look back on past events: *deduce, explain, recall, reflect, remember, review,* and *revise*. Some project into the future: *anticipate, conceive, divine, expect, foresee, imagine, intend, plan, plot, predict, project,* and *scheme*. Others seem mostly concerned with what is going on at the moment (although the present is never entirely free of past or future connotations): *analyze,*

Table 9.6   Key words and phrases in discussing

Focus	Typical words and phrases	
Remind the reader of the issues, briefly.	recap, summarise, revisit, reiterate	
Remind the reader of what you were trying to do.	explore, investigate, examine, illuminate, look at, research into	
Questions and arguments: your own and others'.	ask, posit, argue, aver, suggest, assume, put forward, note, highlight, draw attention to, believe, assess	Moderated throughout by criticality and tentativeness
What you have found?	disclose, reveal, uncover, suggest that, point to	
Has it affirmed?	affirm, agree, verify, legitimate, validate, support, confirm, establish, uphold, sustain, corroborate, endorse	
Has it contradicted?	contradict, disagree with, oppose, deny, challenge, conflict with	
How have your ideas developed or changed?	develop, redevelop, formulate, reformulate, deduce, speculate, construe, conclude, conjecture, guess, hypothesise	

argue, assert, assume, attend, believe, categorize, classify, comprehend, concentrate, conceptualize, determine, empathize, estimate, examine, invent, judge, know, opine, organize, presume, propose, reason, suggest, suspect, and *understand.* (Smith, 1992: 2)

It is important to reiterate some general rules here, since you will be seeking to weave together facets of your research work – ideas, arguments, findings and assertions – in ways that you have not in other parts of your project write-up. Remember always to be critical and to be tentative, as discussed in Chapter 3. Remember the duty of doubt. Be critical of others, certainly, but only when you have good evidence to be so. Be equally critical of yourself in the way that you have done your research, but make sure this is constructive criticism, noting always what you could have done instead.

Drawing out 'theory'

I noted in Chapter 4 the different meanings of *theory* in social research and the tangles that can arise because of the confusion between these meanings. Here, in your discussion, theory is concerned with one of those meanings in particular – to do with seeing links, generalising, abstracting ideas from your data and offering explanations, connecting your findings with those of others and having insights. But in doing this, you don't say 'I am drawing out theory'; rather you provide evidence of the process in your thinking and writing. It is very important that you do this, for the absence of 'theory', as I have noted in Chapter 4, is a major reason for the marking down of a piece of work, particularly at Master's level and beyond.

Drawing out 'theory' isn't just about making links to 'big' theory (such as Marxist or Freudian theory), though it can be about this if you have framed your project around one of these. More importantly, it is about making connections, identifying issues and offering reasoned explanations.

The way that you draw out theory hinges around your own knowledge of your subject and how your findings sit in relation to this knowledge. Your knowledge, your familiarity with your subject, will in turn depend on your reading and understanding of the existing research and debate. Links and associated ideas will have occurred to you throughout your project, and here, in your discussion, you tie up issues, cement connections and make explicit the clusters of ideas in your own work and that of others. These connections may be to existing bodies of knowledge or models of explanation or even to formalised 'theory' (such as Marxist theory, Freudian theory, behavioural theory or construct theory), or they may be to points of interest or 'trouble', as Bruner puts it (see p. 37), in the literature. You articulate continuing paradoxes, or perhaps offer tentative explanations for differences that continue to exist between your own analysis and that of the literature. All of this generalising process *is* the drawing out of theory.

It's as if your head is a giant sorting machine for the mass of data, yours and that of others, that has been pumped into it during the course of your project. It's all swilling around in there, but it mustn't simply swill out onto the paper in front of you. Rather, your head must provide little crystallisation points to which ideas ('theories' if you must) can attach themselves. And these little starting points, these tiny crystals, these inspirations, will – if you work hard at it – grow by the accretion of other ideas and insights. In this process is the development of theory.

There follow two examples of theorisation, with 'theory' conceived of differently, but equally validly, in each.

Murder in the family: an example of theorisation

Amerdeep is working for a Master's degree in forensic psychology, hoping ultimately to be promoted to the rank of inspector in the police service. Her research project centres on the media's presentation of mental instability and illness in the discussion of serious offending. This involves content analysis of newspaper articles about murder and other serious crimes. One of Amerdeep's main sources in her literature review is a Home Office study entitled *Murder and Serious Sexual Assault: What Criminal Histories Can Reveal about Future Serious Offending* (Soothill et al., 2002). Among the rich data she finds in the report is that shown in Table 9.7.

Table 9.7   Murderers by victim–offender relationship

	N	% with previous convictions
Family	119	62.2
Acquaintance	218	69.7
Stranger – male victim	195	70.3
Stranger – female victim	31	61.3
Total	563	68.0

From Soothill et al. (2002).

Table 9.7 reveals that in around two-thirds of *all* murders, including family murder, in the Home Office study the murderer had a previous criminal conviction. This surprised Amerdeep, whose impression from reading the press was that murder of a family member was something of a different kettle of fish from other murder – that it was a crime of passion, motivated by domestic unhappiness, provocation, self-defence or rage. The popular belief – either created by or just reflected in the press – was of domestic murderers being like you and me: ordinary people impelled under extraordinary circumstances to awful acts. But the Home Office research said something different: that 62 per cent of family murder was committed by someone with a previous criminal conviction – i.e. *not* like you and me. Or to put it more accurately, it was committed by a very unusual subset of the population at large: those with a criminal conviction, and in this sense the population of family murderers was similar to the population of all murderers.

Here, in this noticing of something unexpected, was the germ of *theorisation*. It came from an intelligent noticing of a mismatch, an 'angle', a disparity between a common view and the evidence. It enabled Amerdeep to take her analysis beyond mere description and toward discussion of this disparity. Her theorisation involved the integration of a range of 'knowledges':

- her own knowledge as a police officer;
- her knowledge as an ordinary member of the public;
- the data she had accumulated as part of her empirical research;
- her reading of the research literature.

All of this diverse knowledge was available to her in making sense of her observation about murder 'in the family'.

That first step – the seed of the idea, the noticing, the point of crystallisation – took place early on in the project, during her reading for her literature review. She had to hold that seed of an idea with her as she progressed through the rest of her literature review and her data collection. In many ways, the observation of incongruity between the literature and a popularly held view altered the course of her research, and this was to be expected (see the discussion of the *recursive plan* on p. 15). This small starting point, arising from her noticing of something unexpected, gathered other pieces of information to it; it led to new questions; it led to a more targeted search for data that would throw light on it. She could ultimately identify it as one of the major themes of her research.

Given that seed of inquiry, that itch to find out more – the 'trouble' – Amerdeep started thinking, or theorising (see Figure 9.12). She came up with possible explanations for the finding, and sought ways of testing those ideas. For example, was her own idea of 'received wisdom' concerning family murderers wrong? To test this out she could do a small impromptu survey of friends and colleagues. And what did the media tend to say about family murder? She would make a special note to examine this in her own content analysis. Could it be that the highly detailed Home Office study was leading her astray? What was the sample of murderers used? If it was murderers in prison (as it was), it omitted murderers who were not in prison, and these would surely form a special subset – perhaps overrepresented with family murderers. While murder carries a mandatory prison sentence, it may be that family murderers tend to receive much shorter sentences so the population of them in prison is proportionately smaller

Figure 9.12   Murder in the family – theorising around a mismatch

at any one time than that of the non-family murderers – and those of them who are there (in prison) may be there because their backgrounds and histories make them more typical of 'normal' prisoners, making them less likely to receive parole etc. In all of this Amerdeep was reading, asking questions, gathering ideas, 'gutting' other ideas and research findings, questioning explanations, questioning her own beliefs and views, and coming up with new tentative explanations. All of this is theorisation.

Laughing all the way to school: another example of theorisation

Michael is studying for a BA in English, Psychology and Education and has been work-ing during his vacations as a volunteer in a primary school close to his university. He is now able to use the goodwill felt towards him at the school to help him gain access for his double-module interdisciplinary research project. He has an interest in inclusive education and wonders how Year 6 children use humour and laughter to include or exclude other children. He plans to do some informal observations in an ethnographic design frame. He explains this to the staff at the school who are happy with it given appropriate assurances of anonymity and of completely unobtrusive observation, and the head teacher requests support for Michael's study in a letter to parents.

On discussing theorisation with his tutor Michael decides that he needs to review the way that others have understood humour and laughter and their role in creating social capital – in forming the social 'glue' and 'oil' that helps groups to stay together. In reviewing the literature Michael comes across some classic works by Freud and Bergson, and out of these he develops a typology that sees humour being used in three ways by groups:

1. to relieve tension or stress;
2. to assert superiority;
3. to introduce new ideas into a community's thinking by highlighting incongruity.

This typology forms the basis for his *theorisation*. He sees connections to inclu-sion and exclusion certainly in the first two points of the typology – in the ways that certain children may be the object of unkind humour, first to defuse tension in a group by identifying a different 'outsider', and second to strengthen *bonds* in a sub-group by isolating individuals perceived to be inferior. However, he noted that humour may also be used to defuse tension in a harmless way, by not mak-ing a joke at anyone's expense – and in fact in the hands of a socially skilled mem-ber of the group to deflect attention from individuals at times of tension onto an impersonal feature of the situation.

Michael linked the idea of *social bonds* with Robert Putnam's (2000) notions of *bonding* and *bridging* in social groups. Bonding, said Putnam, is a means of strengthening a group by excluding others, with bridging by contrast being a means of easing in new members. As Putnam puts it, 'Bonding social capital con-stitutes a kind of sociological superglue, whereas bridging social capital provides a sociological WD40' (Putnam, 2000: 22–3). Michael related his typology to Putnam's bonding and bridging as indicated in Figure 9.13.

This detailed and thoughtful overview of the literature provided Michael with a strong theoretical framework within which to build and conduct his ethnography – the latter involving observations and interviews. By watching especially in his obser-vation for instances of the use of humour and its use in the relief of stress, the exertion of superiority or the highlighting of incongruity, he could first broadly define its use in his analysis and discussion as threatening or benign. He could then in turn interpret specific instances as examples of Putnam's bonding and bridging. This provided an invaluable lens through which to view examples of humour. Without it, Michael's nar-rative would have been a flavourless set of illustrations: illustrations of what? There needs to be a structure within which these illustrations can be interpreted. This is not to say that the structure cannot in itself ultimately be questioned and reinterpreted or even discarded: this is all part of the process of 'theorisation'.

Figure 9.13 Typology related to Putnam's bonding and bridging

You can see, I hope, that what goes under the name of 'theorisation' and 'theory' takes a variety of shapes and forms in different types of inquiry. The important thing is to use your intelligence to try to understand what is going on – to be *making sense* of your findings.

Overview

This is the most interesting part of your project – the part where you get the chance to think seriously about your own findings and what they mean. The analytical frame that you use, whether it is thick description or some kind of statistical method, will provide a rich source of ideas for your thinking. Now that you are here, analysing the results of all your hard work, it's where you can let yourself off the leash a bit, and make wider interpretations and judgements. The kinds of interpretations that you make will be determined in part by the approach or approaches that you have taken, but it is here that you will set your analysis in the context of everything that has gone before, including your literature review. You will be tying strands together, intertwining ideas, weaving a fabric that is sometimes called 'theory'. If done well, this can be a real contribution to knowledge in a particular area. It may be a small area, but you will have enhanced your own understanding and added to that of others. And you will have developed your own skills along the way.

Further Reading

Analysing words

Coffey, A. and Atkinson, P. (1996) *Making sense of qualitative data.* London: SAGE.
Denzin, N. and Lincoln, Y. (eds) (2008) *Collecting and Interpreting Qualitative Materials.* Thousand Oaks, CA: SAGE.
Comprehensive and thoroughgoing.

Miles, M.B. and Huberman, M. (1994) *Qualitative Data Analysis: An Expanded Sourcebook.* 2nd ed. London: SAGE.
Schwandt, T.A. (2001) *Dictionary of qualitative inquiry.* Thousand Oaks, CA: SAGE.
Actually, this is much more than a dictionary.

http://www.hoopandtree.org/sociometry.htm which gives information on the sociomatrix – one of these is used in Colin Lacey's *High Town Grammar.*

Analysing numbers

Field, A. (2009*) Discovering Statistics Using SPSS.* 3rd edn. London: SAGE.
If you want to go further in using statistics, for which you will need SPSS, you can't do much better than this book. Some funny examples, including lap dancers and ejaculating quails.

Gorard, S. (2001) *Quantitative methods in educational research.* London: Continuum.
Good discussion and advice.

Hinton, P. R. (2004) *Statistics explained: a guide for social science students.* London: Routledge.
A good spread, though more on social science *per se* rather than applied social science.

Salkind, N.J. (2004) *Statistics for people who (think they) hate statistics.* Thousand Oaks, CA: SAGE.
A friendly book on statistics. Lots of cartoons; nicely written. Explains (if you really want to know) the difference between one-tailed and two-tailed tests.

Miles, J. and Shevlin, M. (2001) Applying *Regression and Correlation: A Guide for Students and Researchers.* London: SAGE
Good on correlation.

10

Concluding

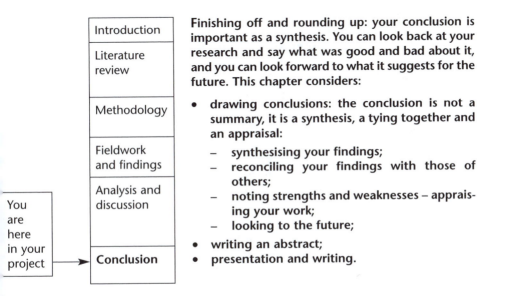

Introduction
Literature review
Methodology
Fieldwork and findings
Analysis and discussion
Conclusion

You are here in your project

Finishing off and rounding up: your conclusion is important as a synthesis. You can look back at your research and say what was good and bad about it, and you can look forward to what it suggests for the future. This chapter considers:

- drawing conclusions: the conclusion is not a summary, it is a synthesis, a tying together and an appraisal:
  - synthesising your findings;
  - reconciling your findings with those of others;
  - noting strengths and weaknesses – appraising your work;
  - looking to the future;
- writing an abstract;
- presentation and writing.

At the beginning of this book I said that your research project is like a story: it needs a beginning, a middle and an end. You are now at the end, and this bit is as important as the beginning. It's important (a) because it performs a set of crucial functions which I'll come on to in a moment, and (b) because, like the introduction, it is the bit that will be read most thoroughly by markers and, possibly, an external examiner. They will of course read the whole report thoroughly and make detailed comments on it, but they will be looking in the conclusion and the introduction for a sense of cohesion and integrity, for a sense of your approach to research, for a sense of your critical awareness and your attitude to knowledge. These are as important, or more important, than what you have actually 'found'.

As this is the place at which you will probably be doing most of your writing and tidying up, I shall include some general points here that in fact apply right through your project work – points concerning audience, the way that you write and the way that you present your work. I shall also say something about the *abstract*, since it is here, at the end of your project, that this should be written.

Writing a conclusion

The good news is that the conclusion doesn't need to be very long. The conclusion and the introduction are the shortest chapters in your dissertation. I'll start by saying what a conclusion is not. It is not a summary. Unlike the introduction, it should not plod through each of the chapters saying what each is about. The reader has read those and doesn't need to be reminded of them. Rather, it is a synthesis that captures for readers what the research was about and leaves them with an idea of your understanding of the field, and your understanding of research, its benefits and its frailties. What should it contain?

First, it should address whether you have been able to answer your question(s) and it should reiterate briefly some of the points in the discussion. It should chart the progress of the change in your questions as the project has progressed. It should say how your interests have changed.

Second, it should summarise *briefly* the main findings – that is to say, in a page or two, and it should outline dilemmas, questions and paradoxes still existing.

Third, it can outline any recommendations for those who have been participants in your research (for example, the school that accommodated you) or for policy more widely. However, there is no *need* for a research project to have recommendations and often when students include these they can seem trite and reveal a lack of understanding about the realities of policy and practice. With this in mind it is as well, if you do want to make any kind of recommendation, to include here some discussion about implementation in the real world. Here, the title of a famous paper comes to mind: *The Myth of the Hero-Innovator* by Georgiades and Phillimore (1975). It makes the point that it is extraordinarily difficult to effect change in an organisation and that if you expect or hope to do this you need to devote a great deal of attention to the workings of the organisation, its structure and its politics.

Fourth, you can acknowledge your project's weaknesses, which you may realise toward the end were quite major. Maybe you should, in retrospect, have used a completely different approach. Do acknowledge this if it is the case; don't try to paper over the cracks, because the reader will realise it anyway. Say that you recognise in hindsight that you should have used a different method, used different tools or adopted a different form of analysis. You will be credited for your perception and understanding in the examiner's marking. After all, part of the criticality of which academics are so fond consists in the ability to be self-critical and to understand the shortcomings and imperfections that almost inevitably exist in research.

Fifth, you can outline points for further research, or how your research leads to further questions. This may be obvious, but if it isn't try the following:

1. *Imagine*. How would things be different if something were changed in 'the system'? Suppose, for example, that you have been researching the curriculum and there were no National Curriculum (you never know, it might happen one day). On the basis of your research, what could you say about such a scenario.
2. *Predict*. How is something likely to look or to be in the future, based on the way you have found it to be in your research? If you are doing research, for example, on the funding of the health service in your region, how would things look if the National Health Service were to accept 'top-up funding' from patients?
3. *Solve*. What tentative solutions can you offer to any broader questions or issues that have been raised in your research? Does it offer any insights on problems that exist today? For example, if you have been undertaking research on the marketing of soft drinks to children, what insights might be offered on the growth in childhood obesity? But remember: be tentative; be modest; think small – your findings may well be relevant, they may be significant, but the hallmark of scholarly research is self-critical caution. Unlike journalists, researchers know – and are proud that they know – that they don't have easy answers. Remember that you are not a journalist.
4. *Compare or draw an analogy*. Find the similarities and differences between your topic of interest and a similar subject, or with the same subject in a different time period or place. For example, how has the introduction of education action zones been mirrored in Europe or the USA?

Writing an abstract

Here, at the *end*, you can write your abstract – though it will be placed right at the *beginning*, on the first page after the title but before the contents page. Your abstract should be between 150 and 300 words – enough to fit onto one side of A4. (It is acceptable to use single spacing for the abstract.) You should spend a lot of time thinking about your abstract because it should encapsulate the whole project and is a first impression to all of your readers – and it is the abstract that will be recorded electronically. If anywhere, it is here in the abstract that you are writing a summary of the project: it should be a balanced review of your questions, methods, findings and conclusions. Don't make the mistake (which many people do) of not saying what you actually found.

I give in Figure 10.1 my own PhD abstract. While a PhD is a lengthier and more complex piece of work than an undergraduate or Master's project, the abstract is essentially the same in each. I have put in the thought bubbles by the side my own reflections now on this abstract. Looking back on it I think it is not too bad, though it is a little pompous in parts and there is a touch of repetition, which I would, if I were writing it again, expunge.

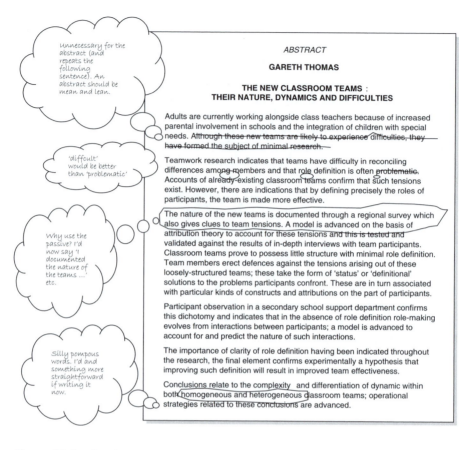

Figure 10.1   An abstract

General points about writing and presentation

Writing

I have talked *ad nauseam* about being critical and telling a coherent story and this is certainly the central current through any consideration about the way that you write. But the writing is more than an articulation of your thought and work; it is also a communication of this to others. Writing is about communicating; it is not about trying to sound clever (and this sadly is not a maxim followed by some academics who write for scholarly journals – I have explored this elsewhere: Thomas, 1994). There are many books on how to write, and you won't have time to read any of them, but in case you do let me point you to one that has helped me: John Whale's (1984) *Put It in Writing*. He gives a number of reminders, such as 'remembering the reader', and 'hear it in your head'.

In other words, read it out to yourself in your head (or, even better, out loud). Does it sound right? Does it make sense? Will the reader understand? Whale also suggests that you should sound like yourself, and this is certainly good advice, with the proviso that there is *register* to consider. 'Register' is the accepted form of writing for a particular audience or forum, and to write your dissertation in phone text would be unacceptable, obviously. There is a certain expectation about a degree of formality that has to surround anything as important as a piece of work which will count in a significant way toward your degree. However, this does not stop you from using your own words and sounding like yourself in your writing. Indeed, it is to be welcomed and admired. George Orwell, in his brilliant essay *Politics and the English Language*, makes the point that there is bad writing that finds its roots in imitation of others (i.e. imitating them and therefore *not* sounding like yourself) and this bad writing actually leads to sloppy thinking:

> [Our language] becomes ugly and inaccurate because our thoughts are foolish, but the slovenliness of our language makes it easier for us to have foolish thoughts. ... Modern English, especially written English, is full of bad habits which spread by imitation and which can be avoided if one is willing to take the necessary trouble. If one gets rid of these habits one can think more clearly. (Orwell, 1969)

Given that one of Orwell's targets is academic language (and you will have come across plenty of bad examples in your own reading), his essay is well worth reading. He comes up with a checklist of what to do and what not to do ...

1. Never use a metaphor, simile or other figure of speech which you are used to seeing in print.
2. Never use a long word where a short one will do.
3. If it is possible to cut a word out, always cut it out.
4. Never use the passive where you can use the active.
5. Never use a foreign phrase, a scientific word or a jargon word if you can think of an everyday English equivalent.
6. Break any of these rules sooner than say anything outright barbarous.

It is worth reiterating that your design frame and approach determine to a great extent the register that you adopt in your write-up. The examples of ethnography that I have given show, I hope, that the kind of writing, the register, that you use in this sort of work will be very different from the write-up of an experiment. The former may be more like a newspaper article or even a novel, while the latter will demand more of the structure and strictures of formal academic writing.

One last point:

Q. Can I say 'I'?

A. Yes. 'I' is a good word. (See p. 226.)

Non-sexist and non-discriminatory writing

Quite rightly, there is the expectation that your writing should not engender or perpetuate stereotypes of any kind, and there are some basic rules here. Do not use any gender-based language (for example, using 'he' when you mean 'he or she'). To avoid it, try using the plural, or if that really won't work, use 'they' as a non-gendered singular pronoun. Some people get very exercised about this ('But it's not correct grammar! ...'), but it has now become an acceptable form of use to avoid sexist writing. Don't use a gendered form if a neutral form is available (e.g. don't use 'headmistress' in preference to 'headteacher').

At the time of writing 'disability' is acceptable, though 'impairment' is preferred by some authorities. 'Handicap' is not acceptable.

In the UK, the term 'black and minority ethnic' (BME) is used by the Home Office to refer to all people who are not white.

Presentation

Draft, proofread and edit; re-draft, re-proofread and re-edit; then re-re-draft, re-re-proof read and re-re-edit ... and so on. Get it right. Maybe I'm oversensitive, but when I am marking and I read something that clearly has not been proofread even once I feel a little insulted. It puts me in a bad mood, and you don't want to put your marker in a bad mood.

Use your Spellchecker and Grammar check, but be aware that they are not foolproof. Words such as 'practice', that change their spelling depending on their use ('practice' when a noun, 'practise' when a verb) will not be picked up by your Spellchecker. So ask someone who is good at spelling to proofread for you. If English is not your first language, ask someone for whom it is if they will read it through for you.

Get your apostrophes right. I know it shouldn't matter to your markers, but sadly it does. When they see *childrens'* it jumps out at them and puts them instantly off their lunch. Given that more than half of students use apostrophes incorrectly, here is my half-page guide.

Apostrophes: Part 1

> *it's and its*
>
> > Use *it's only* as an abbreviation for *it is*
> > for example ...
> > > *It's* a nice day today.
> > > I'm going because *it's* necessary.
> > Use *its* for *everything else*
> > for example ...
> > > *Its* colour is blue.
> > > The dog was cross because *its* dinner was late.
> > (In other words, *its* is an exception to the general rule that a possessive *s* takes an apostrophe.)
> > *Tip*: There is no such construction as *its'*.

Apostrophes: Part 2
  ownership
  Singular nouns – like *cat, tree, Piaget, nut* – take an apostrophe before the
  s when you want to indicate ownership
  for example …
    Piaget's theories have been used for many years in education.
    The ***cat's*** fur is falling out.
  But when those singular nouns have an *s* added to make them plural –
  like *cats, trees, nuts* – they take an apostrophe after the *s* to show ownership
    for example …
    Trees' leaves fall in the autumn.
  However, *plural* nouns – like *people, women, children* – take an apostrophe *before* the *s*
  for example …
    The ***women's*** group meets on Wednesdays.
    Children's clothes are not subject to VAT.

There are one or two other things to consider – but that's for the advanced
course. The above will cover 99 per cent of all cases of apostrophe use.

Other points

There will be regulations and guidelines about the presentation of your
thesis produced by your university department. Clearly, you must conform
to these. Here are a few all-purpose ones:

- *Numbering*. Make sure your pages are numbered. Go to Insert in Word,
  then Page Numbers. The bottom right is the best place for a page
  number in my opinion.
- *Tables and diagrams*. Label tables 'Table 1', 'Table 2', etc., and the same with
  diagrams and pictures, which are called 'Figures'. It is best to label these by
  chapter, so the fourth table in Chapter 3 would be called 'Table 3.4'. Refer
  to tables and figures by their numbers, not as 'in the following table'.
- *Margins*. Use at least 33 mm (1.25 inches) on the left and 25 mm (1 inch)
  on the right, top and bottom. Your university may have its own
  specification, but I've never known any of my colleagues actually get out
  a tape measure when marking. The main thing is to ensure that the
  margins are ample so markers can write in them with a bit more on the
  left to allow for binding.
- *Spacing*. University regulations usually specify double spacing, though
  I'm not actually sure why. I think it is a hangover from the days when
  typesetters needed to write between lines. I personally prefer single
  spacing – and there is a green issue here as well – but of course you
  must follow the guidelines set by your university or department. I
  think 1.5 spacing would usually be acceptable (and it's what I use
  whenever ordered to use double spacing).

- *Quotations*. If you use a quotation of 40 words or longer, indent it. Otherwise, keep it in the text.
- *References*. There is a distinction between references and a bibliography. References are the works that you have actually referred to in the text. A bibliography, by contrast, is a list of works that you may have read but not necessarily mentioned by name. In an academic work of this kind it is *references* that you need (see the Harvard method, pp. 54–6).
- *Hyphens and en dashes*. When you type a hyphen between words, Word autocorrects it into something called an 'en dash' (as long as the appropriate box is ticked in Autocorrect, as it is by default). It looks like this – it's a bit longer than a hyphen and is a 'proper' dash. The only problem is that when you go back to edit material and want to put in a dash and type the hyphen, Word doesn't 'know' what you are doing, so it just puts in a hyphen. This looks messy. To avoid it, use the en dash direct entry when editing (i.e. type Ctrl and the minus sign on the number pad).

Coda

Coda is a pretentious word meaning 'the end'. I'm using it because I don't want to end the book on anything as unprepossessing as a discussion of the use of the hyphen versus the use of the en dash.

I said at the beginning that research can give you a buzz, and I am sure that you will have felt that buzz. You will have emerged from doing a research project with greatly enhanced skills. You will have acquired detailed knowledge about one aspect of education, healthcare, medicine, dentistry, social work or whatever, and you will be something of an authority in this aspect of your subject. You may even have insights on policy and practice that will be valuable in local discussions. But perhaps more importantly, you will have acquired knowledge about how to inquire and do research, having developed a healthy scepticism about the claims of research to be able to discover the truth. You will be able to set different kinds of research against each other and against other kinds of inquiry and evaluate the strengths and weaknesses of each. And, by doing all of this in your own research, you will be able to understand better the research that you read.

I hope you have enjoyed the journey. Good luck.

Further Reading

Writing

Becker, H. S. and Richards, P. (1986). *Writing for social scientists: How to start and finish your thesis, book, or article*. Chicago, IL: The University of Chicago Press.

Thomson, A. (2005) *Critical reasoning: a practical introduction*. London: Routledge.

See especially Chapters 4 and 5 on writing and reasoning. Good especially on how to summarise.

Wolcott, H.E. (2009) *Writing up qualitative research.* 3rd edn. London: SAGE.

AERA (1999) Publishing educational research: guidelines and tips. Available at: http://www.aera.net/uploadedFiles/Journals_and_Publications/Journals/pubtip.pdf Accessed 12th October 2008.
This is mainly intended for junior researchers trying to get published and contains some good advice on writing.

Appendix: Critical Values for Chi-square

	Level of significance		
df	0.1	0.05	0.01
1	2.71	3.84	6.64
2	4.00	5.99	9.21
3	6.25	7.82	11.34
4	7.78	9.49	13.28
5	9.24	11.07	15.09
6	10.64	12.59	16.81
7	12.02	14.07	18.48
8	13.36	15.51	20.09
9	14.68	16.92	21.67
10	16.99	18.31	23.21
11	17.28	19.68	24.72
12	18.65	21.03	26.22
13	19.81	22.36	27.69
14	21.06	23.68	29.14
15	22.31	25.00	30.58
16	23.54	26.30	32.00
17	24.77	27.60	33.41
18	25.99	28.87	34.80
19	27.20	30.14	36.19
20	28.41	31.41	37.57
21	29.62	32.67	38.93
22	30.81	33.92	40.29
23	32.01	35.17	41.64
24	33.20	36.42	42.98
25	34.38	37.65	44.81
26	35.56	38.88	45.64
27	36.74	40.11	46.96
28	37.92	41.34	48.28
29	39.09	42.56	49.59
30	40.26	43.77	50.89

References

Alderson, P. (2004) *Ethics, Social Research and Consulting with Children and Young People*, 2nd edn. London: Barnardo's.

Andreski, S. (1972) *Social Sciences as Sorcery*. London: André Deutsch.

Ball, S. (1981) *Beachside Comprehensive: A Case-Study of Secondary Schooling*. Cambridge: Cambridge University Press.

Becker, H. S. (1998) *Tricks of the Trade*. Chicago, IL: University of Chicago Press.

Bliss, J., Monk, M. and Ogborn, J. (1983) *Qualitative Data Analysis for Educational Research*. London: Croom Helm.

Browne, E., Mehra, S., Rattan, R. and Thomas, G. (2004) 'Comparing lecture and e-learning as pedagogies for new and experienced professionals in dentistry', *British Dental Journal*, 197 (2): 95–9.

Bruner, J. (1997) *The Culture of Education*. Cambridge, MA: Harvard University Press.

Bryman, A. (1998) 'Quantitative and qualitative research strategies in knowing the social world', in T. May and M. Williams (eds), *Knowing in the Social World*. Buckingham: Open University Press.

Burgess, R. G. (1982) *Field Research: A Sourcebook and Field Manual*. London: Routledge.

Burgess, R. G. (1984) *In the Field: An Introduction to Field Research*. London: Routledge.

Butterfield, H. (1931/1973) *The Whig Interpretation of History*. London: Pelican.

Campbell, D. T. and Stanley, J. C. (1963) *Experimental and Quasi-Experimental Designs for Research*. Chicago, IL: Rand McNally.

Coady, C. A. J. (1994) *Testimony: A Philosophical Study*. Oxford: Clarendon Press.

Coles, G. (2000) *Misreading Reading: The Bad Science that Hurts Children*. Boston, MA: Heinemann.

Cremin, H., Thomas, G. and Vincett, K. (2005) 'Working with teaching assistants: three models evaluated', *Research Papers in Education*, 20 (4): 413–32.

DCSF (2007) *Education and Training Statistics for the United Kingdom*. London: DCSF. Available at: www.dcsf.gov.uk/rsgateway/DB/VOL/v000761/index.shtml (accessed 22 September 2008).

Denzin, N. (1978) *Sociological Methods: A Sourcebook*. 2nd edn. New York: McGraw-Hill.

Derrida, J. (1978) *Writing and Difference*. London: Routledge & Kegan Paul.

Descartes, R. (1647/1996) *Meditations on First Philosophy*. Cambridge: Cambridge University Press.

Devlin, B., Fienberg, S. E., Resnick D. P. and Roeder, K. (eds) *Intelligence, Genes and Success: Scientists Respond to the Bell Curve*. New York: Springer-Verlag.

Dewey, J. (1920/2004) *How We Think*. Whitefish, MT: Kessinger Publishing.

Dickens, W. T. and Flynn, J. R. (2001) 'Heritability estimates versus large environmental effects: the IQ paradox resolved', *Psychological Review*, 108: 346–69.

Fairclough, N. (1995) *Critical Discourse Analysis*. Harlow: Longman.

Flanders, N. (2004) 'Interaction analysis', in C. Seale (ed.), *Social Research Methods: A Reader*. London: Routledge, pp. 111–16.

Galton, M., Simon, B. and Croll, P. (1980) *Inside the Primary Classroom*. London: Routledge & Kegan Paul.

Geertz, C. (1975) *The Interpretation of Cultures*. London: Hutchinson.

Georgiades, N. J. and Phillimore, L. (1975) 'The myth of the hero-innovator and alternative strategies for organizational change', in C. C. Kiernan and F. P. Woodford (eds), *Behaviour Modification with the Severely Retarded*. Amsterdam: Associated Scientific Publishers.

Glaser, B. G. and Strauss, A. L. (1967) *The Discovery of Grounded Theory: Strategies for Qualitative Research*. New York: Aldine.

Goffman, E. (1956) *The Presentation of Self in Everyday Life*. Edinburgh: University of Edinburgh.

Gorard, S. and Taylor, C. (2004) *Combining Methods in Educational Research*. Maidenhead: Open University Press.

Gordon, H. (1923) *Mental and Scholastic Tests among Retarded Children*, Education Pamphlet 44. London: HMSO.

Gould, S. J. (1996) *The Mismeasure of Man*. McHenry, IL: Sagebrush Education Resources.

Haldane, J. B. S. (1928) *Possible Worlds and Other Essays*. London: Chatto & Windus.

Hammersley, M. (1992) *What's Wrong with Ethnography*. London: Routledge.

Hammersley, M. (1996) The relationship between qualitative and quantitative research: paradigm loyalty versus methodological eclecticism, in J.T.E. Richardson (ed.), *Handbook of research methods for psychology and the social sciences*. Leicester: BPS Books.

Holton, G. (1995) 'The controversy over the end of science', *Scientific American*, 273 (4): 168.

Hume, D. (1748/1910) 'An enquiry concerning human understanding', *Harvard Classics Volume 37*. New York: P.F. Collier & Son. Also available at: http://eserver.org/18th/hume-enquiry.html.

ICM (2007) *Royal family and War Survey*. Available at: www.icmresearch.co.uk/pdfs/2007_august_daily_mail_royals_poll.pdf (accessed 27 August 2007).

Jenkins, R. (1992) *Pierre Bourdieu*. London: Routledge.

Jones, L. and Brown, T. (2001) '"Reading" the nursery classroom: a Foucauldian perspective', *International Journal of Qualitative Studies in Education*, 14 (6): 713–25.

Jones, S. (1985) 'The analysis of depth interviews', in R. Walker (ed.), *Applied Qualitative Research*. Aldershot: Gower.

Junghans, C., Feder, G., Hemingway, H., Timmis, A. and Jones, M. (2005) 'Recruiting patients to medical research: double blind randomised trial of "opt-in" versus "opt-out" strategies', *British Medical Journal*, 331: 940. Available at: www.bmj.com/cgi/reprint/331/7522/940.pdf (accessed 26 August 2008).

Kellett, M. (2005) *How to Develop Children as Researchers*. London: Paul Chapman Publishing.

Kelly G. A. (1955/1991) *The Psychology of Personal Constructs*, Vol. II. London: Routledge.

Klein, P. (1997) 'Multiplying the problems of intelligence by eight: a critique of Gardner's theory', *Canadian Journal of Education*, 22 (4): 377–94.

Kounin, J. (1970) *Discipline and Group Management in Classrooms*. New York: Holt, Rinehart & Winston.

Kuhn, T. (1970) *The Structure of Scientific Revolutions*, 2nd edn. Chicago, IL: University of Chicago Press.

Lacey, C. (1970) *Hightown Grammar*. Manchester: Manchester University Press.

Lévi-Strauss, C. (1962/1966) *The Savage Mind*. Chicago, IL: University of Chicago Press.

Lewin, K. (1946) 'Action research and minority problems', *Journal of Social Issues*, 2 (4): 34–46.

Lewis, A. (1995) 'Views of schooling held by children attending schools for pupils with moderate learning difficulties', *International Journal of Disability, Development and Education*, 42 (1): 57–73.

Lewis, A. and Lindsay, G. (2000) *Researching Children's Perspectives*. Buckingham: Open University Press.

Lincoln, Y. S. and Guba, E. G. (1985) *Naturalistic Inquiry*. Beverly Hills, CA: SAGE.

MacIntyre, A. (1985) *After Virtue: A Study in Moral Theory*. London: Duckworth.

McNiff, J., Lomax, P. and Whitehead, J. (2003) *You and Your Action Research Project*. 2nd edn. London: Routledge.

Maslow, A. (1966) *Psychology of Science*. New York: Harper & Row.

Medawar, P. B. (1982) *Pluto's Republic*. Oxford: Oxford University Press.

Miles, M. B. and Huberman, M. (1994) *Qualitative Data Analysis: An Expanded Sourcebook*, 2nd edn. London: SAGE.

Milgram, S. (1963) 'Behavioral study of obedience', *Journal of Abnormal and Social Psychology*, 67 (4): 371–8.

Milgram, S. (1981) 'Behavioral study of obedience', *Social and Behavioral Science*, 9: 18. Available at: www.garfield.library.upenn.edu/classics1981/A1981LC33300001.pdf (accessed 25 August 2008).

Newman, J. H. (1960/1852) 'The idea of a university', in M. J. Svaglic (ed.), *The Idea of a University Defined and Illustrated*. San Francisco, CA: Rinehart Press, pp. 15–16.

Oakley, A. (2000) *Experiments in Knowing: Gender and Method in the Social Sciences*. Cambridge: Polity.

Orwell, G. (1969) 'Politics and the English language', in G. Orwell, *Inside the Whale and Other Essays*. London: Penguin. Available at: http://orwell.ru/library/essays/politics/english/e_polit (accessed 2 October 2008).

Patrick, J. (1973) *A Glasgow Gang Observed*. London: Methuen.

Pawson, R. (2006) *Evidence-Based Policy: A Realistic Perspective*. London: SAGE.

Pólya, G. (1945/2004) *How to Solve It*. Princeton, NJ: Princeton Science Library.

Pring, R. (2000) *Philosophy of Educational Research*. London: Continuum.

Putnam, R. (1995) 'Bowling alone: America's declining social capital', *Journal of Democracy*, 6: 65–78.

Putnam, R. (2000) *Bowling Alone: The Collapse and Revival of American Community*. New York: Simon & Schuster.

Russell, B. (1956) 'Galileo and scientific method', in A. F. Scott (ed.), *Topics and Opinions*. London: Macmillan.

Ryle, G. (1949/1990) *The Concept of Mind*. London: Penguin.

Sacks, O. (1996) *An Anthropologist on Mars*. London: Picador.

Smith, F. (1992) *To Think: In Language Learning and Education*. London: Routledge.

Smith, J. and Heshusius, L. (1986) 'Closing down the conversation: the end of the quantitative–qualitative debate among educational inquirers', *Educational Researcher*, 15: 4–12.

Soothill, K., Francis, B., Ackerley, E. and Fligelstone, R. (2002) *Murder and Serious Sexual Assault: What Criminal Histories Can Reveal About Future Serious Offending*, Police Research Series Paper 144. London: Home Office. Available at: www.homeoffice.gov.uk/rds/prgpdfs/prs144.pdf (accessed 24 October 2008).

Spradley, J. P. (1979) *The Ethnographic Interview*. New York: Holt, Rinehart & Winston.

Stake, R. E. (1995) *The Art of Case Study Research*. Thousand Oaks, CA: SAGE.

Tarr, J. and Thomas, G. (1997) 'The quality of special educational needs policies: time for review?', *Support for Learning*, 12 (1): 10–14.

Thagard, P. (1998) 'Ulcers and bacteria I: Discovery and acceptance', *Studies in History and Philosophy of Science. Part C: Studies in History and Philosophy of Biology and Biomedical Sciences*, 29: 107–36. Also available at: http://cogsci.uwaterloo.ca/Articles/Pages/Ulcers.one.html.

Thomas, G. (1992) *Effective Classroom Teamwork: Support or Intrusion*. London: Routledge.

Thomas, G. (1994) 'Write on or write-off?', *British Journal of Special Education*, 21 (1): 12.

Thomas, G. (2002) 'Are eggs the right size for egg cups because of good planning by hens? Where is reading research going?', *Educational Psychology in Practice*, 18 (2): 157–66.

Thomas, G. (2004) 'Introduction: evidence and practice', in G. Thomas and R. Pring, *Evidence Based Practice in Education*. Maidenhead: Open University Press.

Thomas, G. (2007) *Education and Theory: Strangers in Paradigms*. Maidenhead: Open University Press.

Thomas, G. and James, D. (2006) 'Re-inventing grounded theory: some questions about theory, ground and discovery', *British Educational Research Journal*, 32 (6): 767–95.

Thomas, G., Walker, D. and Webb. J. (1998) *The Making of the Inclusive School*. London: Routledge.

Vickers, G. (1965) *The Art of Judgment: a Study of Policy Making*. London: Chapman & Hall.

Vincett, K., Cremin, H. and Thomas, G. (2005) *Teachers and Assistants Working Together*. Maidenhead: Open University Press.

Wacquant, L. D. (1989) 'Towards a reflexive sociology: a workshop with Pierre Bourdieu', *Sociological Theory*, 7: 26–63.

Wells, M. (2005) 'Paxman answers the questions', *Guardian Unlimited*. Available at: http://politics.guardian.co.uk/media/story/0,12123,1402324,00.html (accessed 26 August 2007).

Whale, J. (1984) *Put It in Writing*. London: Dent.

Wheeler, L. R. (1970) 'A trans-decade comparison of the IQs of Tennessee mountain children', in I. Al-Issa and W. Dennis (eds), *Cross-Cultural Studies of Behavior*. New York: Holt, Rinehart & Winston, pp. 120–33.

White, J. (2006) *Intelligence, destiny and education*. London: Routledge.

Wolcott, H. F. (1992) 'Posturing in qualitative inquiry', in M. D. LeCompte, W. L. Milroy and J. Preissie (eds), *The Handbook of Qualitative Research in Education*. New York: Academic Press, pp. 3–52.

Wright Mills, C. (1959/1970) *The Sociological Imagination*. New York: Holt.

Index